FRIDTJOF NANSEN 1893–96

OTTAR CA. 890

THOR
HEYERDAHL
1978

INDIAN OCEAN

ROALD AMUNDSEN 1910–12 (South Pole)

EAN

NORWEGIAN MARITIME EXPLORERS AND EXPEDITIONS

«To all the explorers whose stories were never told»

NORWEGIAN MARITIME EXPLORERS
AND EXPEDITIONS

Published by Index Publishing AS
N-0243 Oslo, Norway

Tel. +47 22 92 63 00
Fax +47 22 92 63 33
E-mail: index@index.no
Internet: www.index.no

1st edition: September 1999
2nd edition: December 1999

Graphic design: Kristine Steen, PDC Tangen Oslo
Graphic production: PDC Tangen
Line drawings and maps: Kristine Steen
Photo credits: page 173

Originally published as Norske Maritime Oppdagere ISBN-82-7217-103-1
Norwegian Maritime Explorers ISBN-82-7217-105-8

English translation: Dahlia Pfeffer, Veronica Harrington Hansen, Richard Lawson

NORWEGIAN MARITIME EXPLORERS AND EXPEDITIONS

OVER THE PAST THOUSAND YEARS

INDEX PUBLISHING AS

PREFACE

In the year 2000 it will be one thousand years since Leif Eiriksson set foot on North American soil. He was the first European to discover America, almost 500 years before Columbus. This is an event that should be commemorated, and both Norway, Iceland and the United States will be arranging celebrations to mark the anniversary. This book, produced by Index Publishing AS, a subsidiary of the Norwegian Trade Council, is one of the Norwegian contributions towards the celebrations to mark the 1000th anniversary of Leif Eiriksson's achievement.

Leif Eiriksson and another Viking named Ottar are the first names known to us in a long line of outstanding Norwegian maritime explorers. They started a tradition of exploration that was to focus in particular on the North and South Poles, but that has also included explorers who preferred warmer climes – among others, Thor Heyerdahl. This book is a tribute to these men and the contribution they have made to our store of geographical and historical knowledge about our planet. At the same time, Leif Eiriksson and the other Norwegian maritime explorers have perhaps done more than any other Norwegian "product" to promote Norway abroad.

In view of Norway's geographical position, the character of its landscape and the way of life that develops in a country so dependent on the sea, it is not surprising that there have been Norwegian explorers all through history. It is not without reason that a line in an old, well-known song, written by one of the most famous Norwegian writers and poets, Bjørnstjerne Bjørnson, claims that wherever there is a possibility of sailing a ship, Norwegians will always be the first to try. Without wishing to blow our national trumpet too hard, it is safe to say that in this song Bjørnson touched upon something very fundamental in Norwegian history. The explorers in this book have sailed all the oceans of the world, confirming the prominent position Norway, a small country, holds as a maritime nation.

Most of the expeditions described in this book can to a certain extent be re-lived by visiting the museums on Bygdøy, Oslo's museum island. Several of the original vessels used in the expeditions are on exhibition at the Fram and Kon-Tiki museums. The Viking Ship museum contains the world's best preserved Viking ships, giving us the chance to view the kind of vessels the Vikings used on their voyages. The Norwegian Maritime Museum, as its name suggests, displays examples of our proud maritime history, providing a background and a historical context for the expeditions.

Explorations and explorers is a subject that will always appeal to the imagination. Many books have depicted the history of the world's explorers, but the story of our most important *Norwegian* maritime explorers has never been presented in one volume. The purpose of this book is to do just that.

We would like to thank journalist Liv Linde for coordinating the project and editing the manuscripts, Director Bård Kolltveit at the Norwegian Maritime Museum for his encouragement and professional support, Kristine Steen at PDC Tangen for the graphic design, Torunn Borthen for her assistance in the hunt for illustrations, and Marit Hagen for helping to proof-read the text.

Finally, our thanks to translators Dahlia Pfeffer, Veronica Harrington Hansen and Richard Lawson for translating this book into English, and to language consultants Jean Aase, Carol Eckmann, Alison Coulthard and Maidie Kloster for their help in editing the English text.

Oslo, August 1999

Øystein Kock Johansen

TABLE OF CONTENTS

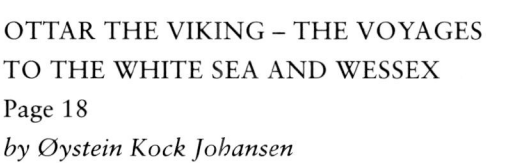

IT BEGAN WITH A BOAT
– AN INTRODUCTION

BY ØYSTEIN KOCK JOHANSEN

People have an innate need to explore the unknown. Explorers are those who do so by discovering new land or exploring unknown territory, such as the many Norwegian maritime explorers through history. Some of them have become universally famous, others are relatively unknown. Countless explorers – mostly those who lived in the earliest times – remain unknown and nameless. An apt explanation as to why so many have risked life and limb to venture into inhospitable environments may be found in the words of one active explorer who described the undertaking as "an obsession. The more I discover, the more I want to know. Unfortunately, I will not discover everything."

Needless to say, explorers are individualists whose motives for embarking on ventures to discover or probe new territories vary from person to person and from expedition to expedition. Nevertheless, there are a number of characteristics – curiosity, an urge to travel, a desire for triumph, achievement and personal success, a wish to satisfy the ego and test physical endurance – which most explorers have in common. The

differences between these inquisitive and intrepid men and women lie in which of these motives is most important, and this is of course a matter of individual personality.

The first travellers and explorers were "primitive" people who spread to all four corners of the world. About 10,000 years ago, when the Ice Age ended, people from present-day Northern Germany, Denmark and Southern Sweden crossed the sea to discover a new land, Norway. They settled here and later became explorers in their own right. During the Stone, Bronze and Iron Ages, they ventured farther by land and sea, a bold people searching for new trading partners and land to settle. The individual leaders of these early expeditions are nameless, hidden in the dark recesses of prehistorical times. Only at the end of the pagan period, i.e. in the Viking Era, do the first Norwegian maritime voyagers enter the arena as explorers with names that became known to future generations.

Ottar was one such explorer who lived at the same time as King Harald Hårfagre, or Harald the Fairhaired. A North Norwegian chieftain and merchant, he is important in

Norwegian history because he is the first truly Norwegian explorer whose name is known. At the end of the 9th century, he made a voyage that was chronicled by English scholars, who thereby immortalized it for all time.

A quick look at a map shows the length and size of Norway and its rugged terrain. Its extremely long coastline has meant that a large segment of the country and its population necessarily turn toward the sea. To the earliest settlers, the sea was a "larder", where they found their most important source of food, and it also served as a vital transport artery, less perilous and faster than travelling overland. Until this very day, *leia*, a Norse word meaning a channel or fairway, means the principal water route for transporting people and goods, a sort of aquatic "Norwegian Highway Number One". Similarly, the old Norse word *farvann*, also still in use, literally means water on which one travels. Until quite recently, Norway's road network was either very poor or non-existent, and *leia* was the lifeline of coastal communities. As a result, people mastered the use of boats, whether they were sailed, rowed or paddled. Boats made life simpler and provided greater mobility. As different types of vessels were developed, people penetrated almost everywhere.

From time immemorial, the sea has been the Norwegians' way out to the larger world beyond. For better or worse, the seas and the oceans set the terms for the men and women whose lives depended on them. This reality left an indelible imprint on the makeup of the coastal population, creating highly skilled sailors whose audaciousness and curiosity further transformed them into explorers driven by a strong urge to find new land. Thus geographical constraints made boats and ships an integral part of most Norwegians' lives. To rephrase the Norwegian poet Bjørnstjerne Bjørnson: the Norwegian sailor is to be found at the ready, wherever a vessel is able to float.

Boats have been the basic tools of all Norwegian maritime explorers, from Ottar and Leif Eiriksson to Fridtjof Nansen, Roald Amundsen, Otto Sverdrup and all the rest. The boat has been as essential for the Norwegian explorer as the space rocket is for the astronaut. They have relied on vessels based on ancient boat-building traditions that had been practised for thousands of years before the Vikings came on the scene. These early craftsmen and sailors are gone and forgotten, but information about their vessels has been obtained by means of archaeological excavations.

FROM THE DUGOUT TO PLANK BOATS

What did the boats of the explorers who discovered Norway look like, and what were they made of? It is impossible to answer these questions with any certainty, because no ancient boat finds have been made in Norway. However, the remains of a dugout have been excavated in northern Holland, at Pesse in the province of Drenthe. The boat consists of the hollowed trunk of a pine tree, measuring three metres long and 36 cm wide. This is presently considered to be Europe's oldest known vessel, dating from the 7th century B.C. It was probably in such simple dugouts that the first explorers found Norway. In all likelihood other types of boats were also in use in early times, for instance skin boats and bark boats.

The dugout is a simple construction. Although Stone Age hunter-gatherers and fishermen varied the shape and finish of their vessels, the point of departure was always a thick tree trunk which was hollowed out in some way, for instance by burning the unwanted wood to produce a shell construction. On many dugouts the traces left on the wood by flintstone axes and adzes can still be seen. In cross-section, a dugout may show a round trunk or have a flattened bottom. In some cases the fore stem is pointed, in others it is either blunt or rounded, while the aft stem is cut across or rounded. Some dugouts have an extra freeboard above the trunk's natural gunwale, which is intended to enable the boat to freight heavy loads in high waves without taking in too much water. The thick bottom of a dugout helped to stabilise the keel-less boat, but clearly this was not always adequate. Stones were therefore frequently used as ballast, weighing the boat down and increasing its stability. Probably Stone Age people also used an outrigger system to further increase stability. Outrigger canoes have been documented as being in use in Norway at a later date.

The dugout was a vessel for use in calm waters. Narrow and unstable, it was not suitable for open seas. Nevertheless, archaeological finds on islands far out to sea indicate that Late Stone Age people did in fact make their way to and settle on these islands. The islands of Hespriholmen, west of Bømlo; Vega and Træna off the coast of Nordland; and Magerøya in the Arctic Ocean, outside the Porsanger Fjord, are all examples of such islands. Indeed the whole of Norway was explored and settled, and even remote islands which are uninhabited today became part of the territory of Stone Age hunters and fishermen.

Between 4,000 and 3,500 B.C., knowledge of agriculture slowly began to spread into the country. In the course of one thousand years, farming and animal husbandry became as important as hunting and fishing. Norway had entered the farming phase of the Stone Age. Although the nature of work changed, there is little indication that new types of vessels came into use; the old, reliable dugouts were still in use. The choice of material and details of shape varied, but the tried and tested methods for processing tree trunks to make dugouts were still used by Stone Age farmers.

In the 3rd century B.C., dugouts were being turned to good account in journeys between northern Jutland and Lista and south-western Norway. It is apparent that the Skagerrak was not regarded as too formidable a barrier, since there was extensive flintstone trade between these areas. In Denmark flintstone was mined and then exported to Norway and other regions. Clearly, the spirit of pioneering and exploration was a characteristic of Stone Age seafarers and tradesmen. The same

Stone Age dugouts were built for quiet waters, not for the open sea.

seafaring flint traders are also known to have operated far into the Gulf of Bothnia and the Gulf of Finland.

The period following the Stone Age, i.e. the Bronze Age, began around 2,000 B.C., and lasted for approximately 1,500 years, until 500 B.C. Since copper and tin, the most important constituents of bronze, were not extracted in Norway at this time, as far as is known, the metal had to be imported from abroad. Therefore all the bronze objects found in Norway are a sure sign of trading activity. Bronze objects arrived from southern Scandinavia and from many parts of Europe. Boats must have played a central role in the bartering system in use at the time. Norway's inhabitants were wholly dependent on boats for maintaining contact with the international network of Bronze Age traders. The Bronze Age may truly be described as a

time of bold mariners and explorers who were on the lookout for new places and people with whom to trade, though they were not averse to getting rich quickly by plunder and piracy.

The bold and enterprising sailors of this epoch were the forerunners of the Vikings in both exploits and achievements. They paddled their boats to the remotest corners of the continent and the British Isles, crossing the sea and navigating rivers. It is unfortunate that no written sources dating from this expansive period are available. They would certainly have told tales of sea voyages of discovery and feats of courage, daring and heroism as impressive as anything related in the Icelandic Sagas.

PICTOGLYPHS OF BOATS CHISELLED IN ROCKS

No Bronze Age vessels have been found in Norway. However, all over the country there are hundreds, perhaps thousands, of pictoglyphs of boats chiselled on rock surfaces. Although the shapes and types of boats represented on these vary, it has been possible to form a general picture of the vessels used by the tradesmen and explorers of the age.

Boats are depicted in many pictoglyphs, showing their importance to Bronze Age people.

The general design was as follows: the boats were a symmetrical constructions fore and aft. As a rule, the gunwale was extended along and beyond the vessel's interior, ending in long, upwardly curved points. The stem extension might be decorated with a wooden animal head, or it could be even higher and more sharply and backwardly curved, ending above the boat's interior. In some depictions, the same type of upwardly curved and pointed extension can be seen below the stem extension, that is from the bottom part of the boat. Sometimes the stem extension is present both fore and aft. The side of the boat, between the extended gunwale and the extended bottom part, may appear in the pictoglyphs either as an outline, without any markings at all, with the space completely filled-in, or with vertical lines, frequently above the gunwale. Probably this is a representation of something novel, a plank-built skeleton or rib-system design.

Reconstruction of a Bronze Age boat. Note the characteristic prow, also shown in rock carvings.

The vertical lines above the gunwale on pictoglyphs of Bronze Age boats provide an indication of their size. The general consensus is that each line represents a person. Thus 30 lines would represent 15 paddlers on each side, which would have meant a boat some 20 – 25 m in length. Bronze Age boats were paddled, not rowed, and there are no indications of the presence of a sail; the boats relied on man-power as opposed to wind propulsion.

The many rock carvings of Bronze Age ships give a good impression of the shape, height and length of the boats and how they were propelled, but no information on either the materials or the technology used to build them. Some scholars believe that the Bronze Age rock carvings show the origins or prototypes of Norway's oldest plank-built boats. Others believe that the rock carvings in fact portray wooden skeleton boats which were skin- or bark-clad. The latter group point to Arctic skin boats, especially the Eskimo *umiak*, as a parallel to

Bronze Age boats. The discussion as to whether the boats were skin- or bark-clad or plank-built has not been resolved, nor will it be unless a fortuitous boat find supplies the answer.

Regardless of materials and shape, Bronze Age boats must have been very functional vessels. Had this not been the case, such a widespread international trading network could never have developed. At several sites, rock carvings depict whole armadas of boats, indicating that sea warfare, seafaring and exploration were the order of the day. How far Bronze Age Norwegians travelled and the shores they reached remain a mystery. However, the find of a bronze axe near Brantford, Ontario in Canada, has caused a reputable Swedish archaeologist to speculate about a "Bronze Age Columbus". He conjectures that the axe from Grand River might perhaps have belonged to a Bronze Age castaway or an explorer from the North. Fascinating as his theories are, they are extremely difficult to prove.

BOAT FINDS IN THE BOG
Around the year 500 B.C. the Iron Age reached the Nordic region. Tools made of iron, especially axes and adzes, must

The Hjortspring boat from 300 B.C. is the oldest plank-built boat found in the Nordic region.

have made it possible for boat-builders to design more advanced vessels. Although the degree to which iron tools revolutionised boat-building remains uncertain, the oldest plank-built vessel known from the Nordic region dates from the 4th century B.C. It was found in a bog at Hjortspring on the Danish island of Als. The boat was a religious offering which was lowered into the bog, carrying on board swords, spears and shields.

The still unique Hjortspring boat clearly shows what boats looked like in early Iron Age Scandinavia. In what follows, it is therefore taken as typical of the kind of vessels to be found in Norway at the time, even though it is unlikely that such large plank-built craft would have been owned by ordinary people. The Hjortspring vessel is a canoe measuring almost 14 m in length and made of lime wood. The shell has a wide, curved bottom plank with a side strake and a sheerstrake on each side. The stems are hollowed blocks of wood which rest on the bottom plank. The bottom plank and the sheerstrakes extend

to the outside of the hull, closely resembling two protruding elephant tusks, one on top of the other. Beyond the hollowed stempieces are strong, vertical oak supports fixed to the upper and lower "tusks" by wooden treenails and a compound consisting of oil and ox tallow. The oak supports reinforce the stempiece structure. The hull itself is supported by thin ribs of hazel which were bent and lashed to the cleats on the strakes. No metal was used in the boat's construction; all the individual parts were either sewn, lashed or mortised into place.

Although the boat appears to be both fragile and unstable, the details show that considerable thought went into the design. Moreover, the craftsmanship is beyond reproach; there must have been a long tradition of craftsmanship behind the building of the Hjortspring boat. The boat-builder or builders put considerable effort into making the boat as light as possible, at the same time not neglecting an elegant appearance. The boat weighed approximately 530 kg, without a crew and equipment, which is extremely light for a craft of this size.

The Hjortspring boat was probably a war canoe. It was neither sailed nor rowed. Several paddles were found in the

boat, showing that it was driven forward by paddling. Probably it carried a crew of 22-24 men, which would correspond to the 20 seats on the brace athwart of the canoe and in addition a helmsman, a lookout and others. It is not certain where the boat carrying the raiders to Als came from nor where it was built, although it is likely to have been from Skåne in Sweden. Clearly, it was not difficult to cross the sea and reach Als in this type of vessel. The cargo-carrying capacity of plank-built boats and the superb seamanship of their crews gave them a far greater range than dugouts, giving easy access to places that could once only be reached with great difficulty.

Although Norway was on the periphery of the known world at the time of the Hjortspring boat, such a vessel would have made journeys to distant parts far easier than in the earlier dugouts. Without doubt, the Norwegians would have known how to make the most of the excellent features of the plank-built boat. But it must be stressed that there is no information in prehistoric sources about the sea voyages and discoveries of the period, at least not those undertaken by Norwegians.

THE DISCOVERY OF THULE

By contrast, remnants of a written manuscript have been found describing a named explorer's travels to Norway. In Marseille, or *Massilia* as the city was known when it was a Greek colony, there lived a scholarly explorer by the name of Pytheas, who wrote the oldest known description of a journey to countries including present-day Norway. He undertook his voyage of discovery at the time when the Hjortspring boat was in use. Around 330 B.C. Pytheas sailed through the Strait of Gibraltar and north along the coastline of western Europe. His voyage followed

the coasts of Portugal and France, from where he rounded the Tin Islands, that is, the British Isles, followed by the Orkneys, before setting out on a northerly course. After sailing for four days, he arrived a land he referred to as Thule, which lay below the Arctic Circle.

Researchers do not entirely agree on Thule's whereabouts, but since Iceland was uninhabited at the time, it is difficult to see what other country than Norway Pytheas could have visited. Thule was inhabited and the land was cultivated. Pytheas says that "...near the cold belt there is an absence of the finer types of fruit...but those who have wheat and honey, make a drink out of these. Since they do not have clear sunshine, they gather the ears of grain in order to thresh them in large buildings, because they become useless (were they to be threshed) in the open threshing places due to the lack of sunshine and the rain showers." This is a testimony to the harsh Norwegian climate at the beginning of the Iron Age. Pytheas also tells the reader his reasons for the voyage: 1) He wanted to visit the places where the Mediterranean countries obtained tin and amber. 2) He wanted to explore the northern settlements and their geography. In other words, his objectives were much the same as those of more recent explorers. Presumably the Norwegians who paddled their Hjortspring-like boats in the opposite direction from Pytheas also had similar objectives.

Pytheas' map from ca 330 B.C. is the first to show Thule (probably Norway).

Reconstruction of the Kvalsund boat from about 700 A.D.

THE FIRST ROWING BOAT

Until now it has been necessary to look outside Norway's borders to learn about the types of vessels used by the nameless discoverers of ancient times. But from the very early years of the first century A.D. onwards, it is no longer necessary to look abroad because local boat finds make it possible to study the vessels the Norwegian maritime pioneers used to reach the outside world.

On Halsn Island in Sunnhordland, parts of a boat dating from the beginning of the first century A.D. have been found. Although not much has been preserved, there are enough remains to show that the strakes were "sewn" together without the use of iron elements. In other words, the underlying construction principle was the same as in the Hjortspring boat. Nevertheless there is a big difference between the two vessels: the Halsn Island boat was rowed. This was a technological advance which must have significantly increased the seafarers' radius of action.

Around 700 A.D. the people of Kvalsund in Sunnmøre sacrificed two boats to the gods, a large ship and a small boat. The large Kvalsund ship measured 18 m in length and was 3.2 m wide. This vessel is a precursor of the Viking ships, without which the Vikings would have been unable to cross stormy open seas to engage in warfare, colonization and exploration. The Kvalsund ship is a double-ender with a sharply-pointed prow and stern. The keel was not yet fully developed and resembles a bottom plank, in other words, a carry-over from the dugout. The prow and stern curve elegantly from the

strengthening lath on the underside of the straight bottom, giving the same familiar profile as the more technologically advanced Viking ships. The Kvalsund ship is clinker-built with rivets fastening the strakes together. The ship is wide enough to have carried a mast and sail, but there is no trace of a mast support. It is thus impossible to be certain that the ship was a sailing vessel, even though the hull seems stable enough in shape to carry a mast and sail. Furthermore, in the Kvalsund ship the earlier, loose steering oar has evolved into a long, fixed side rudder, also a characteristic of the first Viking ships.

THE ADVENT OF THE SAILING BOAT

Carbon-14 dating of the first Norwegian archaeological finds of vessels which bear the traces of a sail and mast place these at the onset of the Viking Era. This is strikingly delayed given the fact that sailing boats had been in use in Egypt and Mesopotamia for more than 3,500 years, and that the Greeks and Romans used sailing boats in southern Europe. The Northerners must have seen such ships, and it is strange that in the windy North no one hit upon the idea of using sails to harness the power of the wind. Nevertheless there are no traces of the adoption of a mast and sail on Nordic vessels until the Viking Era. Researchers are still unable to explain this.

It is, however, important to point out that the lack of sails did not prevent the early Norwegians from crossing the sea to foreign destinations. There is archaeological evidence that people from Norway's Vestland crossed the North Sea to islands further west. In the 7th and 8th centuries there must have been considerable traffic to England, Scotland, Ireland, the Hebrides, the Orkneys, Shetland and the Faeroe Islands.

Long before the first documented Viking raid in 793 A.D., Norsemen travelled to the islands around the rim of the Atlantic Ocean. Some of the seafarers who crossed the North Sea may even have reached Iceland. Archaeological excavations in Herjolfsdallur at Heimaey and in Reykjavik have unearthed finds indicating the presence of a Nordic people, probably western Norwegians who found their way to the distant Atlantic island as early as 600 or 700 A.D. This is 150–200 years before the traditionally accepted date for the settlement of Iceland, around the year 870 A.D. In other words, the lack of a sail did not prevent voyagers from venturing to far away places; the North Atlantic was conquered by pure oar-power.

Some researchers have argued against the theory that there was Norwegian west-bound traffic across the North Sea so early on, because the Norwegians and other Scandinavians did not adopt the sail until the end of the 8th century. They contend that before this, it would have been impossible to cross the vast, open stretches of the stormy North Sea and Atlantic Ocean. This position, however, disregards the archaeological indications that the Norsemen may well have adopted the sail by the 7th century, as, for instance, the Frisians did south of the North Sea. It is possible that the archaeological finds that could settle the matter have simply eluded us in Norway. Furthermore, it would not have been

Picture stone from Gotland showing one of the earliest Viking sailing ships.

The traditional boats from Nordland county are very similar to the old Viking ships.

difficult to cross the sea from Vestland to the islands further west in the North Sea and journey to the Atlantic Ocean with vessels like the Halsn Island and Kvalsund plank-boats, even though they were rowed. These were excellent boats which could get up considerable speed at sea.

By the 8th century, Norwegians had been crossing the Skagerrak by boat for several thousand years. They mastered the turbulent waters along the Norwegian coast and found their way to islands far from the mainland and exposed to the harshest of weather conditions. It is not possible therefore to use shipbuilding techniques to argue that people from Western Norway could not have crossed the North Sea to Britain before the Viking Age. Indeed, there are strong indications that when the first Viking raid took place in 793 A.D., the Vikings were not sailing in unfamiliar waters. The novel aspect of the 793 raid was not that ships reached England from Norway, but that they came with an aggressive and war-like purpose.

NAVIGATION AND MAPS

How the sailors of the distant past found their destinations has challenged the imagination of both laymen and scholars. The compass did not exist. The first compass-like instrument became available in the 13th century, while the earliest maritime chart was produced in 1500. The use of a log to determine the speed of a ship was described for the first time as late as 1577.

The Stone, Bronze and Iron Age explorers clearly navigated by means of various celestial bodies, especially the sun and the North Star. In addition, they used currents, wind direction, cloud formations and seabirds to help them find their course

The Viking house at Borg in Lofoten.

across the sea. Information must also have been handed down from generation to generation by those who knew the waters well. The only technical aid available before the Middle Ages was the deep-sea sounding-lead. A simple tool, but extremely important in northern waters to avoid shoals and underwater skerries, it consisted of a heavy, conical, hollowed piece of lead which was filled with an adhesive material, such as wax, and attached to the end of a line. When the lead was lowered, the adhesive substance caught samples of the bottom sediment, which told the navigator a great deal about his location and warned of potential hazards.

In early times, navigation, or the science of locating the position and plotting the course of a vessel, was mainly based on observations of natural and astronomical phenomena. To label this as "primitive" is not to disparage the accomplishments of the earliest unnamed explorers who found their way to wherever they wished to go. The lack of technical aids and charts only heightens the stature of these skilful mariners.

OTTAR CA. 890.

OTTAR – THE VIKING – THE VOYAGE TO THE WHITE SEA AND WESSEX

BY ØYSTEIN KOCK JOHANSEN

The Vikings' perception of the world differed from that of modern man. The Vikings imagined the world to be as round as a disc. At the centre was Åsgard, the dwelling place of the gods. Surrounding the home of the gods was Midgard, "the farm in the middle", inhabited by the mortals of the world. Utgard, "the farm on the outside", was in the hands of a large variety of giants, trolls, elves and demons who were the enemies of both the gods and man.

*U*tgard was a dangerous region into which even the gods were afraid of straying. Venturing too far into the wilderness of either the forests or mountains meant being in *Utgard*. Seafarers believed that if they strayed from their course and found themselves on the high seas, they were then in the power of the giants. Journeys, and not least sea voyages, were considered dangerous since there was always the possibility of getting lost.

Despite these perils, the Vikings set out to explore the world beyond. They went further than any of their forefathers,

sailing west to North America and east to the Caspian Sea, sailing south from northernmost Norway to the Mediterranean on expeditions known as the Viking Voyages. Why did the Vikings have such an urgent, unique need to explore the outside world? One proposed explanation is that the Norwegian population had expanded significantly and that there was a need for more *Lebensraum,* or living space. Perhaps the Vikings were looking for new trading partners or simply for adventure and challenges. But the most significant prerequisite for their successful expansion was probably the

superiority of the Viking ships and weapons. The importance of their solid, clinker-built, shallow-draught sailing vessels should not be underrated.

The Viking ships known today took shape around the year 800 A.D. By that time the keel had been fully developed, the strakes were relatively thin, and the skeleton was fastened to clamps in the strakes, making the vessels supple and seaworthy. With such vessels driven forward by a square sail, the Vikings could sail hard and fast. A copy of the *Gokstad* ship crossed the Atlantic Ocean in 1893, reaching speeds of up to 11 knots under especially good conditions. Vessels on documented voyages undertaken during the Viking era had an average speed of roughly seven knots on long voyages.

TRADESMEN AND EXPLORERS

The Viking boats were refined to near perfection so that the world was open to those intrepid enough to set sail. The Vikings who did so were mainly driven by economic motivations, such as plunder, trade or settlement. However, many also had a strong sense of adventure and a desire to

This copy of the Gokstad ship crossed the Atlantic in 1893, proving the Vikings' skill as shipbuilders.

explore. Indeed, it was trade and the exploration of new lands which provided the impetus for the voyages of the Viking chieftain Ottar. A Northern Norwegian who lived at the end of the 9th century, Ottar undertook several relatively well-documented voyages, and was the first Norwegian explorer to be identified by name.

Braving the stormy seas and the perils of *Utgard*, Ottar reportedly sighted "new" land along the coast of Northern Norway, the White Sea, Sweden, Denmark and northern Germany, and he even voyaged to Wessex in England. Below follows a translation of his travelogue as dictated to an English chronicler:

Ottar related to his Lord, King Alfred, that he lived furthest to the north of all Norwegians. He said that he lived in the north of the country, by the Western Sea. Moreover, he also said that the land stretched even further to the north from

there, but that it was entirely uninhabited, with the exception of a few places here and there where Laplanders had their camps in order to hunt in the winter and fish in the sea in the summer.

He related that on one occasion he wanted to explore how far north the land extended, and whether or not any people lived north of this desolate stretch. Thus he sailed directly north along the coast. For three entire days, he had the uninhabited land on his starboard side and the open sea on his port side. At that point he was as far north as the whalers went. He continued directly north as far as he could sail for an additional three days. Then the land bent sharply to the east or the sea went into the land – he did not know which of the two. However, he knew that he waited for wind slightly north of west before sailing eastwards along the coast as far as he could in the course of four days. There he had to wait for wind from the north because the land bent directly southwards – or the sea went into the land – he did not know which of the two was correct.

From there he sailed directly south along the coast, as far as he could, for five days. There he found a big river which stretched inland. Then (Ottar and his men) turned upriver, not daring to sail past it for fear of a hostile reception, since the other side of the river was entirely populated. Prior to this he had not encountered any inhabited land since leaving his homestead. The entire way, the land on his starboard side had been uninhabited – with the exception of fishermen, bird-catchers and hunters, all of whom were Laplanders – and the open sea was on his port side.

The Bjarmlanders cultivated their lands very well, but (Ottar and his men) did not dare to go ashore. By contrast, the land of the ter-Finns was entirely uninhabited, with the exception of the sites where hunters, fishermen or bird-catchers made camp. The Bjarmlanders told him many tales about their own land and the surrounding lands, but he did not know if they spoke the truth because he himself had not seen the land. He believed that the Laplanders and the Bjarmlanders spoke almost the same language.

Apart from wanting to learn about the land, he went there first and foremost because of the walruses, since the bone in their tusks was very valuable and their skins were very suitable for making ship ropes. (Ottar and his men) brought some tusks back to the king. (According to Ottar), these whales

(walruses) were much smaller than other whales, no more than seven alen (14 feet) in length. But the best whales were to be found in his own country; these were eight and forty alen (96 feet) long, with the longest reaching fifty alen (100 feet). He related that he and five others had killed sixty of these (whales) in the course of two days.

Ottar was a man who was very wealthy in animals, the riches of his (country). When he visited the king, (Ottar) still had six hundred unsold, domesticated animals, called reindeer. Six of them were decoy reindeer, which were valued by the Laplanders for capturing wild reindeer. (Ottar) was among the most prominent men in the land. Nevertheless he did not have more than twenty cattle, twenty sheep and twenty pigs; and he ploughed his small bit of land with horses.

But (the Norwegians') wealth was mostly based on the tax which the Laplanders paid them. The tax consisted of animal skins, bird feathers, walrus tusks and ship's ropes made of walrus and seal skins. Everyone paid according to his social position. The most prominent had to pay 15 marten (sable) pelts, five reindeer skins, one bearskin, 10 (ambarer) feathers,

---

Ottar's ship was probably a trading vessel like the one depicted here by Karl Erik Harr.

Jewellery and ornaments found at Kaupang (near Larvik), where Ottar once traded.

one bearskin or otter skin jacket, and two ship's ropes sixty alen (120 feet) in length, one of whale (walrus) skin, the other of sealskin.

Ottar related that the land of the Norwegians was very long and narrow. All the land which could be used for either pasture or ploughing lay near the sea, and even this land was very mountainous in parts. The inhabited areas contained desolate mountainous stretches to the east and to the north where the Laplanders lived. The inhabited area was widest in the south, becoming gradually narrower further north. In the south, it was some 60 miles wide as they reckoned it, and in the middle still 30 miles across, but in the north it was as little as 3 miles from the sea to the mountains. In some places the mountains were so wide as to take two weeks to cross, and in other places so wide as to take six days.

Along the southern part of the country on the other side of the mountains was Svealand, reaching all the way to the northern part of the land; and along the northern part of the country was the land of the Kvens. Sometimes the Kvens went on raids across the mountains, and other times the Norwegians

raided them. There were very large lakes everywhere in the mountains, and the Kvens carried their very small, lightweight boats overland to the lakes in order to raid the Norwegians.

Ottar related that the district in which he lived was called Hålogaland. He said that no one lived further north than he. There was a trading town called Skiringssal in the southern part of the country, which he said could not be reached in one month of sailing even if one were to go ashore at night and had fair weather every day. He also said that one had to sail along the coastline. He explained that one first had Ireland on the starboard side, followed by the islands that lay between Ireland and (England). Thereafter one had (England) on the starboard side until one reached Skiringssal, after having sailed all the way with Norway on the port side. South of Skiringssal, a very large lake stretched inland, and it was so wide that no man could look across it and see the other side. Jutland lay right on the other side of the lake, followed by Sillende, and the lake stretched into the country for several thousands of miles.

Ottar said that he had sailed from Skiringssal to the trading town of Hedeby in five days. Hedeby lay between the Wends, Saxons and Angles, and belonged to the Danes. When he sailed there from Skiringssal, Ottar had Denmark on his port side and the open sea on his starboard side for three days. Thereafter, he had Jutland, Sillende and many islands on his starboard side for two days before he reached Hedeby. The Angles lived in these lands before they came to (England). For two days (Ottar also) had the islands belonging to Denmark on his port side.

It is not certain who Ottar was, at least not beyond what can be deduced from his travelogue. Nevertheless, it can be assumed that he was a very important personality: a chieftain, a tradesman and a member of the Viking elite in Northern Norwegian society. Although he described himself as a one of "the most prominent men in the country", he had no more than 20 cattle, 20 sheep and 20 pigs, apart from 600 reindeer, which probably did not impress King Alfred. It is unlikely that the story of his life will ever be complete, as it is even uncertain whether or not Ottar returned to *Hålogaland* after completing

his trading expedition abroad. However, according to comments made during his audience with King Alfred, it is clear that he had intended to return home.

By contrast, it is certain that Ottar undertook his voyage around the year 890 A.D., during the period Harald Hårfagre was the king of Norway. It is not known exactly where he lived, as he did not give any details about the location of his manor, apart from his statement that he came from the northernmost part of Norwegian territory. Much study has been devoted to the possible location of Ottar's ancestral manor. Most scholars believe that it was located in the vicinity of present-day Tromsø. Others maintain that he resided at the *Greipstad* farm on Kvaløy, or in the Hillersøy region. Bjarkøy has been suggested as another possibility. However, nothing is certain.

How were the tales of Ottar's travels and discoveries handed down? Extraordinarily enough, the story was preserved through Orosius' history of the world – a rather unexpected source. The background for this is as follows: at the beginning of the 5th century A.D., the Spanish-Roman prelate Paulus Orosius was given the task of writing a special history. The work was to cover the period from the Creation until 417 A.D. This resulted in a total of seven manuscripts titled *Historiarum libri VII adversus paganos*, or *Seven Books of History Against the Pagans*.

Hedeby (near Schleswig) was an important trading centre where Ottar sold skins and other valuable goods.

ANGLO-SAXON MAP OF THE WORLD,
ca 1000 A.D.
No maps have been found from the time of King Alfred.

Christians did not allow this accusation to stand unchallenged. Orosius was one of many theologians who took pen in hand to present the Christian case. His contribution was intended to be a concise work of history in which he listed all the accidents, wars, and natural disasters that had occurred in the world long before Christianity, the implication being that the old pagan gods had not been able to prevent such events either.

Although not a great scholarly work, Orosius' seven books have gradually become European classics. At the end of the 9th century, the English king, Alfred the Great of Wessex, had the book translated into Old English. The first part of the world history contained a geographical survey, but this only covered the part of the world with which Orosius was familiar, i.e. Europe south of the Alps. Therefore, when the work was translated, Alfred wanted a description of Europe north of the Alps to be added. Thus the description of Northern Europe, including Ottar's travelogue, is an addition to the Orosius' work and not a translation of it. Ottar's report on his discoveries and travels was included in the history because Ottar was able to give first-hand information about the northernmost parts of Europe. King Alfred's scholars could not have acquired this information from any other source. Ottar himself apparently told the story to scholars at Alfred's court when he paid it a visit around the year 890 A.D.

The Old English edition of Orosius has been handed down through a manuscript which was probably written in Winchester between the years 892 and 924 A.D. The manuscript is complete apart from a missing section consisting of Ottar's and another Norse traveller's reports. This gap is filled by the insertion of a copy of another manuscript, which dates back to the 11th century. Both manuscripts are now in the British Museum.

The way in which Ottar communicated with King Alfred and his scholars is not known, but there are several possibilities. Ottar may have spoken Old English very well himself, or King Alfred and some of his people may have acquired a knowledge of Old Norse through the many treaty negotiations with the Danish Vikings. Or Ottar may have used an interpreter, although according to linguistic experts, the texts do not bear this out. In Ottar's time, the two languages were so closely related that many words and phrases were mutually comprehensible.

The explanation for the work's peculiar title lies in the political situation at the time in which Orosius lived. Around the year 400 A.D., Rome's days of glory were past, and many provinces had been conquered by barbarian tribes. On 24 August 410, the antique world experienced the most improbable and incredible catastrophe: the Visigoth general, Alarik, vanquished and plundered Rome. This unthinkable victory gave rise to considerable introspection and self-examination. Many believed that the old gods were avenging themselves for the many conversions to Christianity. The

A KNARR FOR MERCHANT OTTAR

Ottar's ship and his discoveries, travel routes and voyages need some explanation. Ottar's report did not state which type of vessel he used. Layman's language uses the generic term Viking ship, despite the fact that many types of vessels were used during the Viking era. They included a small sailboat known as a *dragon*, a long ship *(langskip)*, a barque *(bard)*, and other ships called *knarr, karv, snekka* and *skeid*. Ottar probably used a merchant ship called a *knarr* for his voyages. These vessels had higher sides than warships, helping them to stay dry and enabling them to carry a considerable cargo with the aid of a relatively small crew. Ottar was primarily a merchant, not a Viking warrior or pirate, and he probably did not sail in a vessel like the *Gokstad* or *Oseberg* ship. Such boats, called *karver*, were built to carry a large crew of warriors and their equipment.

Norwegian, Swedish and Danish archaeological finds of boat remnants help to paint a fairly clear picture of Ottar's ship. Similar ships have been found in the western part of Norway. The *Klåstad* ship, for example, although badly preserved, has served as a model for reconstruction on the drawing board. Dating back to the 9th century, a contemporary of Ottar's vessel, the *Klåstad* ship was an oak merchant ship roughly 21 m long and 5 m wide. It sank with a cargo of grindstones on board. Another, somewhat smaller trading vessel called the *Skuldelve* was found in the Roskilde Fjord. Measuring 16.3 m in length and 4.5 m in breadth, the boat was largely constructed out of pine, indicating that it was built in south-western Norway. The *Skuldelve* could easily have carried a cargo of 15-20 tonnes, which means that its draught was no more than about 1.5 m. The surface of the sail was roughly 100 m^2. Using this type of ship, Ottar would have been able to freight both heavy and lightweight goods in such great quantities that he could earn a great deal of money with just a single voyage a year.

Ottar's ship probably carried a crew of 10 to 12 men. The description of Ottar's personal status indicates

If the wind failed, the crew took to the oars (Ill: Karl Erik Harr.) Below: Old English translation of Orosius' history showing the beginning of Ottar's tale. From a manuscript in the British Library.

ræde hiſ hlaſorde ælfrede kyninᵹe. þæt he ealra
norð manna norðmſþr bude. he cpæð þæt he bude
onþæm lande norðe preapoum. piðða peſc ræ. he ſæde
ðeah þæt þæt land ſy ſpyðe lanᵹ norð þanon. ac hit
iſ eall peſre buton on reapū ſropum. ſacce m ælum
piciað ſinnaſ. onhuntaðe onpinrra. ɟonſu m ɟira
onſiſcoðe beðæhr ræ. he ræde þæt he æt ſumū cyrre
polde ſanðian hú lanᵹe þæt land norð rihre læᵹe
oððe hpæþeр æniᵹ man be norðan þæm peſrene
bude. þa ſor he norð rihre beſæn lande lec him

Ottar – the Viking – must have been a wealthy and important chieftain.

that the men on board were some of his serfs, and that he himself owned both the ship and the cargo. At that time similar trade journeys were also organised as joint ventures by groups of less prominent merchants. Each owned his share of the cargo, which he marketed individually once it was brought ashore.

With his *knarr*, crew and cargo, Ottar set out to the north, south and west. It must be kept in mind that the cultural geography of the Viking era differs from today's. At that time, Northern Norway was divided into two parts: *Hålogaland* and *Finnmork*. *Hålogaland* – where Ottar lived – was the northernmost "county" in Viking Norway, and the land of the *Håløygens,* a Norse people who belonged to the same group that lived further south. *Hålogaland* consisted of the coastal areas in present-day Nordland county, as well as a large part of Troms, and possibly extended as far north as Vanna Island and the Lyngen Fjord. *Finnmork* – where the Laplanders settled –was made up of the interior segments of the fjords and the inland country from Helgeland in the south to present-day Finnmark in the north. The Laplanders' *Finnmork* lay outside the Norwegian realm, and many hundreds of years were to pass before it became integrated into the Norwegian state. The country's northern border was first delineated in the treaties with Sweden in 1751 and Russia in 1826.

INTO THE WHITE SEA

When Ottar went north "to examine how far the land stretched to the north, and whether any people lived north of the desolate stretch of land", he left Norse territory. On a modern map, it is easy to follow Ottar's voyage along the Norwegian coast, rounding the northern rim of the Scandinavian Peninsula, passing the Varanger Peninsula, rounding the Kola Peninsula and entering the White Sea.

It took Ottar six days to reach the North Cape. According to his reports, he found no permanent residents along this stretch of land. The only people to be seen were fishermen, hunters and bird-catchers, all of whom he labelled Laplanders. But his accounts indicate that Norsemen were engaged in economic activity at the North Cape, as he reported sighting Norse whalers there.

After rounding Norway's northernmost point, he sailed to the east, explaining that "the land bent directly to the east or the sea went into the land." He did not know which one was true. This rather strange wording derives from the world view that was prevalent at the time. If it was the land that turned, it meant that one had arrived at the very edge of the world. If, by contrast, it was the sea that cut into the land, then it meant that it was an inland sea such as the Baltic or the Mediterranean. Clearly, the English chronicler found it imperative to clarify

whether or not Ottar had travelled on the earth's outermost edge, and whether or not there was land even further to the north. For that reason it was very important to specify, every time Ottar changed direction, whether the land deviated from its course or the sea penetrated the land.

With a north-westerly wind, Ottar sailed for four days along the Varanger Peninsula and around the Kola Peninsula, arriving at the wide mouth of the White Sea, between Svyatoy-Nos on Kola and Kanin-Nos on the Kanin Peninsula. Again he used the formulation "the land turned directly south, or the sea went into the land". Here Ottar waited on fair winds from the north. When they came, he sailed directly southwards, entering the White Sea and sailing as far as he could for a period of five days before reaching a wide river which extended inland. This was either the present-day Dvina or Onega River. Ottar makes it clear that during the entire

---

Ottar sailed along the shores of the White Sea.

journey the land on his starboard side was uninhabited, apart from the Laplanders whom he did not count as permanent settlers as they were engaged in hunting, catching birds or fishing.

ENCOUNTERS WITH FOREIGN PEOPLES

At the innermost point of the White Sea, Ottar encountered, for the first time since leaving home, a permanently settled people whom he called the *Bjarmlanders*. These people inhabited the meadowlands of present-day Archangel or Severodvinsk. Ottar had borrowed the label *Bjarm* or *Beormas* from the Finnish *permi*. In Finnish dialects, *permi* meant a travelling trader from Karelia who bought goods, primarily fur pelts, from all over northern Russia and sold them to the Bulgarians on the Volga River. The Bulgarians, in turn, sold the furs to the Arabs which is evidenced by several finds of Arabic coins along the *Bjarmlanders'* trade routes.

At the same time as Ottar described the *Bjarmlanders*, he also described the *ter-Finns*, whose land, he concluded, was

Viking swords dating from the time of Ottar.

uninhabited. The *ter-Finns*, or *ter-Finnas*, were a Lapp people who lived on the Kola Peninsula. Unlike the *Bjarmlanders*, they were hunters, not farmers. According to Ottar, the *Bjarmlanders* "cultivated their land very well". After describing the peoples and their land, he explained why he had undertaken such a long voyage. Aside from the desire to explore, he journeyed to the north "first and foremost because of the walruses". Walrus tusks and skins were highly-prized trading goods in southern regions, and Ottar therefore brought a number of walrus tusks home with him for King Alfred. In addition to being an explorer, farmer, reindeer owner and whaler, Ottar was above all a merchant.

Although he combined trade and exploration in his northern voyages, there is enough historical evidence to support the assertion that Ottar's most important contributions were as an explorer and an ethnographer. On his voyages Ottar exhibited a researcher's attention to detail, registering the unique characteristics of the countries, their people and their ways of living. He was objective and factual in his reports on both his northern and southern voyages. His careful and truthful evaluation of the *Bjarmlanders*, in particular, is extraordinary. The *Bjarmlanders* provided Ottar with information for his descriptions in which he forthrightly stated that he did not know which parts of the stories he had heard were true because he had not seen the things himself. He added that it "would appear" as though the Laplanders and the *Bjarmlanders* spoke the same language. His critical attitude toward what he had been told, but was unable to confirm, increases the credibility of his chronicles.

TRADE WITH THE CONTINENT AND ENGLAND

Ottar's travels took him southwards to south-eastern Norway and northern Germany, where he sold the goods that he had secured in the north. Sailing down towards the Oslo Fjord, he explained that on the other side of southern Norway's mountains lay *Svealand*, the land of the *Sveas* or Swedes, and that inland, further north on the Norwegian side, lay *Cwenland* (as it was called in Old English). The *Kvens* were members of a West Finnish hunting, fishing and martial brotherhood, who collected taxes and carried out raids as far north as *Finnmork* from 800-1100 A.D.

Ottar's route was clearly a well-established one that followed Norway's extended coastline south to *Skiringssal*. Located in western Norway, *Skiringssal* was unfortunately the only place name that Ottar provided in his travelogue, indicating that he sailed a known, fixed route. In his chronicle he described the normal duration of such a journey in an unusual, back-to-front manner, stating that he *could not* sail from his homestead to *Skiringssal* in the space of a month despite fair winds and sailing during the day and resting at night, thereby giving the impression that there had been harbours along his route. This peculiar formulation is perhaps best understood as an answer to questions which were put to him, such as, "Could the trip have been accomplished in the course of a month?" To which Ottar probably replied by saying how long it took him not to complete the trip. His answer may have been, "Perhaps I could have done so, but most likely not, not even with fair winds". Then the interrogator or scribe may have paraphrased the answer to give the text that has been handed down.

*Walrus tusks were traded and carved to make
valuable objects such as this beautiful bishop's crozier
from England.*

If the distance from Ottar's estate in *Hålogaland* to *Skiringssal* was roughly 950 nautical miles, or 1,750 km, his average speed would have been 2 knots had he sailed for 16 hours a day for 30 days. But given the length of the voyage, it is uncertain if even such a modest average speed could have been sustained. Ottar also provided another odd bit of information regarding his journey southwards along the Norwegian coast: "On the starboard side, one first had Ireland, followed by the islands that lay between Ireland and (England). Thereafter one had (England)on the starboard side until one reached *Skiringssal*." It would have been impossible for Ottar to have seen Ireland, the Orkney Islands, the Hebrides or England from his vessel since he was following the coast southwards. Apparently this piece of information was inserted in order to help Englishmen understand the text and travel route.

The trading town of *Skiringssal* has been rediscovered in modern times. Known as Kaupang because it is located on the grounds of the Kaupang farm at Viks Fjord southeast of modern-day Larvik, archaeologists have found objects which stem from the British Isles and the European continent, demonstrating the important role Kaupang held as a centre of trade. Commerce must have been flourishing when Ottar visited *Skiringssal*, which was an important harbour for the

export of soapstone products. Apart from bartering Arctic products, it is not unthinkable that Ottar passed through *Skiringssal* to pick up a cargo of soapstone, which he knew could easily sell in the northern German town of Hedeby and in England.

Indeed, he set a course for Hedeby and then England from *Skiringssal*. Crossing the outer Oslo Fjord, he probably headed towards the Hvaler Islands, thereafter following the Swedish Bohuslän and Halland coasts in a southerly direction. He described the Oslo Fjord as follows: "South of *Skiringssal*, a very large lake stretches inland. It is wider than any man can ever look across and see the other side. And *Jutland* lies directly across on the other side and thereafter comes *Sillende*. This lake stretches into the land for many thousands of miles." The geography is quite well described, but the text's reference to *Sillende* has posed problems for researchers. Some believe that *Sillende* is modern-day Sjælland, while others contend that it coincides with the southern part of *Jutland*, or modern-

day Sønderjylland. Careful analyses of other chronicles indicate that the latter is correct.

Ottar said that it took five days to sail from *Skiringssal* to Hedeby, which was located at the head of the Schlei Fjord in southern Schleswig-Holstein, not far from present-day Schleswig. Ottar makes it clear that for three days he had Denmark on his port side, and the open sea on his starboard side. Apparently, in Ottar's time, Swedish Bohuslän, Hallan and Skåne were Danish possessions, as his unambiguous reference to having had *Denamearc* on his left-hand side while sailing down the Oslo Fjord cannot be interpreted in any other way.

After three days' sailing along the western coastline of modern-day Sweden, Ottar had to travel for two additional days before reaching Hedeby. He had probably crossed over

Skiringssal near Larvik was another important trading centre for Ottar.

towards Sjælland at Skälderviken and Kullen in Skåne, and then sailed northwards around the headland Sjællands Odde. It is uncertain on which leg of his journey he passed the island of Fyn. Either he sailed through the Storebælt strait or the Lillebælt strait. Today it is impossible to determine which course he selected. In any case, he journeyed toward the mainland, following the Schlei Fjord to Hedeby.

In the Viking era, Hedeby was the largest trading town in the Nordic region, and served as a junction for all the goods in transit between the North Sea and the Baltic Sea. For Ottar and his men, Hedeby must have appeared to be a very large town, and very different from *Skiringssal*. The houses were wooden, rectangular structures with storage sheds, workshops and, in some cases, rows of byres for cattle, and their gables faced the sea. The main and side streets were either at right angles to or parallel with the town brook. One of the main streets had a wooden bridge traversing the brook. Surrounding the town were formidable defensive earthworks erected by its inhabitants. The centre of the town – and of trade – was the marketplace. Hedeby's layout was similar to that of many towns in the late Middle Ages.

In his travelogue, Ottar said that *Hedeby* "lay between the Wends, Saxons and the Angles" and was a Danish possession. He stated that the Angles had lived in Denmark before settling in England. The Saxons, or *Seaxum* as they were called in the Old English text, had been the most important people of northern Germany since the 6th century A.D. The Wends, or *Wineda*, were a West Slavic people who inhabited a region in present-day Germany bordering on the Elbe River.

OTTAR'S UNKNOWN FATE

The fate of Ottar and his men after their visit to Hedeby is not reported in his chronicles. Did Ottar sail directly to England from Hedeby? Or did he return to King Alfred's court in connection with another trading voyage? It is likely that he sailed a direct route from his homestead in Hålogaland to Wessex, England. Perhaps the route was deemed too well known to mention in the travelogue.

The last certain traces of Ottar's travel route are found in Hedeby. If his travels to the White Sea, *Skiringssal*, Hedeby and Wessex are added together with at least the same number of days for his return journey, then he must have spent six months on his vessel. Ottar, the first Norwegian explorer to be identified by name, was clearly a man of the sea. Although he is largely unknown to the general public, he is nevertheless the first in a long line of important Norwegian maritime explorers.

Ottar disappeared from history after he presented his report to King Alfred. The story of Ottar was described exclusively in the text reproduced in King Alfred's Old English world history. Ottar is not mentioned in any of the later sagas. He was one of many traders who "discovered" and journeyed to foreign lands during the Viking era, but whose birth, childhood, family life and fate have been forever veiled by the mists of history. There is evidence that not even the saga writers of later periods had heard about Ottar.

GREENLAND

NORWEGIAN SEA

Disko

BAFFIN ISLAND

Hellu-
land

Vesterbygd

DAVIS STRAIT

Austerbygd

Brattalid

Kapp Farvel

ICELAND

Reykjavik

Torshavn

NORWAY

Markland
(Labrador)

L'Anse aux Meadows

NEW
FOUNDLAND

Dublin

London

Paris

Boston

?

ATLANTIC OCEAN

Rome

AFRICA

LEIF EIRIKSSON CA. 1000.

LEIF EIRIKSSON AND THE DISCOVERY OF AMERICA

BY ØYSTEIN KOCK JOHANSEN

Land emerged slowly from beyond the horizon. At first it seemed like a distant mirage, a vague outline that could easily be mistaken for far-off clouds. The crew gathered on the gunwale at the cry of "Land ho!", rubbing their eyes to make certain that what they saw was not an apparition. Some doubted the lookout's proclamation, while others agreed that it really was land on the horizon.

Doubt turned to certainty as the wind filled their sails and the boat drove forward towards the distant outlines. Land it was. Now they could all see the tall mountains and glittering white glaciers. The ship's owner and skipper was the young Leif Eiriksson. He could hardly contain his joy and relief at seeing the unnamed land that he had set out to find.

Leif decided to make landfall and cast anchor. Upon reaching a suitable landing spot, he ordered one of the tenders lowered, and went ashore with some of his men. However, they were not enthusiastic. According to the *Greenlander Saga*, Leif found the land too barren to settle, with no grazing for their livestock. From the beach to the snow-clad mountains stretched a vast, barren plain. Leif was nevertheless satisfied to

have gone ashore, and told crew that he intended to name the place *Helluland* (Stone-slab Land). Then he and his men reboarded their ship and sailed south.

After sailing for a few days, they sighted new land. They had heard of this unnamed place too, but as far as they knew it had never been visited by anyone before. Once again a tender was lowered, and when the captain and crew reached the shore they met a flat, forested landscape. As far their eyes could see there stretched a glistening white sandy beach and shallow waters. As before, the captain decided to name the land. According to the *Greenlander Saga*, Leif Eiriksson said, "I name the land for characteristics, and call it *Markland* (Land of Forests)". This was not a tempting place to settle either, so they made haste to continue their journey.

With a north-easterly wind, the captain and his men had fair weather and continued on a southerly course. Two days later, they sighted land yet again. They went ashore for the third time in beautiful weather. They looked around, nodding to one another, agreeing, "This is a good land!" Here they found game, salmon in the lake and river, and lush meadows of grass for their livestock. The sun's rays were reflected on the dewy grass. Some of the men bent down and collected the dew in their hands. Sipping it, they agreed that they had never tasted anything so sweet, and decided to settle there.

As soon as the tide rose, they floated the ship up river and cast anchor. They were eager to start work on a settlement. Swiftly they carried sacks ashore, let the livestock loose and began building a roof over their heads. Somewhat later Leif decided, in council with his men, that he wanted to stay the winter. So during the autumn they built large, warm homes, insulating the roofs and walls with the plentifully available turf. They explored the land, but went no farther than a day's march in order to return by evening. One day, one of the men, behaving as though he were drunk, claimed that he had found wild grapes. When spring came, they made their ship ready, stocked it with grapes and timber, and commenced their journey home. Before they left, their leader gave the land a name evocative of its bounty, *Vinland* (Wineland).

ARE THE SAGAS TRUE?

Although the description above owes a good deal to the imagination, the sagas provide objective and realistic written evidence of the discovery of North America. This took place around 1000 AD, and the man who led the expedition was called Leif Eiriksson. His voyage, however, has been shrouded in myth and uncertainty until quite recently. Are the sagas true? Was the land that the Viking chieftain Leif Eiriksson discovered present-day North America? And if so,

The ruins of Leif Eriksson's childhood home Brattalid on Greenland are still visible.

An amulet found at Brattalid decorated with Tor's hammer, proof that Leif's father Eirik Raude was a heathen. Leif's mother was a Christian and she had had a church built outside the farm's boundary fences.

have disagreed on his nationality, and both Norway and Iceland claim him as a native son. The chronology in this very early period of history is so uncertain that Leif could have just as well have been born in Norway as in Iceland. It is less likely that he was born in Greenland given that his father, Eirik, is thought to have fled to Greenland in 985–986 A.D. This would have made Leif Eiriksson a mere 15 years old when he discovered *Vinland* in the year 1000.

At all events, his father, Eirik the Red, came from Norway and brought his Norwegian culture and traditions with him into exile. Leif grew up in a Norwegian environment and as a member of an undisputedly Norwegian family. However, it is clear that by the time he discovered *Vinland,* he was considered a Greenlander. The written records give Greenland as the point of departure for the expedition.

Not much is known about Leif except that as the hero of the *Vinland Saga* he is described as good-looking, tall and strong. The way he planned and carried out the first voyage to *Vinland* shows considerable intelligence. The sagas also describe him as wise, exercising moderation in everything he did. After Eirik the Red's death, Leif inherited his father's social status and became the most important leader in Greenland. He enjoyed both wealth and honour, and his nickname meant "happy" or "lucky". Since nothing is mentioned in the sagas, it is likely that Leif died of old age in Greenland.

Perhaps the most important cause of the uncertainty surrounding Leif Eiriksson's *Vinland* voyage is that there are

where do *Helluland, Markland* and *Vinland* lie? Who was Leif Eiriksson? Where was he from? These and related questions have preoccupied both laymen and scholars for many years.

The man who is regarded as the discoverer of the New World was, as his name indicates, the son of Eirik, nicknamed "the Red" (*Eirikr raudi* in Icelandic or *Eirik Raude* in Norwegian). Eirik the Red was a pugnacious man from Jæren in south-western Norway. After committing murder, he had to flee his homeland for Iceland, where he settled. A few years later, in about 985-986 AD, the hot-tempered Eirik had to flee Iceland because he had again committed several murders. He sailed westwards and discovered a new land he called Greenland, where he settled.

No one knows when or where Leif Eiriksson was born. Since his father lived in three different countries, researchers

The controversial map of Vinland from ca 1200 AD, showing Leif Eiriksson's journey.

sagas, the *Greenlander Saga* and *Eirik the Red's Saga*, both written in the 13th century, are regarded as the most complete and important sources.

The oldest sources are the least detailed. *Vinland* is first mentioned in Adam of Bremen's work, *Gesta Hammaburgensis ecclesial* (*The Archbishop of Hamburg's History*), which was written around the year 1075 A.D. In it, the scholar Adam, giving the Danish king Svend Estridssøn as the source, states that many people had found an island called *Winland*. The island was named after the wild grapes that grew there. *Winland* was also said to have an abundance of wild wheat. Adam does not specify who discovered *Winland*, so that Leif Eiriksson's name does not appear.

The oldest Icelandic information about *Vinland* is found in the *Islendingabok* (*The Book of Icelanders*), written by Are Frode around 1130 A.D. *Vinland* is mentioned in passing when the author, describing the colonisation of Greenland by Eirik the Red, writes that Eirik and his men found traces of an indigenous people whom they believed to be similar to the inhabitants of *Vinland* and whom they called *skrælling*. It is rather striking that the oldest Norwegian history – *Historia Norvegiae* – which was probably written towards the end of the 12th century, makes no mention of *Vinland*, although there is a reference to islands in the far west of Europe, not far from Greenland.

The *Greenlander Saga* and *Eirik the Red's Saga* give most information about the discovery of *Vinland*, but are difficult to interpret for various reasons. The written manuscripts are based on older sources, which themselves were written down some two hundred years after the events that they describe. The texts must be read with a critical eye, as folklore such as the sagas may well be altered in the telling from generation to generation. The difficulties are not lessened by the fact that the *Greenlander Saga* and *Eirik the Red's Saga* give two different versions of the discovery of *Vinland*. Despite these problems, it seems proved beyond doubt that the Norsemen did discover North America about a thousand years ago.

With this starting point, the written sources and the archaeological evidence can be further examined to learn more

several chronicles about the land and its discovery, and they do not always agree. This has given rise to uncertainty and confusion. Archaeological finds in the past few decades lend support to some of the assertions in the chronicles. Quite apart from written and archaeological proof, it would seem to be common sense to assume that sooner or later, Norse seafarers of the Viking era would have discovered North America, whether by accident or purposefully. When Norsemen found Greenland and established a settlement there, North America became their closest neighbour. From Norway to Greenland is a distance of roughly 1,500 nautical miles across the treacherous North Atlantic. By contrast, the Davis Strait between Greenland and North America is only 250 nautical miles wide at its narrowest point. Given the geography and the Vikings' taste for adventure, it would have been almost impossible for Greenland's adventurous Norsemen *not* to have discovered and set foot upon the North American continent about a thousand years ago.

HOW RELIABLE ARE THE WRITTEN SOURCES?

Some of the written sources are rather fragmentary, while others are much more complete and detailed. Two Icelandic

"Land ho!" Perhaps this is what Leif and his crew saw.
Below: A page from the Greenlander Saga.

about the discovery of North America and narrow down the possible areas where Norsemen first went ashore. The *Greenlander Saga* is the older of the two sagas, probably dating from 1200 A.D., while *Eirik the Red's Saga* was probably written in the second half of the 13th century. The *Greenlander Saga* recounts five expeditions to *Vinland*, but *Eirik the Red's Saga* mentions only two. According to the former, an Icelandic merchant, Bjarni Herjolfsson, and his men were the first to discover the new continent, without going ashore, when they were blown off course in 986 A.D. Bjarni's information about the new land to the west was the reason for Leif Eiriksson's deliberate search for it. Leif Eiriksson is considered to be the real discoverer of North America because he and his men went ashore and over-wintered. *Eirik the Red's*

Saga, on the other hand, attributes the discovery of *Vinland* directly to Leif Eiriksson, describing how he was blown off course while sailing from Norway to Greenland. Bjarni Herjolfsson's observations are not mentioned.

Thus, there are two versions of the discovery of *Vinland*, but Leif Eiriksson is the main protagonist in both chronicles. In the older version, his discovery is based on an earlier sighting of the country. Below is a brief summary of both texts.

THE GREENLANDER SAGA

1. Bjarni Herjolfsson sailed from Iceland for Greenland in A.D.986 , but was driven off course. After several days at sea, he sighted unknown coasts. He sighted land three times, but did not go ashore. Afterwards he found his way to Greenland.

2. Leif Eiriksson bought Bjarni's ship. With a crew of 35 men, he set out around A.D.1000 to find the land Bjarni had sighted. He discovered *Helluland*, *Markland* and *Vinland*. He built several houses in *Vinland*, spending winter there. The following year he returned to Greenland.

3. Leif's brother, Thorvald, set out for *Vinland* with a crew of 30. He settled in the buildings that Leif had built. Thorvald and his men remained in *Vinland* for two years. Thorvald was killed by *skrælling* (indigenous people).

4. The Icelandic chieftain Thorfinn Karlsefni was married to Leif's sister Gudrid, and travelled to *Vinland* with a contingent of 60 men. They settled in Leif's house. During the course of their two-year stay, they traded and fought with the *skrælling*. Thereafter they returned to Greenland.

5. Frøydis Eiriksdottir, another of Leif's sisters, equipped an expedition headed for *Vinland*. Internal dissent and a murder led to their return to Greenland after one year.

EIRIK THE RED'S SAGA

1. Leif Eiriksson sailed from Greenland to Norway to visit the court of Olav Tryggvason, who bestowed great honours upon him. The king asked Leif to introduce Christianity to Greenland. On his return voyage to Greenland, around A.D. 1000, he was blown off course and tossed around on the stormy sea, at last finding an unknown land where grapevines and fields of wild wheat grew. The same year he continued his voyage to Greenland, saving the lives of a shipwrecked crew on the way. Leif took the men to Greenland and christened the population. From then on he was called Leif the Lucky.

2. Icelandic Thorfinn Karlsefni decided to travel to *Vinland* because he had heard of the good conditions there. He equipped three ships and manned them with a complement of 160 men and women as well as livestock. He discovered and named *Helluland* and *Markland,* and established a colony at the head of a fjord that he named *Straum Fjord*. Thorfinn sailed southwards until he reached a land he named *Hop,* where wild grapes and wheat grew in abundance. There the colonists traded and fought with the *skrælling*. They stayed for three years and finally left for Greenland because of hostilities with the indigenous people.

These two summaries clearly show the differences between the accounts. *Eirik the Red's Saga* claims that Leif Eiriksson was the first person to discover the "New World", while the *Greenlander Saga* states that Bjarni Herjolfsson was the first Norseman to sight North America's east coast. However, both texts assert that Leif Eiriksson was the true discoverer of North America because he was the first to go ashore.

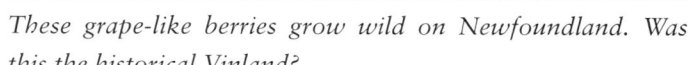

These grape-like berries grow wild on Newfoundland. Was this the historical Vinland?

THE GREENLANDER SAGA:
AN IMPORTANT SOURCE

Today, researchers largely agree that the *Greenlander Saga* is the original and most accurate rendering of the discovery of *Vinland*. There is much to indicate that the author of *Eirik the Red's Saga* knew about the *Greenlander Saga*, but deliberately omitted any mention of Bjarni Herjolfsson to ensure that Leif Eiriksson and no other became known as the discoverer of *Vinland*, on a voyage from Norway. The claim that Leif was asked to bring Christianity to Greenland is dubious, and probably stems from the *Olav Tryggvason Saga*. It was probably incorporated into *Eirik the Red's Saga* in order to ensure the king's fame. As the *Greenlander Saga* is regarded as the most accurate historical source, a translation of the section recounting Leif's discovery of North America follows below.

Leif, the son of Eirik the Red of Brattahlid, sought out Bjarni Herjolfsson and purchased his ship. He then hired a crew of 35 men. Leif asked his father Eirik to head the expedition. Eirik gave in to Leif's urgings and, when they were almost ready, set out from his farm on horseback. When he was a short distance from the ship, the horse that he was riding stumbled and threw him, injuring his foot. Eirik then spoke, "It is not my fate to find any other land than the one where we now live. This will be the end of our travels together."

Eirik returned to Brattahlid and Leif boarded his ship with his 35 companions. One crew member was a man called Tyrkir who came from a more southerly country (Germany). Once the ship was ready, they put to sea and found the land that Bjarni and his companions had seen. They sailed up to the shore, cast anchor, lowered a boat and rowed ashore. They found no grass; large glaciers covered the highlands and the landscape was like a single flat slab of rock from the glaciers to the sea. The land seemed of little use to them. Leif proclaimed: "At least we have gone ashore, unlike Bjarni. I shall now name this land and call it Helluland." Then he and his men rowed back to their ship.

They sailed on and found another land. Again they rowed ashore. The landscape was flat and covered with forests, and there were white sandy beaches and shallow waters as far as the eye could see. Leif spoke: "This land shall be named for what it has to offer. I call it Markland." Then they returned to the ship without delay.

They sailed on with a north-easterly wind for two days before sighting land again. They sailed towards it and came to an island to the north of the mainland. The weather was good and they went ashore, noticing that there was dew on the grass. Some of the men bent down to collect the dew in their hands. Tasting it, they agreed that they had never tasted anything so sweet. They re-boarded their ship and sailed into a sound that lay between the island and the headland that stretched northwards from the mainland. They rounded the headland and steered westward. There their ship was stranded in the shallow waters of the low tide, and the sea seemed very far away to those on board.

Their curiosity to see the land was so great that they could not wait for the incoming tide to float their stranded ship, and ran ashore along a river that flowed from an inland lake. When the tide came in, they took their boat and rowed to the ship, moving it up the river to the lake, where they cast anchor. They carried their sleeping bags ashore and built shelters. Later, when they had decided to spend the winter there, they built large houses.

Salmon was plentiful in both the lake and the river, and it was larger than any salmon they had ever seen. It seemed to them that the land was so bountiful that the livestock would need no fodder during the winter. The temperature never dropped below freezing and the grass only withered slightly. The days and nights were fairly equal in length, unlike in Greenland or Iceland. In the depth of winter the sun was aloft by mid-morning and still visible at mid-afternoon.

When they finished building their houses, Leif spoke to his companions, "I want to divide our company into two groups, as I want to explore the land. One half is to remain at home by the houses while the other half explores the land. They must never go any farther than they can return the same evening and no one is to separate from the group." Leif sometimes accompanied his men, and other times remained by the houses. He was a large, strong, striking man, and he was wise and exercised moderation in all things.

One evening the southerner Tyrkir was missing from the company. Leif was very upset, as Tyrkir had spent many years with him and his father, and had treated him very affectionately as a child. Leif criticised his companions harshly, and prepared to go and search for Tyrkir, taking 12 men with him. When they had gone only a short way from

At L'Anse aux Meadows on Newfoundland, Anne Stine and Helge Ingstad found what may be the remains of Leif Eiriksson's settlement. Inset: A spinning wheel, proof that the Vikings settled in Canada.

the houses, Tyrkir came towards them and they welcomed him gladly. Leif soon realised that the companion of his childhood was pleased about something. Tyrkir had a protruding forehead and darting eyes, with dark wrinkles in his face; he was short of stature and frail-looking, but was a master of all types of crafts. Leif asked him, "Why are you so late returning, foster-father, and how did you become separated from the rest?" For a long time Tyrkir only spoke German, his eyes darting in all directions and his face contorting. They understood nothing of what he was saying. After a while he said in Norse, "I had gone only a bit farther than the rest of you. But I have news to tell you; I have found grapevines and grapes." Leif asked, "Are you really sure of this, foster-father?" To which he replied, "I am absolutely sure because where I was born there was no lack of grapes or grapevines."

They went to sleep, and the following morning Leif spoke to his crew, "We will divide our time between two tasks, picking grapes and cutting vines one day, and then felling trees to take back home the next." It is said that the tender drawn behind the ship was filled with grapes, and that the ship itself was filled with timber. When spring came they made the ship ready and set sail. Leif named the land for its abundant vineyards, calling it Vinland. They headed out to sea and had favourable winds, sailing until they sighted the mountains beneath the glaciers of Greenland.

(*The Complete Sagas of the Icelanders,* Vol. I, Gen. Editor, Vidar Hreinsson, Leifur Eiriksson Publishing, 1997, pp. 22-23. The above text was translated from Icelandic into Norwegian by Finn Hødnebø.)

OUTSTANDING SEAMANSHIP

Leif and his companions were excellent mariners. Norse seamen were probably the most skilful sailors of the western world at that time. Many hundreds of years passed before equally talented and courageous mariners crossed the world's oceans again. The voyagers who explored Greenland, Iceland and *Vinland* navigated treacherous waters with unfailing precision. The exploits of Leif Eiriksson's successors, who found their way to *Helluland*, *Markland* and *Vinland* and even located the original settlement, were no less impressive. Sailing in open ships rigged with square sails, they defied all types of weather in daring expeditions which included women, children and livestock. They were in fact taking calculated risks, as the Viking ships were exceptionally seaworthy and their crews relied on long traditions of seamanship.

The names that the Norse Greenlanders gave to the parts of North America they discovered are no longer in use, which makes it difficult to pinpoint exactly which areas were discovered. Scholars have tried for years to locate *Helluland*, *Markland* and *Vinland*. Today there is a general consensus that *Helluland* is probably present-day Baffin Island, while *Markland* is Labrador's eastern coast. Both areas fit the descriptions in the sagas. The Norwegian archaeologist Helge Ingstad has even specified where he believed Leif Eiriksson made landfall. The Cape Aston area is in all probability what Leif called *Helluland*. Located on the east coast of Baffin Island, across from Greenland's Disco Island, Cape Aston is a wide, flat plain strewn with grey rocks, stretching from the sea to a high mountain chain with glaciers glittering in the background. It is situated at 70° N, where the Davis Strait is narrowest, and closely resembles the description of *Helluland* in the *Greenlander Saga*.

No area fits the Saga's description of *Markland* better than the Cape Porcupine region on Labrador's east coast. The land is flat and covered by pine forests right down to the shore, and the coastline features long white beaches. The *Greenlander Saga* relates that Leif went ashore on a flat,

forest-clad coast with white sandy beaches and shallow waters. Coming from a treeless country where timber for shipbuilding had to be imported from Norway, the Greenlanders must have been impressed by apparently endless forests, where game such as reindeer and bears wandered down to the water's edge. However, *Markland* was unsuitable for settlement because it lacked grazing for livestock. The Greenlanders therefore continued southwards until they came to *Vinland*.

VINLAND'S LOCATION ON NEWFOUNDLAND

It has proved more difficult to ascertain the location of *Vinland*. The suggestions have ranged from Hudson Bay in the north to Florida in the south. Strong arguments have been put forward for placing *Vinland* in New England, particularly the Boston area, or in Nova Scotia or around the Gulf of St. Lawrence. Researchers have generally considered theories that place *Vinland* far north on the continent to be the most more acceptable and scientific. However, the eminent Norwegian archaeologist Professor Anton W. Brøgger has rejected this. "(Such a standpoint) is unmethodical and illogical considering what we know of the Viking era. Once these young seafarers had found their way to America, there was nothing to stop them from travelling further southwards. There is no reason why they could not have reached both Virginia and the Carolinas, and even places further south."

Despite this, it has been accepted that *Vinland* was located on present-day Newfoundland. Anne Stine and Helge Ingstad located a settlement site at L'Anse aux Meadows, and ensuing excavations revealed remnants of Norse buildings, supporting the theory that Newfoundland was Leif Eiriksson's *Vinland*. The Ingstads uncovered remains of eight buildings, six of which were constructed of turf and up to 24 m in length. In addition, there were two smaller, partly subterranean houses, one of which was a forge. The turf houses are unmistakably Norse in character, and are related to Icelandic and Greenlander houses dating from the 11th century. Objects found in the settlement area, such as a spinning wheel and a ring-headed pin, prove that this was a Viking settlement. Carbon dating indicates that the site was used around the year 1000 AD, the time of Leif's discovery of *Vinland*.

Norse silver coin showing Olav Kyrre (1065-1080), found in Maine, USA

OTHERS FOLLOWED

It is hard to believe that this is mere coincidence. The homesteads at L'Anse aux Meadows are probably the last traces of Leif Eiriksson's settlement, but, as with most archaeological theories, this is very difficult to prove conclusively. Whether or not the settlement at L'Anse aux Meadows was Leif Eiriksson's, it is certainly irrefutable evidence that Norse seamen found North America and settled there around 1000 A.D.

Leif's discovery whetted the appetites of other explorers, among them Thorfinn Karlsefni. Thorfinn made a serious attempt to colonise the land, but gave up after encounters with the fierce indigenous people. Written sources document considerable traffic between Greenland and North America, particularly during the 13th century, as easy access to timber enticed the Vikings to journey to America. There is also solid archaeological evidence that Norsemen visited the New World after Leif Eiriksson. For example, a Norwegian silver coin from the reign of King Olav Kyrre (1066-1080) was unearthed in Brookline, Maine. There is absolutely no sign that the coin had been planted or of any other kind of fraud. In addition, a number of objects that are unmistakably Norse in origin have been found in North America, mainly in Canada.

NAVIGATION IN THE VIKING ERA

The sagas and archaeological finds leave no doubt that Norsemen made their way to North America during the Viking era and the Middle Ages, overcoming formidable obstacles to do so. Such voyages required skilful seamanship, a good deal of courage and, above all, navigational skills. The Viking explorer Ottar sailed mainly along the coast, repeatedly indicating in his travelogue that he had land either on his port or starboard side. As long as they followed the coastline or kept in sight of land, it was fairly easy for the Vikings to navigate. Once they ventured into the open sea the situation became much more difficult.

At sea, the Norsemen continued to use the traditional knowledge gained during coastal voyages and handed down from generation to generation for hundreds of years. They used indicators such as seabirds flying out to fish in early morning, the colour of the sea and the temperature of the water. The route to Greenland lay between the Faeroe Islands and Iceland, close enough to land to see birds and whales. Sightings of mountains, such as the inland ice of Greenland, were also important navigational aids.

THE EARLIEST TOOLS

An important new development during the Viking age was the compass card, a disc-shaped wooden instrument with a hole in the middle. On the underside of the hole was a vertical rod used as a handle, and on the top a vertical stick used for navigating. On the edge of the disc, which could be rotated round the handle, were 32 notches corresponding to the 32 markings on a compass. In overcast weather, the Vikings used a *solarstein*, a mineral called calcspar. When held vertically, this caught the sun's polarised rays, making it possible to determine the direction of the sun. The Vikings also used a traditional deep-sea sounding lead to stay on course, and even relied on ravens as guides to lead them to shore.

Anyone who has crossed the North Atlantic in winter must wonder how the Vikings managed to sail the stormy ocean in open boats with women, children and livestock on board. The answer is that they did not sail during winter. All voyages in northern waters came to a halt in the winter due to unpredictable weather, gale-force winds, treacherous seas, ice floes and sub-zero temperatures, and the danger of

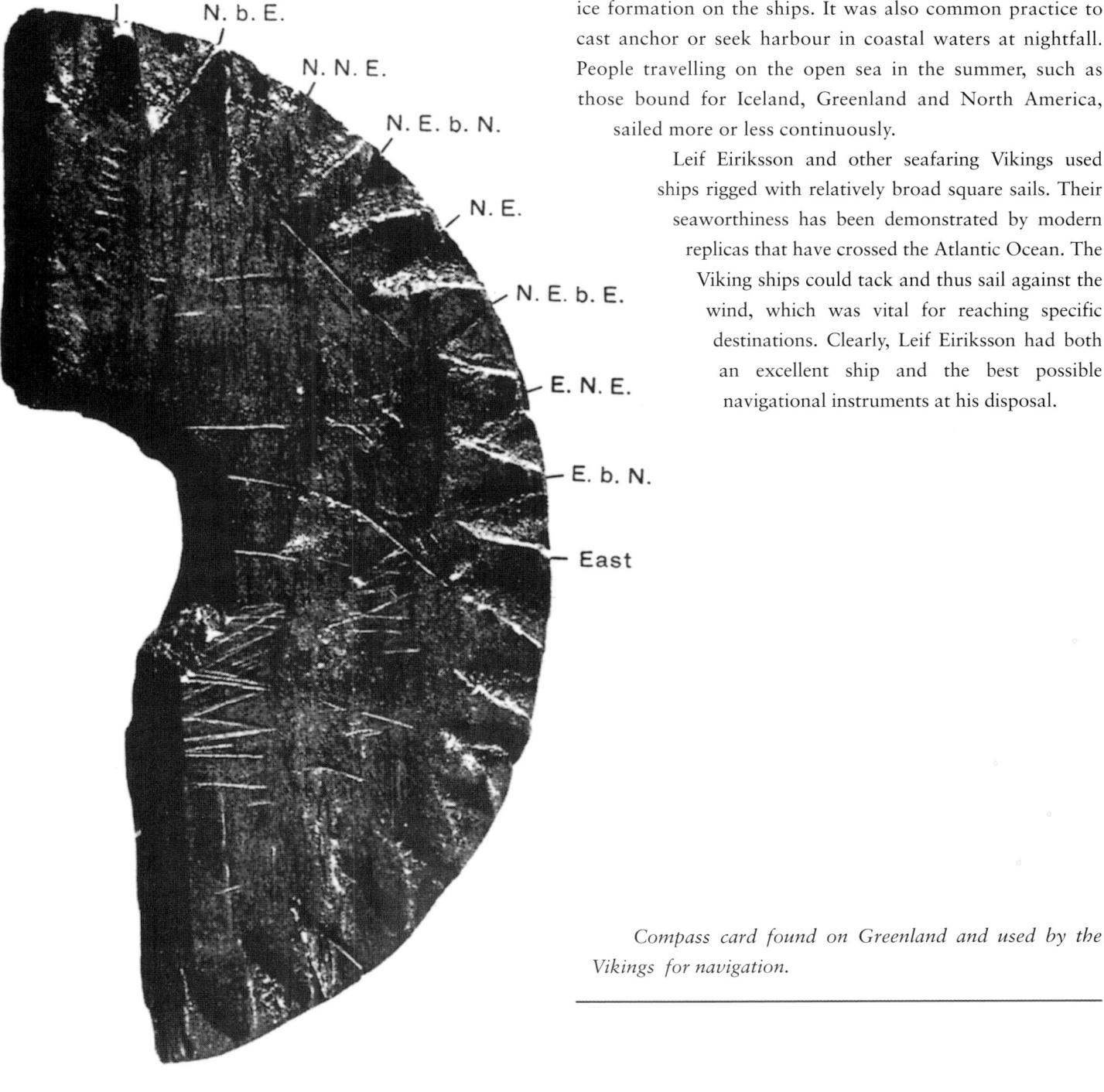

ice formation on the ships. It was also common practice to cast anchor or seek harbour in coastal waters at nightfall. People travelling on the open sea in the summer, such as those bound for Iceland, Greenland and North America, sailed more or less continuously.

Leif Eiriksson and other seafaring Vikings used ships rigged with relatively broad square sails. Their seaworthiness has been demonstrated by modern replicas that have crossed the Atlantic Ocean. The Viking ships could tack and thus sail against the wind, which was vital for reaching specific destinations. Clearly, Leif Eiriksson had both an excellent ship and the best possible navigational instruments at his disposal.

Compass card found on Greenland and used by the Vikings for navigation.

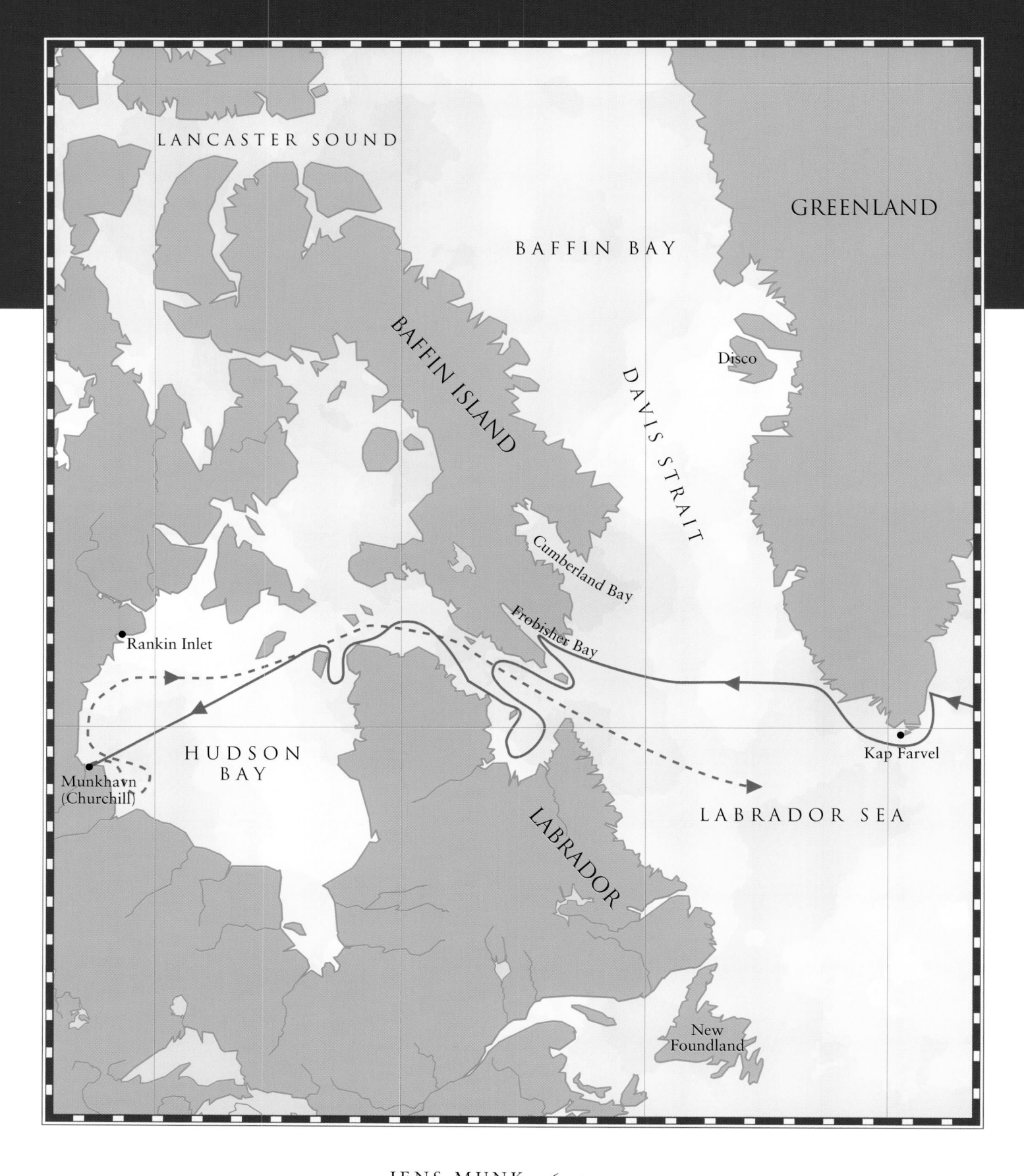

LANCASTER SOUND

GREENLAND

BAFFIN BAY

Disco

BAFFIN ISLAND

DAVIS STRAIT

Cumberland Bay

Frobisher Bay

Rankin Inlet

HUDSON BAY

Munkhavn (Churchill)

Kap Farvel

LABRADOR SEA

LABRADOR

New Foundland

JENS MUNK 1619–20.

JENS MUNK AND THE HUNT FOR THE NORTHWEST PASSAGE

BY HENRIK ULVEN

The treacherous sea to the east and north of Canada has tempted merchants, pirates and adventurers from the time of Italian-Englishman John Cabot who was forced to abort his expedition at 56 degrees latitude N. Cabot returned to England alive, but members of a great many expeditions did not. The sea in the area has been described as a labyrinth of shallow sounds, underwater shoals and violently whirling waters. Stormy and dark most months of the year, this stretch of water, which lies in North America between the Atlantic and the Pacific Oceans, drew adventurers looking for a shortcut to the riches of the Far East. One of the many who attempted to find a passage through the ice-bound wasteland was a Norwegian called Jens Munk, who risked life and limb for the Danish King Christian IV.

The year was 1620. The Arctic winter had not loosened its hold on Hudson Bay. It was June and temperatures remained below freezing, depleting the lifeblood of the last few members of the ship's crew. Out of 65 strong, hardened men only the captain, Jens Munk, and the sailmaker were tenuously holding onto life in the *Einhiørning's* (the *Unicorn's*) cabin. Munk was under the impression that a total of 63 men had died. Painful death by scurvy had turned life during the winter months at Hudson Bay into hell on earth. What was to have been a triumphant voyage to the Pacific Ocean through the Northwest Passage, to the silk, pearls and spices of China and India, had turned into desperate isolation in a deserted wasteland on which Western man had never before set foot. The last of the fish oil used to light the ship's lamp was burning. Soon it would be liberatingly cold, dark and silent. Jens Munk marshalled the last of his remaining strength and reached into his coat to take out his inkpot. Looking for his goose quill, he reached for his

Fortunately, Jens Munk would prove to have been overly hasty in taking his leave. By incredibly good fortune, he managed to return to civilisation and publish the account of his hunt for the Northwest Passage in 1624, in a book titled *Navigatio Septentrionalis*. His exploits and accomplishments place him unquestionably among the heroes of Norwegian maritime history.

FROM PRINCE TO PAUPER

Who was Jens Munk? He was a rather quiet, but nevertheless authoritative and fearless leader. Born on 3 June 1579 to a distinguished Danish family on the Barbo Estate near Arendal, Norway, his father, Erik Munk, was a powerful overlord. He, too, was a bold captain, and had assumed command of naval vessels along the Norwegian coastline and in the Polar Sea in many battles against the English. As a young man he had been the palace bailiff in Vardøhus in northernmost Norway, a county where he spent most of his life. But Erik Munk's aristocratic rank would become the bane of Jens Munk and his family. Since Munk's mother was neither an aristocrat nor legally married to his father, they ran afoul of the Reformed clergy 's laws. When Jens was the tender age of seven, Erik Munk was thrown into the infamous Dragsholm prison just outside of Copenhagen. The once-proud aristocrat was exposed to years of humiliation, and finally took his own life in prison in 1593. At once Jens Munk's social status plummeted, and he was considered a bastard. However, having known wealth and pride, it became his ambition to regain the splendour of his former life.

Jens Munk spent his early years at Fredrikstad, hanging about on the pier where schooners from far-off places docked. There were almost no roads in 17th-century Norway, and most transport of goods took place by sea. Jens had heard stories about Columbus and his expeditions to the New World. More than once he imagined his dinghy turning into a caravel carrying 20-pound cannons and sailing to Denmark to liberate his father, before setting course for the New World. Jens' mother was intent on giving her son an education. He spent two years at Aalborg, Denmark at the home of his paternal aunt who was married to the mayor. But he was homesick for Fredrikstad. He missed sailing in the Hvaler archipelago and he missed the sea breeze that would eventually lead him to faraway, uncharted places.

Jens Munk at an audience with Christian IV, King of Denmark. Only two likenesses of Munk exist, and neither gives us any real idea of what he looked like.

diary, a leather-bound volume embossed with the title, *Captain Jens Munk's Description of the Voyage of 1619*. In deep concentration, he whispered to himself as he wrote the following sentences in a delicate hand:

Because I no longer have any hope of continuing to live in this world, I ask, for the sake of God, that in the event that any Christian men should chance to come here, may they bury my poor remains in the earth along with the others who are here on the ship and on land. God in heaven will reward them for this. And I ask that my diary be brought to the attention of my most gracious Lord, the King. Each word found in it is true. May my poor wife and children benefit from my exertions and hardships and pitiable death. With this I bid the world goodnight and lay my soul in the hands of God.

When Munk returned to Fredrikstad in 1591, he was a well-mannered twelve-year-old who had completed primary school. Since his mother was unable to support him, he quickly found out that he had only himself to rely on. He was hired on a Frisian ship, which happened to be at the harbour ready to sail for Portugal with a cargo of wheat, stockfish and herring. From the ship he waved goodbye to his mother, whom he would never see again. From then on the sea would be the place where he would make his impact on the world. During seven years at sea, he literally learned the ropes, absorbing as much about seamanship as he could.

Jens Munk's next base was Copenhagen. A city of 20,000 inhabitants, it had a world-wide reputation as an urbane place. Munk advanced quickly, becoming the commander of a unit in the Danish Royal Navy. He had always had a keen interest in the northernmost seas. His father had told him about the enormous populations of whale and walrus off of Norway's northern coast. At the time, both sea mammals and fish were growing in commercial significance. Even King Christian IV

Copenhagen at the time of Jens Munk, approx. 1600.

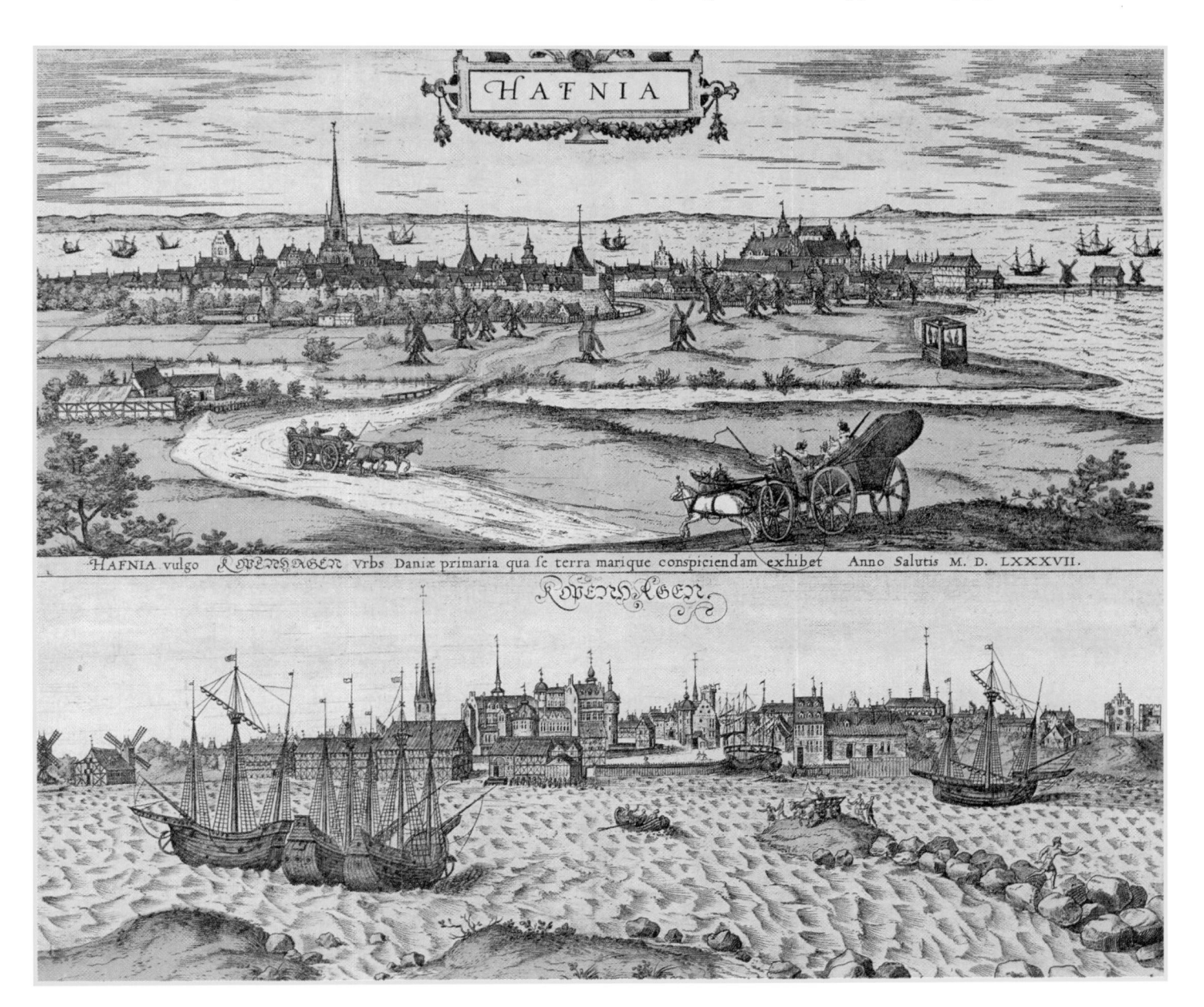

This portrait of King Christian IV is from 1612, around the time when the King was first introduced to Jens Munk.

---

had voyaged to Vardøhus to inspect conditions for himself. At this time Munk's reputation began to grow as tales of the ambitious 30-year-old captain's bravery were spread. Among them was the account of his miraculous rescue of the entire crew of a ship that had gone down when crushed by Barents Sea pack ice near Novaya Semlya. Hearing the account, the King concluded that Munk was the right man to chart the presence of whales, walruses and other sought-after natural resources in northern waters.

Munk and the Danish monarch were, in fact, thinking along the same lines. An underlying idea behind commission was the hope of locating the Northeast or Northwest Passage in order to find a shortcut to China. In the 16th century, Portugal and Spain controlled the shipping lanes to Southeast and Southwest Asia. For some time Asia had been a veritable

goldmine for Europe's maritime nations. The trade in silks, spices, pearls, porcelain and other precious goods yielded huge profits. The problem was that the journey around Africa's Cape of Good Hope was long and perilous, as well as under Portuguese and Spanish control. Thus the search was on for a passage in the northern latitudes which would provide a shorter route to the Asian continent. There had been several attempts to find such a waterway. One took place in 1607 when the English captain Henry Hudson discovered Svalbard, an unknown land, where he found a large population of whale. Inspired by his account, both English and Dutch vessels stepped up their exploration of the northern regions. King Christian IV also took up the challenge, fully intent on demonstrating the Danish-Norwegian kingdom's interest in these territories.

In May of 1610 the naval ship *Angelibrand* set a course for Novaya Semlya with a commission from the King to find the Northeast Passage and to hunt for seal and walrus, as well as to survey the number of whales. On board was the skipper Jens Munk and a 16-man crew. Passing Vardøhus, Munk followed an easterly course toward uncharted territory, supposedly in the direction of China. The winter had been unusually cold, and drift ice covered the water. They passed Kildin Island, forcing their way through the ice as far toward land as possible. Finally, Munk had to yield to the overwhelming superiorioty of the pack ice. He understood that it was terribly important not to lose a major naval vessel, and thus fall out of favour with the monarch. Not having sighted whales and returning with only stockfish, the expedition was a complete failure.

HUNTING FOR PIRATES

Shortly after this debacle, war broke out with Sweden, and Christian IV was forced to concentrate on other pressing matters. The King assigned Jens Munk to carry out an important task, and Munk distinguished himself during the siege and conquest of Gothenburg. Later he was commissioned to protect the northern Norwegian coast from the pirates who were hunting whales for their valuable oil. After a dramatic chase, the most infamous pirate of all, Jan Mendoza, and his gang of 60 freebooters were taken prisoner off the coast of the Kola Peninsula. Jens Munk's skilful negotiations and wisdom decided the outcome of the encounter. The description of the

Many maritime nations sent whaling expeditions to the seas off the coast of Northern Norway (17th-century painting.)

intrepid Mendoza makes for a tale in its own right. A swashbuckling buccaneer, Mendoza dressed in a silk uniform with gold embroidery on his jacket and shoes! Even in the Polar Sea, rules of elegance were not set aside. With the capture of Mendoza and a number of other whale-poachers, Jens Munk seized seven large ships filled with valuable fish and whale oil, gold, and sundry objects. He was given a hero's welcome upon reaching Copenhagen, while Mendoza became

the first man to hang on a gibbet. Munk was paid a sizeable bonus for his booty, and for the first time in his adult life, he was a rich man.

In 1616 the Danish East India Company was founded, and King Christian IV's earlier plans to send Danish ships to India were ressurrected. In 1619 Christian IV bestowed an extraordinary honour upon Jens Munk, commissioning him to lead an expedition to India. In the end, however, Munk was unceremoniously set aside in favour of Ove Giedde, a young inexperienced nobleman. Giedde was given five ships to sail around Africa's Cape of Good Hope. Munk's consolation prize was two ships with which to find a sea passage north of the

American continent. A difficult task, Munk regarded it as a race to see who would reach India first.

Ove Giedde's crew numbered several hundred men. Jens Munk had to be grateful for his 60-some men and two vessels, the *Enhiørning* armed with 12-pound bronze cannons and the *Lampren* (*the Lamprey*), a small but fast sloop. The combination of the two vessels was ideal for the expedition. The *Lampren,* with which Munk was familiar, was perfect for reconnaissance and navigation in difficult shallow waters.

PREPARING FOR THE EXPEDITION

The 61 members of the crew were carefully selected. Munk knew the significance of an expert company of men, as the sinking of his vessel at Novaya Semlya had taught him a valuable lesson. Despite the plague and other obstacles, in April of 1619 he managed to sign on a good complement composed of toughened seamen who came from all parts of Denmark and Norway. Some were so young and agile that they could easily climb the masts to reef the topmost square sails. The battery manning the cannons was selected for their ability to assemble the cannons below deck, should the need arise in the event of a pirate attack. These were men who had sailed before, and some had even been to China. Due to the Black Plague, Munk found it difficult to locate a clergyman or a barber. The latter was a very important crewmember who combined cutting hair and beards with amputations and other types of surgery. Two German barber-surgeons, Kaspar Kasparsen and David Volske, came on board at the last minute. They each had considerable experience attending to battlefield casualties, but they had never sailed before nor dealt with the insidious effects of scurvy. Munk selected two Englishmen to serve as mates, William Gordon as first mate and John Watson as mate. Both had sailed in Arctic waters, and Watson may well have been on an earlier expedition to Hudson Bay. Also on board was Munk's nephew, Erik, whom Jens Munk wanted to help onto a career in the Danish navy, which was sadly short-lived.

No drawing of the Enhiørning remains, but the vessel was very similar to this frigate, the Norwegian Lion.

The provisions and stores were brought on board. Worn-out shoulders carried sacks of flour, dried white and green beans, barrels of ship's beer, honey, mustard, salt-cured meat and herring. Fresh water was available only during the first weeks of the voyage. For the remainder, everyone had to content themselves with drinking unprocessed seawater. Jens Munk planned the expedition with great care. He made certain that the supplies included extra compass needles, wooden planks for ship maintenance, tools, axes, fishing nets and hooks, harpoons, hourglasses, gunpowder, cannon balls, extra ropes, tar, wax candles and whale oil, in sum, anything which he thought might prove to be useful in an unforeseen emergency. An important part of the cargo was made up of mirrors, bells, gilded decorative ornaments, glass beads, scissors and other objects which Munk had learned appealed to the Chinese, and with which hoped to barter were the expedition fortunate enough to reach China. Standing at the side of the ship with a list of provisions and stores, he crossed off items as they were borne on board. He did, however, underestimate one vital aspect of the journey. He did not view it as a rugged Arctic voyage. He, like many others of his time, assumed that the Northwest Passage would be found south of 62 degrees latitude N, roughly on a breadth with Bergen, Norway. There was no knowledge of the Gulf Stream and its warming effect. Although Hudson Bay *does* lie on the same latitude as temperate Bergen, it has a Siberian climate. After a brief church service in the presence of the King, the crew was given a blessing, and the expedition was on its way to the Northwest Passage.

On the other side of the ocean waited a land that few people knew well. The archipelago between the Canadian mainland and Greenland is the size of Europe and filled with bays, treacherous currents and underwater skerries. The Vikings who lived in Greenland had sailed this stretch of water, which they regarded as their own, but Jens Munk was unaware of this fact. He had undoubtedly heard about Henry

Hudson's travels, and most likely had an on-board copy of the 1612 map drawn by the Dutch geographer Hessel Gerritsz and based on Henry Hudson's voyages. However, the southern section of Hudson Bay was still uncharted territory.

CASTING OFF

Whitsun, 1619: Jens Munk was finally on his way. His mission was clear: the King wanted him to sail to Hudson Strait and into Hudson Bay. At some point along the southwestern coast of the bay, he would hopefully find the Northwest Passage. On 25 May the ships arrived at Lista on the southern coast of Norway, but the *Lamperen* was taking

in water and needed to be repaired in the town of Stavanger where a few new hands signed on. The final complement of men totalled 65 and they embarked on a fateful voyage on which just about everyone lost their lives. The day before Jens Munk turned 40 they passed the Shetland Islands. From then on Munk was travelling in unknown waters. On 15 June they sighted land for the first time. First Mate William Gordon

---

This painting shows two ships at Novaya Zemlya. The double sun is a well-known Arctic phenomenon, and is also mentioned in Munk's diary.

Jens Munk's vessel in the Hudson Strait, first at Caribou Sound, where he met the Eskimos, and then at Hare Sound. The Eskimos are depicted naked because the artist did not know what kind of clothing they wore.(Navigatio Septentrionalis, 1624)

confirmed that this was the eastern coast of Greenland, north of Cape Farewell, where he had been seven years earlier. (This was one of the reasons Munk hired him.) They had to break away from the strong ice drifts along the coast and cross the Davis Strait to North America.

At that point Jens Munk fully realised his serious miscalculation of the climate. It was an Arctic climate like the kind he had experienced in the Barents Sea, despite the fact that they were further south than the Barents Sea. The difference in nighttime and daytime temperatures was extreme. Munk wrote in his diary: *"At night there was so much fog and bitter cold that icicles formed during the night, one quarter long (15 cm), so that none of the people could protect themselves from the cold. But on the same day, before three in the afternoon, the sun shone so hard at the same point that the people threw off their (coarsely-woven) blouses and undershirts."* The vessels stayed at a safe distance from the enormous ice masses that were in the process of breaking up. Some of the newly formed glaciers were more than 75 m high. After 39 days, they reached the North American coast. Breaching the ice barrier, the two mates, Gordon and Watson, were certain that they had located

Hudson Bay. Munk, however, was unconvinced. The islands that signalled the approach to the bay were marked on the map, but they were not to be seen. After numerous errors, the crew discovered that they had been sailing in a deadend and proceeded to sail along the coast in a southerly direction.

In time they reached the southernmost point of present-day Resolution Island. Finding the islands at the mouth of the Hudson Strait; they were still ignorant of the fact that this was merely the approach to the bay. Jens Munk named the site Munk Headland, and went ashore in order to find water and shoot game. He shot three birds, but his weapon exploded in his face *"and took the rim in front of (his) hat"*. Lacking a secure haven for the ships, they cast off in order to escape the ice that had ominously beset the vessels during their short stop. It was too late: ice floes covered the entire bay, effectively closing it with no chance of breaking out. As the ice began to press against the sides of the two ships that were tightly lashed together, the level of tension on board rose palpably. The situation was critical. The ice masses pressed unremittingly, damaging the *Enhiørning*, although not beyond repair, which the carpenters were quick to undertake. Slowly, the ice began to yield and they were able to sail along its edge. But after two days, they again had to seek haven behind some islets in order to guard themselves against the ever-present ice floes. They went ashore to hunt, shooting some much-welcome caribou and naming the site Ren Sound. To their great amazement, a group of Eskimos appeared on the other side of the bay. Munk greeted them and they turned out to be peaceful hunters on the lookout for birds. Munk examined their very simple weapons and they exchanged gifts, at which time Munk gave away one of the mirrors. In return, the crew received birds and seal lard. Shortly thereafter, the Eskimos disappeared as silently as they had come. Later, Munk regretted not having attempted to ask for advice about coping with conditions in the region, and he even made an effort to find them again, but to no avail. This was the only time they met indigenous people on their voyage.

THE CLOSE EMBRACE OF THE ICE

Returning to their ships, they were again beset by the unyielding ice masses, although this time the consequences and drama were far more appalling. A gale-force storm blew up, and the ships, still lashed together, drifted helplessly wherever the tide took the pack ice. The pressure of the ice was so severe that the *Lampren*'s keel soon became visible above the waterline and the *Enhiørning*'s rudder was crushed. The vessels drifted between a number of islets and the mainland. *"More than ten pilots would have been needed to tow the ship,"* observed Munk in his account of the event. During the next few days, the ice did not yield its tight grip on the ships, and a break-up seemed imminent. The hull, lined with strong oak strakes, was like an eggshell held tightly in a clamp. The ice was so brutal that it was absolutely impossible to go ashore. They prayed for deliverance, and their prayers were answered. The currents pulled the ships into a bay that lay behind an islet, but the vessels nearly foundered when a mammoth iceberg calved in two, creating huge waves that washed over them. A few days of calm followed, during which the men hunted for hare, christening the place Hare Sound.

Unfortunately, a great deal of time had been lost. Winter was gaining on them, and it was imperative to complete their mission and find the Northwest Passage. First Mate William Gordon was now convinced that they were at the western end of Hudson Bay, and set a south-westerly course. Gordon was wrong, and they lost even more precious time. Munk was forced to intervene. It is not difficult to imagine that an ordeal of such magnitude must have created considerable fear, if not sheer panic, among the crew. After all, the men on Henry Hudson's ship had mutinied. However, Munk was undoubtedly a person who inspired confidence and trust. Before long the map and terrain were identical – they had arrived at Hudson Bay, at waters known as *Novum Marum,* or the New Sea.

Then the unthinkable happened. In dreadfully stormy weather with low visibility, the *Lampren* disappeared from view. It was impossible to search for her in the foul weather. The ships had a common course and a common point of rendezvous, so Munk stayed put. Without the *Lampren* to scout, any further travel was too hazardous. In this totally uncharted and unknown territory, Munk again displayed his superior seamanship. After a days-long crossing, they made landfall. Skilfully navigating the heavy ship through the hostile breakers, Munk sailed across Hudson Bay to a sheltered cove at present-day Port Churchill. Experienced captains have stated that they find it unfathomable that Munk succeeded in his manoeuvres. Even today, with the waters charted, surveyed and marked, this is considered one of the world's most difficult ports of call.

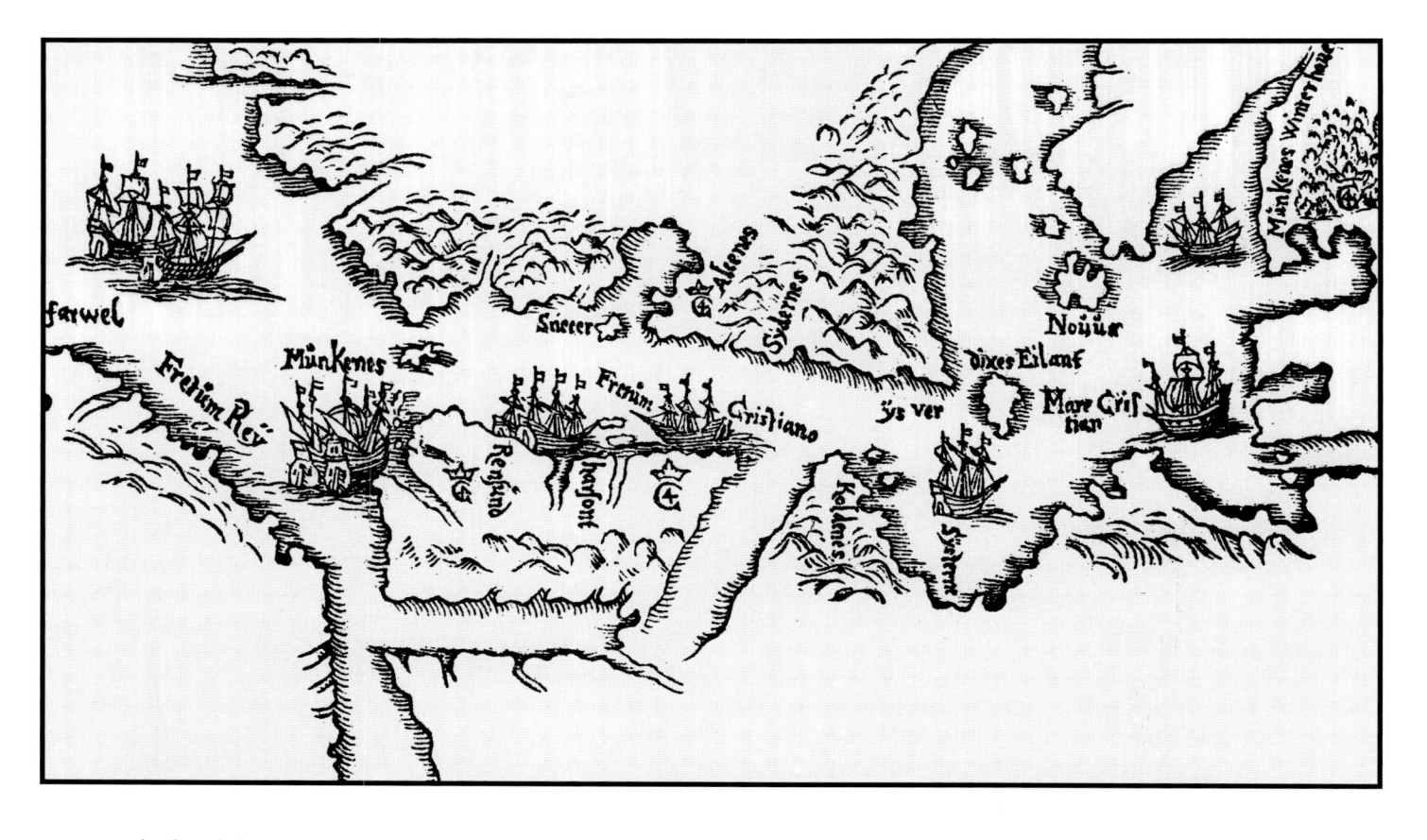

Jens Munk's hand-drawn map from Cape Farewell (Greenland) to the Hudson Bay, from the north. Munk Headland, Caribou Sound, Hare Sound and Munk Haven are all pinpointed. Munk has also drawn in the western coast of the Bay with a possible opening - a last hope of the existence of the Northwest Passage. (Navigatio Septentrionalis, 1624)

Once on shore, Munk ordered the lighting of a beacon to guide the *Lampren*. A huge bonfire was lit on a rock, and an entire night passed without a sign of the sloop. Finally the morning watch caught sight of a rig on the horizon, and the *Lampren* and the *Enhiørning* were reunited. The *Lampren*'s crew was in dismal shape, with many sick men. The early stages of scurvy were becoming apparent. Munk took the situation seriously. Since salted food was the mainstay of the men's diet, he had the sick brought on shore and fed them cloudberries and cranberries. They also managed to shoot a polar bear that supplied them with fresh meat for a few days, and gradually the men began to recover their strength. The date was 9 September and the search for the Northwest

Passage had to be undertaken immediately. The fact that winter was around the corner was becoming obvious with every passing day. They were one month behind schedule and it was clear that continuingthe journey would be much too hazardous. After a few days' reconnaissance to find a more secure harbour, the fateful decision was made: they would attempt to overwinter at what was quickly christened Munk Haven.

THE FATEFUL WINTER

The crew became very busy with the many preparations for staying the winter. The ships had to be secured and were brought up the Churchill River. The dramatic differences in ebb and flow, up to 10 m, caused the *Enhiørning* to rest on its keel. To prevent the ship from being wrecked, the men dug a dock out of mud and stones on which it could rest. The carpenters chopped logs for six large supports that were filled with stones to act as a buffer and relieve the pressure of the pack ice on the ship's sides. The *Enhiørning* was converted into winter quarters. The cannons were borne into the storage room, the ports shuttered and sealed, and the battery deck

Jens Munk's drawing of the winter harbour with the barracks on land. The scene includes men chopping trees, a corpse is being buried and a polar bear hunt. (Navigatio Septentrionalis, 1624)

transformed into a saloon for the crew. The men were divided into three groups of more than twenty. Each group was assigned tasks such as tending the fire in the fireplaces, melting snow, hunting, cooking and keeping watch. Finally, two lookout posts were built on a level with the ships. It took one month before they were ready to face the winter. They finished their work just in time: sub-zero temperatures had become a reality.

Munk kept hoping to meet indigenous people with the aim of securing some much-needed guidance about local conditions. But he saw none, finding only traces of deserted campsites. This was probably fortunate because the region was inhabited by the belligerent Chippewa and Cree tribes who were most likely keeping a close watch on the Danish-Norwegian intruders. One day the sailors shot what they believed to be a fox, but which turned out to be a dog, a clear sign that human beings were in the vicinity. During the autumn, the men enjoyed hunting the many ptarmigan, foxes and other small game which were a welcome supplement to their diet. They even had an opportunity to enjoy a few festive meals accompanied by the normally strictly-rationed wine and beer. Some took out their clay pipes and spirits were high. Up to that point they had performed well.

In mid-November winter was slowly but surely on its way. The first snowstorms made hunting impossible. They lacked fur clothing to protect them from the wind, as well as skis to inspect the traps that they had set on land. However, it was one event which more than any other struck fear into Jens Munk's heart: on 21 November one of the boatswains died. Munk made no mention of what carried the boatswain off. He did not have to, as it gradually became apparent which disease was beginning to rear its head. On 12 December, three weeks after the first fatality, David Volske, the barber cum surgeon, died. There could be no more doubt that scurvy was spreading among the men. A second coffin was constructed, and Minister Rasmus conducted the funeral service on land. *"The cold was so bitter that blisters froze on noses and chins,"* wrote Munk in his diary. He felt a genuine concern for his subordinates. Attempting to keep the crew's spirits up, he ordered them to prepare for Christmas. Thanks to a few days of good weather, they resumed hunting and chopping wood. Once the Christmas meal was secured, the barber shaved and cropped the crew's beards and hair, and the men changed into their cleanest blouses. With fires crackling in the wooden stoves and oil lamps glowing on the battery deck, the minister read the Christmas gospel. Then they all settled down to a Christmas meal of hare and ptarmigan, accompanied by beer served in tin mugs. The sense of foreboding was kept at bay for a little while.

Jens Munk wrote uninterruptedly in his diary about everyday life on board. The cold was so unbearable that even a Rostock barrel of water was frozen into a solid block of ice in the course of one night.

THE RAVAGES OF SCURVY

Death by scurvy, a disease caused by an acute lack of vitamin C found in fruits and fresh meat, is a dreadfully painful way to die. The first signs are fatigue and apathy, followed by bleeding mucous membranes and painful swelling of the gums and mouth. It does not require a very inventive mind to imagine the unbearable pain of chewing salted food under such conditions. The first symptoms are complicated by swelling of the joints and loosening of the teeth and nails. Death ensues shortly after, most often due to malnutrition or internal bleeding. The entire process takes place over a period of several miserable months.

On 8 January another boatswain passed away. The fateful months that passed and the indescribably painful symptoms

that were visited upon the men were carefully observed in Jens Munk's diary, illustrating his strong will to survive. The fact that his account was handed down is fortuitous; many travel diaries have never returned to the place from which their authors embarked on their journeys. Jens Munk's account is deposited at the Royal Library in Copenhagen. Among his observations, are the following:

10 January: Minister Rasmus Jensen and Surgeon Master Kasper Kaspersen took to their beds because they had been terribly sick for a long time. Thereafter there were daily outbreaks of disease among the people, (the outbreaks) becoming more and more predominant. On the same day my best cook died.

18 January: These days have been as mild as they sometimes are in Denmark at this time of year. Therefore all the healthy people were out in the meadows. Everyone had his task to accomplish, especially hunting to provide some ptarmigan for the sick.

23 January: My first mate, Hans Brok, died.

24 January: I had First Mate Hans Brok's body buried. I had two falconettes fire two salvos as a final display of honour. Then the pegs of both falconettes shot out, and the fellow who fired the cannons nearly lost both his legs; this is how fragile the iron had become after the very bitter, extreme cold.

27 January: Jens Helsing, boatswain, died.

2 Februar: There was a terrible frost. The people who were on land got hold of two ptarmigan, which were very welcome (nourishment) for the sick.

5 February: A boatswain named Laurits Bergen died.

13 February: I am passing on a message to the effect that every person should have a measure (2.4 dl) of wine at every meal during the day and a whole measure of spirits in the morning, in addition to the ordinary ration.

4 March: The weather was mild. Today we shot five ptarmigan in the woods and meadow. They were a very welcome sight. I had a soup made of these ptarmigan and had it dispensed to the sick. But they could not eat any of the meat because the inside of their mouths had been destroyed by scurvy.

Nearly every day people died of scurvy. One after the other, they were ceremoniously buried on land. On 17 February, 20

members of the crew died, and only seven survivors were able to get water from shore. The remainder lay dying, spread about on the battery deck and in the cabins. Again temperatures plummeted below zero, preventing the survivors from going ashore to bring vital water and wood on board.

Jens Munk's demonstrative display of care and respect for his subordinates went far beyond what could be expected of a captain of his time. He gave priority to tending the sick and was the first to try to help when others failed to do so. It was very clear to Munk that without a crew to sail the ships back, they were lost.

In mid-March there were a few days of mild weather, but most of the men suffered from sheer exhaustion and could not go on land. Therefore Jens Munk went ahead to look under the loose snow for cranberries and cloudberries. He found small quantities, not enough to stop the development of the disease. Nevertheless, he shared these with the men on board the ships.

On 30 March the freezing temperatures returned in full force, and the weakest men died one after the other. It was now difficult to bury the dead who were left to lie on the deck for several days. In April there was still no sign of spring, only a bitterly cold polar freeze. When May arrived, only Jens Munk and the cook's assistant were able to get out of bed. On 6 May John Watson died, the last of the mates. On 22 May, the weather warmed and they managed to shoot many wild geese migrating from the south. The geese provided a badly-needed meal for the seven surviving men, and a sign that spring was approaching. The ravages of scurvy were so great that crew's bodies turned blue and brown from excessive loss of blood, their teeth and nails were loose, their mouths bled, and all their strength was drained. On 28 May three more men died, leaving only four.

THE TURNING POINT

On 4 June Jens Munk had not eaten for four days, and lay under his bearskin in order to keep warm. Two men had left for shore, but had not returned. The only other survivor was a sailmaker, and he was dying. It was the first time that Munk conceded that the battle had been lost. Writing his last will and testament, he ended it with this pious wish: *"May my poor wife and children benefit from my exertions and hardships and pitiable death. With this I bid the world goodnight and lay my soul in the hands of God."* Unexpectedly, this was the turning point. Almost miraculously, spring came in full force. The wind turned southerly and blew away the remaining snow. In the cabin Munk gradually regained his strength, writing in his diary that he had crawled onto the deck on his bloody hands

Jens Munk's diary of the expedition and his last will and testament are in the archives of the Royal Library in Copenhagen.

that had lost their nails, and to his great surprise he had seen the two seamen who had gone ashore. It is difficult to say with any amount of certainty who these men were, since the crew list has been lost. But by using the list of the dead in Munk's diary, historian Thorkild Hansen has deduced that one of the two was probably Niels Skoster.

Now the three survivors had nothing to lose. Munk searched in vain for the berries that would provide them with the necessary vitamin C. Instead, they carefully sucked and chewed the roots of the green vegetation that was beginning to sprout, which would turn out to be their salvation. They regained some strength as the ice masses in Munk Haven began to loosen their hold on the ships. With great good luck, they manage to catch six magnificent trout in a net they found on the *Lampren*. They even had some wine left over and soon life looked a lot brighter. Somehow, though, it seemed to Munk a useless exercise to have saved their lives when the odds of their returning home were very slim. Their only chance would be to launch the small *Lampren* on the water and sail for home. When they had originally set out, the sloop had been manned by a crew of 16, and the larger boat by a crew of 65. Nevertheless, they wanted to try their luck. In two weeks they emptied the ship of its cannons, anchors, ballast stones and chests with sore and bleeding hands, until their energy was completely depleted. But the ship would not budge. At last, the forces of nature came to their aid: with the next full moon the tide came in and the ship slowly but surely began to budge. Jens Munk was once again a captain, even though his crew was reduced to two. Their boat rigged and ready to set sail, they gathered their provisions and bade farewell to the *Enhiørning* and their dead shipmates. Finally, they exited the fjord with their dinghy in tow, sending Munk Haven a last goodbye. But the way home would take longer than they could imagine.

Only one day after departure, the sloop was again in the grip of pack ice. The crew lost their dinghy and thus their means of reaching land to hunt and get water. A storm blew up and the sloop was almost crushed against the ice masses. At the very last minute, they managed to throw an anchor onto a close-by block of ice, which served effectively as a floating anchor. Their wounded hands smarting intensely as they worked the salty ropes. On 1 August they finally managed to free themselves from the pack ice; it was imperative that they

find their way out of the labyrinth before winter set in once again. Skerries and shallows hampered their progress; they had to constantly sound the waters in order to avoid running aground. They gingerly made their way through the ice, passing through narrows to emerge into the Hudson Strait. A favourable wind facilitated the sailing of the entire length of the strait in two days, a stretch that had taken them several months to cross on their way in. They passed Munk Headland at the entrance of Hudson Strait and arrived at Cape Farewell on the southern end of Greenland in fair, windless weather. For three days they relaxed before a hurricane blew in from the north. Its force was such that they had to tie themselves to the ship in order to prevent being swept out to sea. Bailing water with the ship's defective pumps, the tremendous winds blew them into open waters, where they floated like a cork. Exhausted, soaked to the bone and lacking nights of sleep, the symptoms of scurvy again began to manifest themselves. Fortunately, the currents, waves and wind were in their favour, and they make good speed to the south and Iceland, even though their mainsail and foresail were torn. Yet another storm rose, and this time the damage was more serious. First the topsail sheet tore, then the square sail was rent to shreds and finally the stay frayed. The catastrophe was complete when the mast went over board with a tremendous crash as they reached the Shetland Islands. *"This was an entirely embarrassing event for the three of us,"* Munk observed dryly in his diary. The peculiar thing is that on 9 September, the very day that the mast fell into the water, another boat was sailing west from Portsmouth, England, carrying 102 passengers, and battling the same storm that Jens Munk was riding out. Her name was the *Mayflower*, and she was bringing the first colonists to the New World.

FINALLY RAISING NORWAY

With its shredded sails fluttering in the wind, Jens Munk navigated the *Lamperen* through yet another stormy sea, soberly entering into his diary: *"On 20 September we saw Norway."* Approaching the Sogne Fjord, his and his crew had logged 67 days on the sea, most of which had been spent struggling to overcome the impact of frost, rain, storms, malnutrition and disease. Toothless and in ill health, they were badly ravaged by a second bout of scurvy. A farmer who happened to row past the ship was so terrified by the sight of

the three sailors – who no longer resembled men but wild animals – that he quickly rowed in the opposite direction. In a final desperate act, Munk seized his musket and threatened the man to help them ashore. The ship was tied up and the three collapsed on land, totally exhausted and drenched in tears.

Jens Munk's fate after the horrendous expedition to find the Northwest Passage was not much better than the voyage itself. Arriving in Bergen, Munk visited Knud Gyldenstjerne, a royal overlord who had never forgotten the son of his archrival, Erik Munk. Begging for mercy, Jens Munk was thrown into the Bergenhus prison, the terrible state of his health making no impression on Lord Gyldenstjerne. King Christian IV heard about the event and immediately ordered his release. Sending for Captain Munk, the King became furious upon hearing his report.

The loss of the *Enhiørning* was unacceptable to the King, and he ordered Munk to equip a new expedition in order to salvage the ship and colonise Hudson Bay. Fortunately, there was no return voyage to Munk Haven, but Jens Munk continued to serve his king until his own death in 1628. He led several other expeditions, and in 1624 he published his diary under the title, *Navigatio Septentrionalis*. Although his expedition was technically a failure, Jens Munk remains a significant maritime pioneer. He charted many parts of Hudson Bay's unknown western coat, and narrowed down the area of the possible location of the Northwest Passage. He actually returned from his journey, navigating homeward across one of the most perilous stretches of water in the world. Indeed, the discovery of the Northwest Passage claimed numerous lives.

The city of Bergen in 1620, close to the time when the exhausted Munk returned. The city was a teeming metropolis with 15,000 inhabitants.

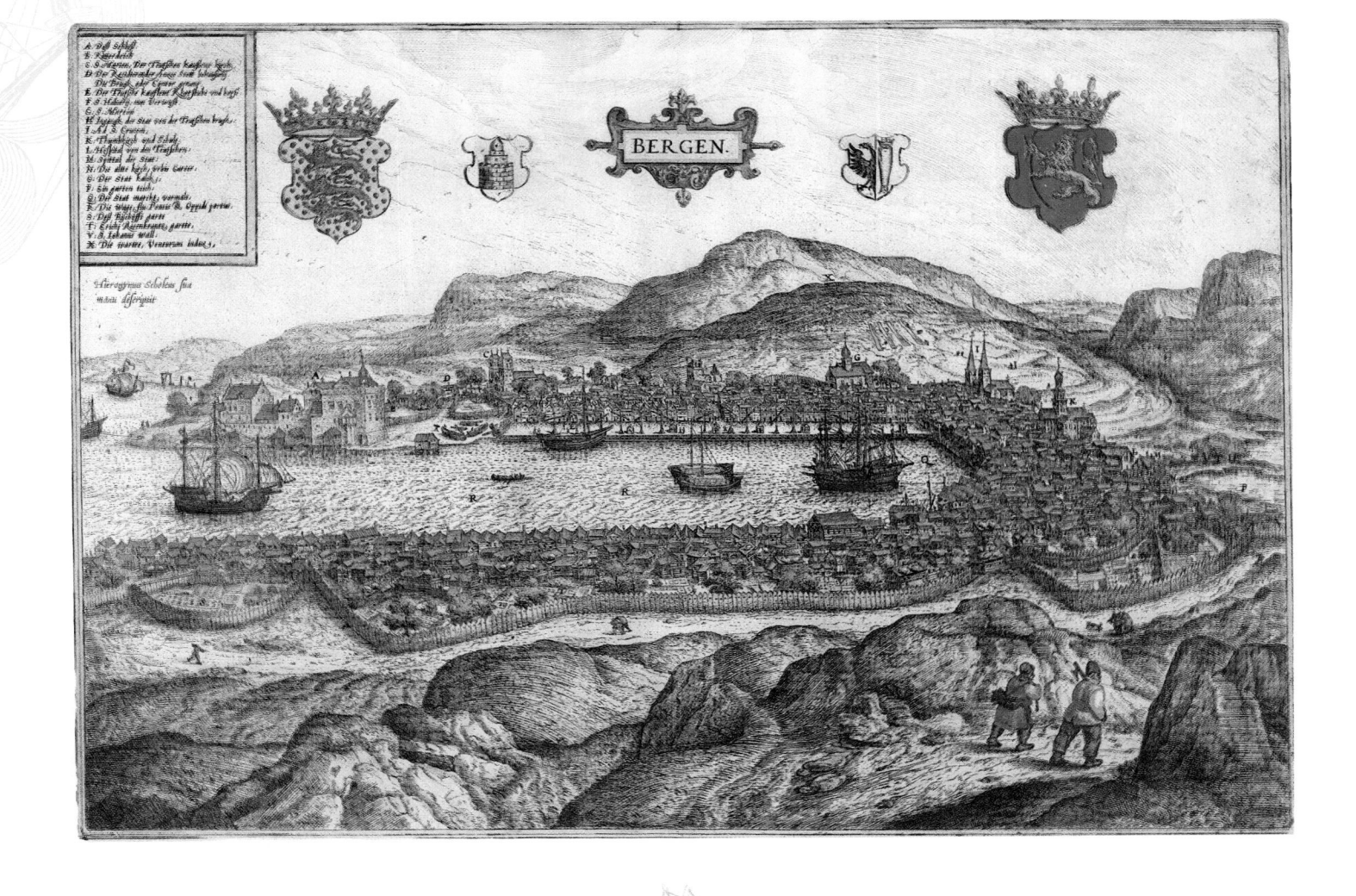

Jens Munk begs the King to be merciful and not send him back to the Hudson Bay to retrieve the Enhiørning.

EXPLORING THE NORTHWEST PASSAGE AFTER MUNK

Almost 300 years would pass before another Norwegian, Roald Engelbregt Amundsen, would find his way through the Northwest Passage. Jens Munk was not the first 17th-century explorer to search for this waterway. A number of English and Dutch expeditions had set out to do the same and many of these explorers, as well as those who came after, paid with their lives in the icy wastelands. Their memory lives on in the names which mark the many bodies of water in the region: Hudson Bay, Baffin Island, Davis Strait, Frobisher Strait, Ross Strait, Bewechey Island, McClure Strait. Already in 1616, the Englishmen Bylot and Baffin discovered the entrance to the Northwest Passage, Lancaster Sound, albeit without knowing it, as they believed the sound was a fjord. The man who came closest to the goal was a tragic figure called Sir John Franklin whose 1845 expedition cost the lives of 130 men who starved and froze to death on a strip of ice only a few nautical miles from completing their voyage through the Northwest Passage. Robert McClure, who was on a mission to look for the Franklin expedition, was the first man to sail through the Passage in 1854. However, it was not in the boat in which he had set out. His ship had been beset by ice on the north side of Banks Island, which is located furthest west in the Northern Canadian archipelago. McClure and the surviving members of his crew were rescued by another expedition sent in an easterly direction to find Franklin.

Around 1880 the Nordic countries joined together to explore the polar territories. The renowned Swedish-Finnish polar researcher, Adolf E. Nordenskiöld, found the Northeast Passage north of Siberia and journeyed around all of Eurasia. In 1906, about 300 years after Baffin and Bylong discovered the entrance to the Northwest Passage, Roald Amundsen was the first to sail through the passage in the same ship, proving that it was possible to do so. With the *Gjøa*, a tried and tested small polar vessel of 47 dwt and a crew of six, Amundsen managed to accomplish what all the other major expeditions had not.

(Amundsen's objective descriptions of the *Gjøa's* travels leave the reader with an impression of an ordinary voyage rather than an expedition into unknown territory and treacherous waters. Amundsen and his men stayed two winters at Gjøa Haven, a small, sheltered bay on the southeastern corner of King William Island. Here the expedition made contact with the Inuit who lived in the area, acquiring important knowledge about survival methods in polar regions. This would become valuable to Amundsen when planning and executing his voyage to the South Pole a few years later. On 26 August 1905, Amundsen encountered the first ship to come from the west, an American whaler. At this time, the *Gjøa* was at Nelson Head, the southern point on Banks Island, facing the Beaufort Sea. Due to the ice, the expedition overwintered with the American whaler at King Point near the mouth of the McKenzie River. First in the new year, 1906, was Amundsen able to report to the world that he had sailed through the Northwest Passage.)

Roughly 50 large and small craft have sailed through the Northwest Passage since Amundsen. As late as 1969 there was a last, major attempt to make commercial use of the passage with the US ice-breaking tanker, *Manhattan*. (The idea was to freight oil through this waterway, but the results of the experiment were inconclusive and the idea was dropped.) The Northwest Passage was conquered in the end, but it never had any pragmatic significance. Too shallow and narrow for commercial exploitation, it can only be concluded that many tragic explorers throughout the centuries suffered in vain.

NEW SIBIRIAN ISLANDS

1894

LAPTEV SEA

SIBIR

SEVERNAJA SEMLJA

Tajmyr

7-4-1895

KARA SEA

85°

1896

Wintercabin 1895

Kapp Flora

FRANZ JOSEF LAND

Jalmal

GREENLAND

NOVAJA SEMLJA

80°

SPITSBERGEN

75°

BARENTS SEA

24-7-1893

Vardø

20-8-1896 Skjervøy

Tromsø

ICELAND

NORWAY

FRIDTJOF NANSEN 1893–96.

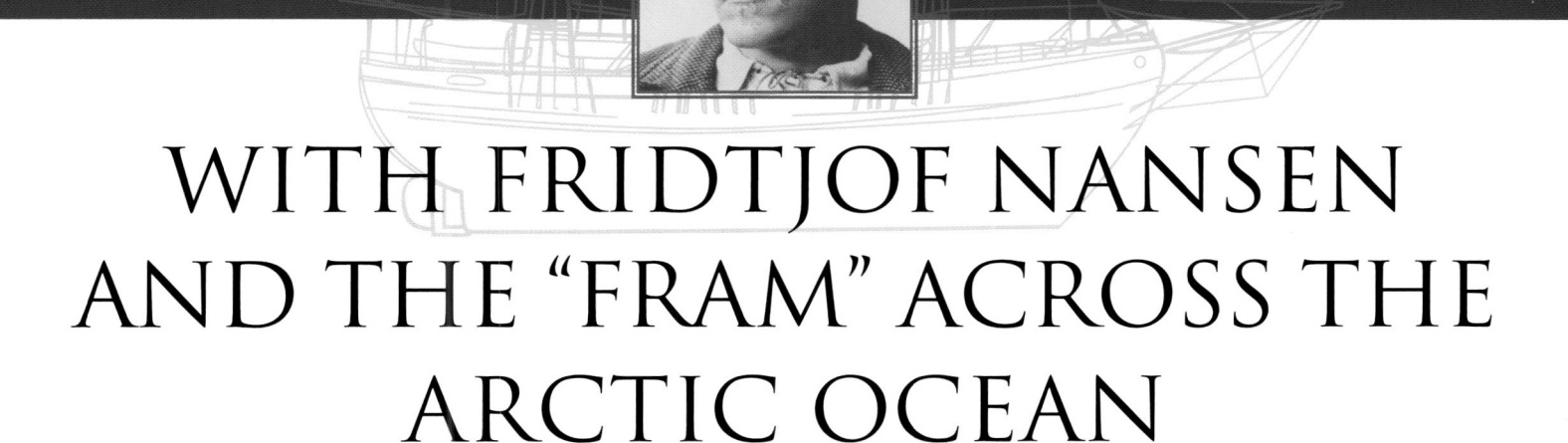

WITH FRIDTJOF NANSEN AND THE "FRAM" ACROSS THE ARCTIC OCEAN

BY KÅRE BERG

Does the Arctic current flow to the north and west of the New Siberian Islands, and does it reach Greenland's eastern coast? Is there an open passage between the waters east of Greenland and north of Asia? To test this theory, Fridtjof Nansen and 12 men entrusted their fates to the ice, winds and sea currents, allowing the Fram to freeze into the pack ice and drift with the elements for three long years. Most considered the exploit to be courage bordering on the foolhardy. No one had voluntarily ventured into the ice before. Many vessels had been crushed by the ice close to the North Pole. However, most daring by far was Nansen's and Hjalmar Johansen's decision to leave the ship and strike out for the Polar Point on skis and by sledge.

Fridtjof Nansen was born on 10 November 1862 on the island Store Frøen, not far from Kristiania, today's Oslo. From his very early years, he showed a keen interest in outdoor life and sports, excelling in both skating and skiing. Never doing anything by halves, in 1884 he took a train from Bergen to Voss from where he skied a distance of 360 km, crossing the mountains to Kristiania in order to participate in the Huseby (Winter) Races. That year, however, cross-country skiing, at which Nansen specialised and for which he had been training, was dropped from the list of athletic disciplines. Therefore he simply turned around and skied back to Bergen. Although he was a first-rate athlete and an avid supporter of athletics in general, in an address to the Pedagogical Society he observed that "athletics has lost some

of its value because the contest has become overly dominant, thus transforming athletics into sport, and everything called sport and records are not positive in nature. Instead of creating healthy, independent men, sport breeds vanity. The objective of athletics should after all be to educate and strengthen body and soul, while bringing us into the outdoors. But many of our athletes have become muscle machines, race horses, who strive to break records at competitions and reach the finishing line a few metres ahead of the other person."

Having taken his *Examen Artium,* the school-leaving exams, in 1880, Nansen decided to study zoology. Robert Collett, Professor of Zoology at Kristiania University, advised Nansen to sign up on a sealer to study polar fishing. The sealer *Viking* left in the spring of 1882 and returned in the autumn. While in the Arctic, the *Viking* was caught in the ice off the coast of Greenland for 24 days. Nansen became fascinated by what he witnessed, and the idea of skiing across Greenland probably began to germinate at this time.

Safely back from the sealing voyage, Nansen was offered the position of curator at the Bergen Museum by Prof. Collett. In Bergen he worked on his doctoral thesis, examining the nervous system of the hagfish. He made significant discoveries, which went unnoticed by his contemporaries, but would later secure him a place among the founders of neurology. In 1888, the University of Kristiania granted him a doctorate.

Five years earlier, in 1883, Finnish-Swedish polar explorer N.A.G. Nordenskiöld landed on the Greenland ice accompanied by two Laplanders. At this juncture, scientists had varying perceptions of Greenland's interior. It was said to be free of ice, arable, and with a relatively warm climate, a view Nansen did not hold. He decided to find out for himself, and by 1884 he had made plans to ski across Greenland. Although preoccupied with his dissertation, he nevertheless found the time to work out the details of the enterprise. He would ski across the Greenland ice sheet from the uninhabited east coast to the west. In other words, no retreat would be possible. Nansen wrote: "I have always thought that the much praised line of retreat is a trap for people who really want to reach their objective." Thus there was only one way – *Fram* – or, forwards.

The entire plan was met with considerable scepticism, even regarded as the idea of a madman. Nevertheless, Nansen selected five companions, among them Captain Otto Sverdrup. In the future, Otto Sverdrup would become one of Nansen's closest associates. Boarding the sealer *Jason,* they sailed along the coast of Greenland, disembarking on 17 July 1888 in two rowing boats at the Sermelik Fjord. Then occurred the first of many unanticipated events. In the course of ten days, they drifted 400 km to the south which meant having to backtrack by oars and sail in order to reach the place from which they had planned to set out on skis. On 10 August they finally pulled their boats ashore at Umivik, and began their journey on 15 August. They reached an altitude of 2716 m above sea level, where the temperature was as low as 46°C. Suffering from thirst, because Nansen's cooker was ineffective and did not produce enough water, they also realised that their pemmican had the wrong composition, lacking fat. A craving for sugar added to their discomfort. Nansen and Sverdrup reached Godthåp on 6 October, after building a small rowing boat. Unfortunately, by this time the last ship had left for Copenhagen.

During the winter he spent on Greenland, Nansen lived with the Inuit people. His book, *Eskimo Life*, provides the best description available on the lives of the Greenland Eskimos at the end of the 19th century. Both the experience of crossing Greenland on skis and the stay among the Inuit were to become invaluable sources of information for the next chapter in Nansen's life.

THE THEORY BEHIND THE FIRST FRAM VOYAGE

Upon his return from Greenland, Nansen addressed the Christiania Geographical Society on 18 February 1890. He reported on the basis for his theory that "there is a current somewhere between the Pole and Franz Josef Land from the Siberian Arctic Ocean toward the coast of Greenland." This theory was based on facts, the most significant of which were:

1. Cargo and wood from the shipwrecked American bark, *Jeanette,* were found off Greenland's south-western coast. The ship was crushed by the ice off the New Siberian Islands in 1881, and items from the *Jeanette's* wreckage were found two years later.

2. Driftwood of a type found in eastern Greenland and plant species from the same area were identical to those found in Siberia.

3. Mud found on the Greenland drift ice indicated that the ice came from Siberia. Sixteen varieties of silica had been identified on Greenland's east coast and at the Bering Strait; in all likelihood, these too originated in Siberia.

Nansen concluded that there had to be a navigable passage between the seas east of Greenland and north of Asia. His theory was that the driftice finds its way across the unknown Arctic Ocean through this open link. Nansen believed that, "On this same ice it ought to be possible to bring an expedition along the same route."

About the expedition, he said: "In brief, the plan is as follows: I intend to have a vessel built that is as small and as strong as possible; it shall be just large enough to hold coal supplies and provisions for 12 men for five years. A vessel of about 170 gross tons would probably be adequate. It will be equipped with an engine which is strong enough to do six knots, but will also have sails."

He also addressed the National Geographical Society in London, where his plan met not only with strong objections, but also nearly unanimous condemnation. To date no one had willingly gone into the ice, and many of the vessels which had been caught in the ice had been crushed by its pressure.

THE BUILDING OF THE FRAM

The die, however, were cast and the only question remaining was who could build a vessel according to Nansen's specifications. The choice was obvious: Colin Archer, Norway's foremost builder of wooden-hulled ships. A close collaboration was established between Colin Archer, Fridtjof Nansen and Otto Sverdrup. By early September 1891, the work was in full swing, and the world's strongest vessel was beginning to take shape on the stocks. A number of modifications would be made along the way, but the vessel was completed and launched in Rekkevik near Larvik on 22 October 1892, after more than one year's construction.

Archer was convinced that an upright-sided hull, even if made of steel, would not be strong or supple enough to withstand the pressure of the pack ice. The hull was therefore constructed with rounded sides and bottom. A cross-section of the ship bore a close resemblance to a coconut shell with its top half missing. The purpose of the design was to enable the ship to rise on top of the ice as it pressed against her sides, and

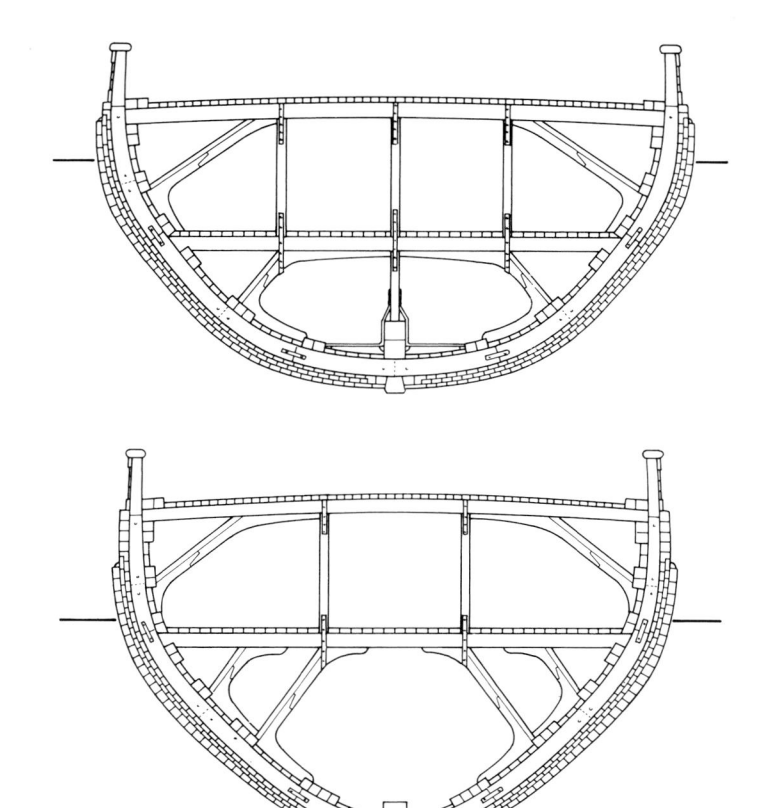

The Fram was specially designed to withstand the pressures of the pack ice.

thus avoid being crushed. To ensure that the ice did not damage the rudder and propeller, these could be hoisted on deck through a bilge well.

Mainly built of Italian oak, the vessel measured 39 m from stem to stern and was 11 m in the beam, with the width of its sides varying from 70–80 cm, i.e. three to four times thicker than that of an ordinary vessel. Fore and aft, the *Fram* was reinforced with steel. Her electrical system was based on batteries charged by a generator which, in turn, was operated by a steam engine. When the steam engine was switched off, the generator was operated by a windmill or, alternatively, by hand.

The craft had eight boats on board: four lifeboats (of the type used by sealers as their work boats), a tender and a motor boat, the latter proving to be more an irritant than a boon, and two large boats. The large boats could hold the entire crew and provisions and stores for several months, in the event the ship had to be abandoned. Nansen believed that if the ship

were to go down, there would be enough time to transfer provisions and equipment to the large boats.

The mainmast was 32 m tall, providing the lookout in the crow's nest with a superb overview of the ice conditions ahead. Six cabins surrounded the saloon. Built for comfort, the vessel was intended to provide a warm and safe home. To that end, stoves were installed, with the paraffin lamps in the cabins giving off additional warmth. In one corner of the saloon there was even an organ.

This masterpiece of shipbuilding was launched on 26 October 1892, although her name was still a mystery. *Eva*, Nansen's wife's name, was mentioned as a likely choice or, perhaps, *Norge*. At the official ceremony, Eva Nansen mounted the small platform, and breaking the bottle of champagne across the ship's bow, she declared, "You shall be called *Fram*"(Forwards). Nansen did not believe in lines of retreat, something he made clear when he crossed the Greenland Ice Cap from the eastern coast. The same would be true when he set out for the Arctic Ocean. This was probably the reason for the choice of the name *Fram*.

The engine was installed at the Akers Mekaniske Verksted yard. The *Fram*, her rigging in place, embarked on her fabled voyage on Midsummer's Day, 24 June 1893. She withstood the many trials of journeying through the icy Arctic waters, returning to Kristiania in September 1896, after an absence of three years.

The overall cost of the expedition at the time of its departure in 1893 was NOK 444,339.36, or some NOK 23 million, in 1999-kroner. The expedition was financed by funds raised by the triumvirate of merchant Thomas Fearnley, Consul Axel Heiberg and brewery-owner Ellef Ringnes. The three gentlemen also made large personal contributions. King Oscar II sent a gift of NOK 20,000 and, after a heated parliamentary debate, the Norwegian parliament, the *Storting*, allocated NOK 200,000, later supplemented by a further NOK 80,000. Baron Oscar Dickson covered the cost of the electrical system and Nansen made up the outstanding sum in order to balance the accounts.

THE PROVISIONS AND THE CREW

A great deal of care went into planning the provisions for the expedition, since scurvy was the foremost threat to the health of the crew. All the physiological aspects were thoroughly reviewed with Professor Torup, the expert on nutrition at the University of Kristiania. It was concluded that the preservation of meat and fish by salting, smoking or incomplete drying was inadequate, even objectionable, for lengthy Arctic expeditions. The choice of stores was based on the principle that the provisions were to be prevented from decomposing either by careful and complete drying, or sterilisation by heat.

The *Fram* had enough provisions to last five years. In addition Nansen expected to be able to supplement them with fresh food by hunting game. Great emphasis was put on the importance of provisions being nutritious and healthy. It was also important to ensure a varied diet.

Among the provisions selected were:
All types of tinned meat and fish
Dried fish
Dried and tinned potatoes
Dried vegetables. Large quantities of preserves and marmalades
Sugared and unsugared condensed milk
Preserved butter
Dried soups
Norwegian ship's biscuits made of rye and wheat, as well as British ship's biscuits
Flour for baking fresh bread

All the foodstuffs were chemically analysed, and their packaging in soldered tin cases to keep out moisture was closely supervised. Beverages for breakfast and supper were hot chocolate, coffee, tea and, at times, milk. For the first six months there was also bock beer from Ringnes. Later they had to make do with lime juice mixed with sugar or syrup.

Despite all the warnings and the general assumption that the ship would be crushed by the pack ice, there were more than 100 applicants who wanted to join the expedition. Apart from Nansen, the selected members of the crew numbered 12 men. Otto Sverdrup was appointed the ship's skipper and First Lt. Sigurd Scott Hansen was second-in-command. Fredrik Hjalmar Johansen was one of the last to join, finally taken on as stoker after numerous applications. Excluding the doctor, Henrik Greve Blessing, the crew consisted of sailors, several of whom had served in the Navy, who were also good craftsmen. This was a combination which Nansen greatly appreciated.

THE DEPARTURE FOR THE ARCTIC OCEAN

Taking leave of his wife, Eva, and their 6-month-old daughter, Nansen and a close to over-loaded *Fram* sailed from Kristiania on Midsummer's Day 1893. The first stop was Horten where explosives were brought on board in the event there was a need to break up the ice masses. From here the *Fram* headed for Larvik to bid farewell to Colin Archer and hoist on board the large boats and lifeboats. Continuing their voyage, they ran into a storm off Lindesnes, the southernmost tip of Norway. At the time, the *Fram* still had a low foredeck which posed no obstacle to the towering waves breaking on her deck. The deck cargo was precariously close to slipping its ropes, but a dense fog made it difficult for the ship to reach a harbour. Eventually the *Fram* dropped anchor in Lister Fjord, and the freight was secured. In Tromsø they loaded jackets and boots made of reindeer skins (called pæsker and *kommager* by the indigenous Lapp, or Sami, people), finnskoe (reindeer skin slippers which the Sami wear over their boots), sennegress (used as insulation against the cold) and reindeer meat, and bunkered coal.

Their final port of call in Norway was Vardø where the *Fram*'s bottom was scraped and the crew underwent a

Lithograph titled SIBERIAN NORTH COAST – by Fridtjof Nansen.

celebratory rite of purification, that is, they took a sauna and bath "... worthy of the devil himself, and all the while one is whipped with birch rods by young Kven girls. Afterwards one is rubbed, washed and dried, charmingly and lightly...I am led to ruminate on whether Old Father Muhamed has managed to institute something similar in his paradise." Nansen, however, was very unhappy with the fact that a large number of the crew had been on a drinking binge just before the day of departure, 24 July.

The *Fram* now crossed the Barents Sea, with Khabarova in the Yugo Strait as her goal. Here the half-Norwegian Aleksandr Trontheim from Riga waited with the 34 dogs which he had driven across the Ural Mountains. The *Fram* and her crew waited to bunker new supplies of coal from the coaster *Urania*, but the latter was taking her time in arriving. Since the Kara Sea was open and inviting, Nansen decided to leave on 3 August, and enjoyed a relatively uneventful passage.

Scientific research. Collecting deep-sea samples.

They were now in the North-East Passage, which was first navigated by Nordenskiöld in 1878. The Kara Sea was rather shallow, however, and it was imperative to take regular soundings the entire time. Even so, the *Fram* ran aground twice, although without serious consequences. The men soon felled their first polar bear and hunted seals, walruses and reindeer; with 34 dogs on board more food was needed. Since dogs can also be afflicted with scurvy, the dog food had to be well-balanced and fresh, although frozen meat is a good source of vitamin C.

On 11 September the ship passed the old Furthest North at Cape Chelyuskin. With a milestone passed there was good reason to celebrate with a salute, toasts and music. Now the Laptev Sea lay ahead, open and free of ice. It almost seemed as though the waterway would be passable all the way to the North Pole. The men were infused with optimism, until ice came into view. Growing more and more compact, it forced the *Fram* to a halt on 22 September. They made fast to a large block of ice, and in Nansen's own words: "It seems to me that this will be our permanent harbour." They were now in the

vicinity of the New Siberian Islands where the *Jeannette* had foundered, and began counting on the same drift which carried the *Jeannette*'s wreckage to the south-western coast of Greenland. In the course of their voyage, they learned that Nordenskiöld's charts were far from complete. Discovering a number of new islands, they christened these Sverdrup Island, Heiberg Island and Ringnes Island. The waters, too, were inadequately charted, causing them to run aground on the many unmarked shoals.

Upon leaving Khabarova, they discovered the presence of the most unwelcome of stowaways, lice, which were a health hazard, major inconvenience and irritant. In their war on lice, which began while the ship crossed the Kara and Laptev Seas, many strategies were tried, including steaming the parasites to death. But since these continued to thrive and multiply, a bright spark, out of sheer desperation, suggested making use of the bitterly cold outdoor temperatures. Bedding and clothing were spread on deck, whereupon the war was won: the lice succumbed to frostbite!

The long winter nights had set in, and the drift phase was about to commence. All apertures were sealed, and to light the interior, the windmill was installed. The *Fram* was now at 78(30'N.

THE DRIFT

The drift, however, did not go in one fixed direction as Nansen had predicted. Instead the *Fram* drifted in the right direction for a few days, only to backtrack to her point of departure. Often there was no progress at all for several weeks, driving Nansen and the crew to distraction. Nansen's theory that there must be a current from the east toward the north and west had been dealt a serious blow. It was generally assumed that the Arctic Ocean was a shallow body of water, possibly with a mainland at some point. Nansen based his theory on the idea that the Gulf Stream which flowed into the Barents Sea, and the overflow from the principal Siberian rivers, must have a decisive influence on the direction of the current which emerged between Svalbard and Greenland.

As the crew took regular soundings of the sea bottom, the measurements indeed pointed to a shallow polar basin, but this was only true initially. As the drift took the *Fram* away from the coast, the waters increased in depth. From measurements of 100 fathoms, 200 fathoms, 500 fathoms, the

depth plunged to 1000 fathoms and after a while the bottom fell away to 4000 fathoms. When the sounding line could be lengthened no more, Nansen admitted that his theory of the current was not as valid as he had thought. Given the enormous volumes of water in the Arctic Ocean, the supply emanating from the Gulf Stream and the Siberian rivers could only have a minimal effect on the current. Nevertheless the drift did flow to the north and west. He concluded that a combination of current and prevailing winds were the forces influencing the behaviour of the current.

Caught in the ice, the *Fram* now felt the first dreaded shudders which signalled a build-up of pressure against her sides by the massive pack ice. This caused great alarm among the crew. Would the vessel really be able to withstand the pressure? The ice generally churned twice a day, and gradually everyone grew accustomed to its ominous rumblings. Of course, the men were watchful of even the minor crushing of ice floes against each other, since the collisions resulted in their being pressed out of the water and forming a kind of icy pileup which pressed against the hull and could damage it. But no damage was done. The *Fram* herself had been pressed upwards by the constant collisions, and the voyage continued with the ship and her crew travelling on the ice.

EVERYDAY LIFE

Everyday life onboard the ship consisted of gathering scientific data, hunting and tending to the dogs. The crew made skis, sledges and kayaks. In the morning all the men assembled at 0800 hrs, when they ate a breakfast of coarse bread – freshly baked thrice weekly – butter, cheese, canned meats or bacon, cod liver roe, anchovy roe, biscuits and various types of marmalade. They drank coffee and hot chocolate on alternate days. Every man took his turn in the galley to help the cook for a week at a time. Lunch was served at 1300 hrs, normally a three-course affair, comprising soup, meat or fish, and dessert. The meat dishes were also accompanied by potatoes or macaroni, and vegetables. At dinner time juicy stories and bock beer were also served up until the latter ran out at the end of 1893. After dinner the men retired to the smoking saloon which also doubled as the galley. Supper was served at 1800 hrs and was similar to breakfast.

Birthdays, the anniversary of the *Fram*'s launching , crossing latitudes, Norway's national day, the 17th of May, and any

There was no lack of nourishing food on board. Several crew members put on weight.

other dates which could justifiably be celebrated were honoured with special meals, such as Christmas Day 1893, when the menu featured oxtail soup, fish pudding with potatoes and drawn butter, reindeer roast with early peas, cut beans, potatoes and cranberry sauce, cloudberry porridge with cream, almond wreath cake and marzipan. For supper there was coffee, pineapple pie, honey cake, vanilla cakes, coconut macaroons, and much more, concluding with figs, raisins and almonds. Not surprisingly, double chins and extra "tyre rings" gradually began to manifest themselves on faces and around waists. On Monday, 5 February, when the cook served the last dinner accompanied by Ringnes bock beer, the meal was dubbed a "wake". From now on, the beer would be replaced by a mixture of lime juice and sugar. In fact the crew's health was so good that Dr. Blessing's duties were changed from caring for the men to collecting micro-organisms and attending to the health of the dogs. Nansen, however, worried about the men's weight increase, which could also endanger lives if they were forced to abandon ship, and he now ordered a regimen of daily ski tours.

The organ in the saloon was the type which would play melodies when a roll of music, of which they had 100, was inserted and the pedals were worked. But it also functioned as an ordinary piano, which Nansen and two of the others were able to play. Hjalmar Johansen had his accordion and Mogstad his violin; the trio constituted the ship's entertainment team. On festive occasions the organ was played and the men even danced. Nansen describes one time when spirits were so high that he and the blacksmith, Lars Pettersen, felt the urge to waltz and do a polka: "We executed several truly elegant *pas de deux* on the small dance floor. Finally Amundsen too was carried away by the dancing, while the others played cards." On another occasion the blacksmith danced a solo and Nansen commented in his diary that he had considerable potential as a ballet dancer.

Hanging on the bulkheads in the saloon and in the cabins were paintings by Werenskiold, Munthe, Kitty Kielland, Skredsvik and Eilif Petersen. The *Fram* had a library which stocked several hundred volumes of books, and there were other forms of entertainment, such as a variety of games, although card-playing was the most popular activity.

The entire crew was keenly interested in the drift and its direction. Holes were drilled in the ice and lines were dropped into them. By watching the lines the men could judge the direction in which the vessel was drifting. The general mood of the crew could be read by looking at the position of the line. With a near-total lack of privacy, the uniformity of life and claustrophobic closeness resulted in a few unfortunate episodes, including fist-fights. Nansen was not the most popular member of the expedition. Prone to depressions, he was a difficult man to deal with. On the whole, however, morale on board was good.

Time was now nearing to learn the skill of driving dogs. Harnessed to a sledge, the animals took off, ignoring Nansen's signals for them to halt. The truth be told, the dogs ran Nansen, who cursed and swore, trying in vain to rein in the team. Falling off the sledge, he was first dragged toward blocks of ice jutting out of the water, and from there to the ship, furiously vowing to break the ribs of every single dog. The performance continued, with the dogs calling all the shots. The one thing which made Nansen happiest was the absence of onlookers.

As 1893 ebbed out, the drift continued to be unsatisfactory. On Sunday, 10 December, the motto on Nansen's calendar was:

"He is happy whose circumstances suit his temper; but he is more excellent who can suit his temper to any circumstance." Nansen comments: "Very true, and just the philosophy I am practising at this moment."

"...WOULD LIKE TO TAKE THE POLE AT THE SAME TIME..."

Christmas and the new year, 1894, arrived, and the *Fram* had drifted to 79°19'N. The drift, in other words, was not as predicted. Nansen, finding it hard to contain his frustration, burst out: "Columbus discovered America by a miscalculation that was not even his own. God knows what my miscalculation will mean for me. I say once again that the Siberian driftwood off Greenland cannot lie and we must go in the same direction as these." He calculated that given the nature of the drift, they might spend anywhere from five to eight years in the ice. On 30 April the *Fram* had reached 80°44' N, and the drift continued in a westwardly direction. Nansen now arrived at the conclusion that the drift would definitely last for three years.

Toward the end of May Nansen was no longer in doubt that the expedition would ultimately succeed, but believed that the *Fram* was unlikely to drift higher than 85°N, depending on how far to the north Franz Josef Land lay. In the circumstances, Nansen decided that he was not prepared to give up the Pole, "even though it is basically a matter of vanity, only foolish pranks in comparison with what we are doing and hoping to accomplish, but nevertheless, I must confess that I am a big enough fool to want to take the Pole at the same time..." Upon leaving Norway, he had given assurances that such an exploit was out of the question. He now began to lay plans which entailed leaving the *Fram* and going to the Pole without her.

The sound of the ice blocks crunching and cracking was part of everyday life; temperatures of -50° were no longer sensational. In the spring of 1894, Nansen summed up the situation as follows: "I laugh at scurvy, no sanatorium is better (than the *Fram*). I laugh at the force of the ice, we live in an impregnable fortress. I laugh at the cold, it is nothing. But I don't laugh at the wind to which every will bends."

The interest in measuring the thickness of the pile of ice blocks in which the *Fram* was encased returned. Having drilled down to a depth of 30 ft, roughly 10 m, the men had

to abandon their hopeless undertaking. The *Fram* rested on top of the ice. A 10 ft thick floe lay above the surface of the water and the *Fram* reposed on an additional 3 ft of ice above the floe.

SCIENTIFIC RESEARCH

Besides the depth soundings, a large amount of data was recorded. Water temperatures were measured, hundreds of water samples were taken at different depths and the thickness of the ice was measured. The ice was thickest, 2.49 m, in July. This is explained by the fact that fresh water from the Russian rivers flows on top of the salt water, the temperature of which is below zero, and the fresh water freezes faster than the surface of the ice melts. Samples of plankton, algae and other organisms were collected. The temperature was measured at the top of the mast and on the ice four times a day, and the force and direction of the wind was recorded. On 6 April 1894, an eclipse of the sun was observed. Measurements of the magnetic field were made and the Northern Lights were studied. These and many other measurements formed the empirical basis for the six volumes of scientific analyses published after the voyage.

The Fram endures a test of strength in March 1895.

On Friday, 19 October they crossed the long-awaited 82nd latitude, reaching 82°27'N. The *Fram* had set a new record, and was farther north than any other vessel before her.

Autumn arrived and Nansen was bored. There were no more scientific investigations to conduct; and were he to leave the ship in the following year, he could count on coming home one year before the *Fram*. The gathering of scientific data could continue in accordance with the guidelines which they had followed to date. The stay on board no longer offered any challenges. The practical man that he was, Nansen designed what was probably the world's first oil-fuelled galley because coal had to be rationed. Immediately after the oil-fuelled galley was put into operation, a dull bang was heard from the galley. Lars Pettersen emerged, black-faced as a chimney sweep and angry. The galley had "exploded" in his face. He had merely wanted to make certain that the newfangled contraption was burning properly, and the thing blew up in his face. He had allowed air to enter, and thereby caused an explosion. The new appliance worked perfectly for the rest of the voyage.

PREPARATIONS FOR THE JOURNEY TO THE NORTH POLE

Nansen continued to plan the trip to the North Pole. If the ship reached a position as far north as 84°N, or better still, 86°N, he would set out at the beginning of February or end of March. In November he revealed his plans to Sverdrup, who immediately volunteered to accompany Nansen to the North Pole. Declining the offer, Nansen told Sverdrup that he would be needed to lead the expedition after Nansen left the ship and bring the *Fram* safely back to Norway. The choice of companion fell on Hjalmar Johansen, a hardy outdoorsman, renowned as one of Norway's best gymnasts, perhaps the very best. Nansen assessed the requirements for the journey, concluding that they would need a total of 1050 kg of provisions and equipment. They would also need the 28 dogs on board. Among the potential obstacles, he envisaged the following: 1. The ice might prove more impenetrable than believed. 2. They might encounter land. 3. The dogs might not prove satisfactory, fall sick or freeze to death. 4. Nansen and Johansen could develop scurvy. Once the obstacles had been analysed, the conclusion was to go forward with the plan. On Tuesday, 20 November, Nansen addressed the crew, informing them of his decision, and explaining the plans he had worked out for reaching the North Pole while they returned to Norway.

In December there were incidents that might have been construed as omens of what was in the offing. A number of inexplicable thuds spread unease among the men. Christmas was nevertheless celebrated, and indeed just before the holiday,

they passed 83°N. The Christmas meal was sumptuous and the cakes served were traditional Norwegian Christmas cakes: deep-fried crullers, honey cake, macaroons and the like. There was even champagne, "Polar Champagne 83 Degrees".

THE GREATEST TEST OF STRENGTH

New Year's Eve 1895 was celebrated appropriately, but on 3 January violent vibrations shook the boat to her core. A mammoth hummock of sheets and blocks of ice lay a mere 30 paces from the *Fram*. (The highest pileup of ice floes and blocks that Nansen measured during the drift was 25 ft, or 8 m.) As the menacing structure began edging toward the ship, the sledges, kayaks and provisions were readied on board for evacuation. The ramming which the ship had experienced in December was repeated, and now the ship's hull began working, with all manner of uncanny knocking and creaking sounds emanating from her. For safety's sake, the dogs were brought on board. Past midnight, on 4 January, the ice pack appeared to have settled somewhat. But soon the huge structure continued its relentless approach of the ship. On Saturday, 5 January, as the sinister sounds produced by the wave of ice seemed to herald the coming of doomsday, snow and blocks of ice heaved up, toppling onto the deck from high above the ship's railing and falling over the awning which had been stretched over the ship. The port side passage was completely clogged; indeed, to port, the *Fram* was entirely buried under a mass of ice and snow. All men were ordered on deck and confusion ensued. The members of the crew brought up their personal effects in duffel bags, and some began to eat up their reserves of sweets, cakes, chocolates, raisins, dates, and the like. The first mate was seen hauling a huge duffel bag with numerous cups dangling from it. Later in the evening he strutted about with various objects – mittens, knives, cups – all tied to articles of clothing and swinging and clanking noisily. When Nansen got around to taking a head count, he found that one man was missing: the skipper. Sverdrup, who had been washing himself in the galley, calmly explained that he wanted to finish his bath since it might be a long time before he could have another. The ship had withstood the onslaught of the wave of snow and ice. Huge blocks of ice lay on deck,

The Fram is dug out of the ice masses which toppled over her.

including a three-metre-thick floe. The ship was listing badly, but when the *Fram* lifted herself with not a scratch on her, it was apparent to all that they had been spared a calamity. It took several months to remove the ice from the deck and dig the ship out from under the ice.

The preparations for the assault on the North Pole, which had been well under way in the autumn of 1894, continued now with renewed vigour. Two kayaks and three sturdy sledges were made ready. The sledges had been designed by Nansen who based his construction on the Østerdal sledge with skis for runners. To this day the Nansen ski-sledge is still used by many dog-sledding clubs. Among the provisions and equipment were large quantities of pemmican and dried liver pâté which were readied for loading on Wednesday, 13 February. The pemmican and pâté were packed in blocks to form a platform on which the kayaks were placed on the sledges. The first trial overnighting was not successful despite the fact that the temperature, according to Nansen's observations, was "only" -37°C. Sverdrup apparently derided Nansen for being "thin-blooded" because Nansen used mittens when working in -30° C. Finally the date of departure was set for 20 February.

Nansen and Johansen prior to departing for the North Pole.

The date arrived, but their departure was postponed once again, this time to 26 February. However, as soon as they left it was clear that the sledges were not sturdy enough. Their next departure took place on 28 February, but hampered by too many sledges and too much cargo, they were back on board the ship by 6 March. They decided to reduce their cargo and the number of sledges to a total of 763 kg, loaded on three sledges. The 28 dogs weighed a total of 725 kg. There was enough food for 100 days and dog provisions for 30 days. Weighing each dog, Nansen determined that by feeding the dogs the meat from their companions, which would be slaughtered along the way, they would have enough dog food for 80 days. Yet another farewell feast was organised and on 16 March the voyage to the North Pole finally commenced to the accompaniment of salutes and cheers.

The journey did not unfold as anticipated. The temperature was a constant -40°C, but their fur clothing had been left behind since prior experience indicated that it would be too

warm; in the future there would be many opportunities to regret the decision. Nansen and Johansen were clad in wool garments, and the rigours of the journey were enormous: they regularly had to lift the sledges over tall piles of churned ice. During the day their clothes were drenched with perspiration, while in the night's sub-zero temperatures, their clothing froze into icy suits of armour. The first thing they did when entering the tent in the evening was to get the Primus fire going, managing to raise the temperature to a few degrees above zero. They had to remove their footgear, drying the insulating sennegress and their mittens either between their thighs or on their chests as they slept. As for sleepwear, they slept fully clad in reindeer skin sleeping bags. Johansen had a tendency to snore, and Nansen remarked in his diary that he had to kick him to get him to stop. The snoring ceased briefly, only to continue again, Nansen remarks dryly, "but in a different key".

The food tasted good and the evening meal became the day's single solace. Soon the first dog had to be slaughtered. It was stabbed to death, and the carcass was skinned and butchered. Although sceptical at first about their new food, the dogs soon downed it with great relish. Later when dogs were slaughtered, they were not skinned, but simply divided into suitable chunks; the other dogs did not object, eating with a hearty appetite. Clearly, the dogs could have been shot, but saving ammunition was an important priority.

As has already been pointed out, the ice moved in many directions, which meant that on some days almost no progress was made due to the drift. There was no lack of frustrations: on one occasion Johansen fell through a crevasse in the ice. He wanted to stop and recover, but Nansen's reaction was, "We're not womenfolk, are we?", and thus they continued their journey. On that night Johansen froze in an especially solid armour of ice and felt considerable bitterness toward Nansen.

The physical strain of lifting the sledges over huge piles of ice as well as avoiding the many holes in the ice, which often meant circumventing them, took its toll and Nansen now understood that he had to turn back, while they still had a chance to make it back. On Monday, 8 April the surface of the ice was so broken and uneven as to be impassable, precluding any further travel to the north. "At this northernmost tent site, we consumed a huge festive meal consisting of lobscouse (stew), bread, butter, dried chocolate, lingonberry pudding, ...and a hot Serin drink...more than replete, we finally crawled into our beloved sleeping bag, our dearest friend and shelter..." The temperature was -36° C. The latitude was 86°13', 36°N; a new Furthest North record had been set.

THE WAY HOME

The way home would prove to be both long and excruciatingly fatiguing. Spring was on its way and the temperatures became more hospitable. Unfortunately, both Nansen's and Johansen's watches had stopped working, which would affect the accuracy of their navigation, preventing them from fixing the degree of longitude. They expected to tread on their first dry land at Petermann Land, and were greatly puzzled when they could not locate Petermann Land. The explanation lay in the fact that although drawn on the map, it did not exist. Initially, they made good progress; there were few hummocks and holes to negotiate. But once the holes began to reappear, their pace was severely impeded. The dogs were slaughtered when there was a need for dog food, or when the animals were so exhausted that they were no longer fit to pull the sledges. Their provisions were beginning to run low which also meant that their sledge load was lightened. However, their return journey began so far to the north that there was still no wildlife. The kayaks were in a bad state of disrepair, riddled with gashes after all the rigours of crossing the ice. It was

time to mend them to enable the men to paddle across channels in the ice.

Around 20 May, they observed polar bear tracks; in other words, fresh meat was now within reach. June arrived and the dreary grind of their return journey continued unabated. Now the crevasses were posing a greater obstacle than the ice ridges and piles of ice blocks. They set to work on repairing the kayaks which would soon be needed on the water; it was becoming much too difficult to bridge or circumvent the many holes in the ice.

On 8 June the kayaks were fit for use. Sighting two seagulls, Johansen shot them, thus providing the first fresh food the men had consumed since leaving the *Fram* in March. The food was weighed, and estimated to last 35-40 days. On 16 June only three dogs were left: Kaifas, Suggen and Haren. Nansen did not write that they were eating dog meat, but they did collect the blood from the butchered Storræven to make "blood pudding". Their store of food had reached the point where it needed to be strictly rationed. The situation was precarious.

By 22 June, they had reached 82°N. It was summer; the snow was partly melted, making it impossible to move forward. However, wildlife was now more prevalent. Nansen's entry reads: "Half past eight in the morning, after a splendid breakfast of seal meat, liver and soup." Johansen had killed a bearded seal, and the food crisis for both man and dogs was temporarily over. The seal blubber tasted exceedingly good both raw and fried. For their dinner they fried the meat, and no meat served at Kristiania's Grand Hotel had ever tasted better, although a tankard of bock beer at this time would have been rather wonderful, they mused; they ate blood pancakes for supper. Here, at Homesickness Camp, the name they gave their summer residence, they remained for several weeks, unable to journey on. The warm summer temperatures which had broken up the snow were now the greatest hindrance to their progress.

On Wednesday, 10 July, they shot a she-bear and two cubs, which they dubbed piglets. Wonderfully warm furs were spread on the floor of the tent, and with fresh food in their bellies, they slept for an uninterrupted 24 hours. Invigorated, they began to prepare for the continuation of their journey. They devoted more attention to the state of the kayaks since these had to be reliable. Fully expecting to reach home in the same year, they left a great deal of their equipment at Homesickness Camp. They did, however, bring along a sack of dried seal and bear meat.

A polar bear attacks Johansen. "Now you had better hurry, if it is not to be too late," Johansen says.

"We are thoroughly plucked of any excess(baggage), and there isn't as much as a wooden stick to find, were one to need a small knob at the end of one's tow rope." They departed on 22 July.

LAND IN SIGHT

The following day they sighted land. In fact, this was the same land they could see from Homesickness Camp, but they had mistaken it for banks of clouds. Counting on setting their feet on terra firma that very same day, they believed a new life was about to begin. They celebrated with a meal of pemmican stew, made of sliced dry bear and seal meats, sliced bear tongue, potatoes and dessert made of butter and bread crumbs fried in bear fat, topping the meal off with a piece of chocolate. However, the ice was now drifting away from the dry land, and it would be 14 days before they went ashore. During this time, Nansen developed a slipped disc and Johansen nursed him back to health. On one occasion during this period, Nansen proved to be equally invaluable to Johansen. While attempting to reach the elusive and distant stretch of land, Nansen suddenly heard Johansen bellow, "Get the rifle." Turning around, Nansen caught sight of an enormous bear lunging at Johansen. The rifle lay on the foredeck of Nansen's kayak which was in the process of slipping out to sea. Johansen had a grip on the bear's neck,

The "Winter Lair" was Nansen's and Johansen's home for 233 days.

AT WINTER QUARTERS

On the journey back, they paddled along the shore, at times sailing, their kayaks lashed together and the sledges mounted athwart the kayaks' foredeck. They survived frightening attacks by walruses as well as foul weather. They also encountered pack ice which forced them to reach shore by walking on ice floes, while pulling the kayaks and sledges behind them. The hope of reaching Svalbard dimmed as time passed, and on 27 August they conceded defeat. They built a tiny stone shelter, so small that Nansen's legs protruded through the door. Having recently shot a bear, they had a warm skin for a floor. Otherwise there were gaps in the stone walls, even though they laid their jackets over the entrance in a feeble attempt to protect the shelter from the elements. As they could ascertain on the following day, the route to the south was blocked by ice. Nansen decided that they would spend the winter there.

Now the pace of their activities picked up. They had to build a dwelling and stock food and fuel for the winter. The area abounded in walruses, seals and bears, and Nansen counted on having plenty of walrus blubber for fuel. Their first priority was the hut, which was made of stone and moss and roughly six sq m. Digging it down some 50 cm, they built walls which were 1.70 m high; Nansen could not stand upright inside the structure. For a spade they used one of the sledge runners and a shoulder blade from a walrus carcass. For a pick they resorted to using a walrus tusk mounted on a shaft. Fortunately, they found a large log of driftwood which became an excellent ridge beam, over which they stretched two walrus skins for a roof, now using a bear skin for the entrance door. When the latter quickly froze, it formed a sort of trapdoor. For heating and cooking they used a lamp. They had not had any paraffin for some time, and walrus blubber would have to do. A chimney was shaped out of ice and with part of the bear skin they also made a kind of fireplace hood, which channelled most of the cooking fumes out of the hut. Their dwelling was fittingly re-christened "The Winter Lair". Responsibility for making meals alternated between Nansen and Johansen, each taking

while the dogs barked, distracting the bear's attention. As Nansen was struggling to get hold of the rifle, he heard Johansen's calm voice, "Now you must hurry, if it is not to be too late." Nansen threw himself around and shot the animal dead from a sitting position. "The only injury caused (Johansen) was that the bear scraped a bit of dirt from Johansen's right cheek, so he walks around with a white stripe now…"

Finally, on 7 August, they reached land, standing at the edge of the ice. A bleak fate awaited the last two dogs, Kaifas and Suggen. They had outlived their purpose and would have to be put down now. For the first time they sacrificed one bullet per dog. The sledges, which now carried only the basic necessities for their survival, had long since been shortened. After all, they expected to reach home in the same year. Landing on their first island, they christened it Eva, after Nansen's wife. The second island received the name Liv, after Nansen's daughter. The land was rife with wildlife and bear tracks. They set out to sea again and paddled along the shore. On 16 August, for the first time, they established camp on dry land. Here they raised the Norwegian flag and prepared a festive meal. Nansen had no idea where they were: was this Franz Josef Land, he wondered? If so, was it its western or eastern side? Could they be on Giles Land? (Known today as White Island, it is the island furthest north-east in the Svalbard Archipelago.) This uncertainty lasted until their ski trip finally came to an end.

one week at a time. These tours of duty served as a way of marking the passage of time. It remains a mystery how they managed to thaw the frozen meat and prepare it. Probably, it was eaten raw, which meant that they consumed enough vitamin C.

They hunted successfully, although not without running into dangers and problems. A total of 13 polar bears were downed, several of them cubs. Living off the land, they learned to waste nothing: walrus and bear tendons were carefully extracted for later use as sewing thread.

On 28 September they moved into the Winter Lair. Since their mattress was made of stone, they now sorely regretted having left behind their reindeer skin sleeping bags. After sewing two sleeping bags out of wool blankets, they soon realised that they would stay warmer if the single bags were made into a double bag. They had previously used polar bear skins as bedding, but they could not get the skins to dry and they soon began to rot. In time, however, the hides became sufficiently dry to be turned into a two-man sleeping bag, helping Nansen and Johansen maintain a good level of warmth. The temperature in the hut varied between a few degrees above zero to freezing. Polar bear meat and blubber were virtually their only source of nutrients and sustenance. Many hours were spent in the sleeping bag, up to 20 hrs at a stretch. Nansen missed not having reading material, the only thing he had to look at were the navigation tables which he learned by heart. It was at this time, however, that he began to give thought to taking an expedition to the South Pole. During the time at the Winter Lair he became remiss about writing in his diary; there was too little to write about.

For Christmas the hut was cleansed of all grime and dirt. That is, "...Johansen has undertaken a thorough washing of the hut, mainly entailing scraping the ashes out of the fireplace, collecting bones and bits of meat and throwing these out, and chopping up the ice, which is frozen with all manner of trash and rubbish which lay in a thick layer on the floor, lowering the ceiling in here." Christmas came, and Nansen thought of previous Christmases at home, writing in his diary, "But we, too, are having a celebration in a shabby fashion. Johansen has turned his shirt inside out, even wearing his outermost shirt on the inside. I have done the same, but then I have also changed underpants and put on

my second pair, which I washed in warm water. And I have also washed my body with a quarter cup of water, using the other pair of underpants as a sponge and towel...". It has been claimed that on that Christmas Eve Nansen proposed that they should address one another in the familiar form of address, i.e. the second person singular pronoun, *du*. To this Johansen is said to have replied, "May I be permitted to think it over?"

New Year's Eve arrived, accompanied by -41.5° C. Only on Christmas Eve and New Year's Eve did they touch their sledging food. "On New Year's Eve Nansen and I said *du* to one another," Johansen wrote in his diary. Winter faded and spring came. Now they shot five bears and there was no lack of walruses. Unfortunately, it turned out that all their travel provisions had been spoiled. From now on, their only food, also during the journey home, would have to consist of bear meat and blubber. Their clothes were threadbare and they made new garments out of the woollen blankets in the sleeping bag. They also sewed a double sleeping bag made of selected, light bear hides. The most important part of their equipment, the rifles and ammunition, was in order.

With two kayaks lashed together, Nansen and Johansen paddled the "catamaran" along the coast toward Svalbard. The trip nearly cost them their lives.

NORWEGIAN MARITIME EXPLORERS AND EXPEDITIONS

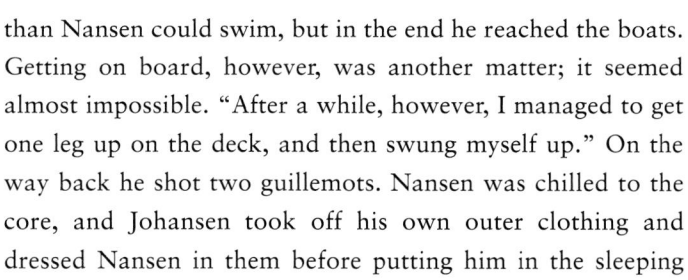

Nansen meets Jackson at the Cape Flora base on Franz Josef Land. Photo to the right: Johansen in front of Jackson's hut.

SOUTHWARD BOUND

On Tuesday, 19 May, after having spent 233 days at the Winter Lair, they were ready to depart. Nansen was still in doubt as to their location. He left a report behind at the Lair, in which he concluded that "We believe we are on Gile's Land." The report was placed in the cylinder of the Primus and nailed to the ridge beam. They hauled their sledges as far south as possible, and then sailed in their kayaks toward Svalbard. The trip was not uneventful. They travelled harnessed to their ski-runnered sledges, at times paddling or sailing their kayaks. On one occasion they tied up at the edge of the ice and went ashore. Suddenly, they saw their makeshift catamaran, their two lashed kayaks, gliding away to sea. On board was the entire basis for their survival – food, equipment and weapons. Nansen tore off his jacket, threw his watch to Johansen and jumped into the Arctic Ocean to swim after them. At first, the kayaks drifted faster

than Nansen could swim, but in the end he reached the boats. Getting on board, however, was another matter; it seemed almost impossible. "After a while, however, I managed to get one leg up on the deck, and then swung myself up." On the way back he shot two guillemots. Nansen was chilled to the core, and Johansen took off his own outer clothing and dressed Nansen in them before putting him in the sleeping bag to warm up.

On 15 June, as they were paddling along the coast, a walrus came up unexpectedly. Charging the kayak so that it nearly turned over, it then drove its tusks into the foredeck. Nansen paddled to the edge of the ice where the kayak sank. All their equipment – weapons, food and camera – was drenched and had to be dried while the kayak was repaired. On 17 June Nansen arose to make breakfast. Going out, he suddenly heard dogs, first faintly and later more strongly. He called Johansen, who also heard dogs barking. Nansen began walking in the direction of the sound. First he saw a dog and then a man, whom he heard speaking to the dogs. The man was the British polar explorer Frederick G. Jackson, whom Nansen had met on a previous occasion. A classic Livingstone-

Stanley situation then ensued. Nansen raised his hat, the two men shook hands, exchanged "How do you do's" and continued their conversation. Jackson: "I am damned glad to see you." Nansen: "Thank you, I also." Jackson: "Have you a ship here?" Nansen: "No, my ship is not here." Jackson: "How many are there of you?" Nansen: "I have a companion at the water's edge." They walked together toward Jackson's base on Cape Flora. Suddenly Jackson stopped and said, "Aren't you Nansen?" "Yes, I am," Nansen replied. "By Jove, I am devilish glad to see you."

Nansen and Johansen were now in the care of people who welcomed them back to civilisation, which they had left behind 462 days ago, during which time they mainly lived off the land. When they left the *Fram* they had provisions for 100 days. They discovered that in the time they spent at the Winter Lair, Nansen had gained 10 kg and Johansen 6 kg. Polar bear meat and blubber are clearly very nutritious.

THE HOMECOMING

Johansen and Nansen remained at Jackson's base until the latter's expedition vessel, the *Windward*, arrived. They arrived in Vardø on the *Windward* on 13th August. On the same day, the *Fram* freed itself from the grip of the ice around Svalbard, having spent 1,056 days in its clutches. The *Fram's* drift brought her to 85°57'N. The voyage had proceeded in an orderly manner, with the scientific studies carried out as planned. On 20 August the *Fram* entered Skjervøy Harbour where Sverdrup learned that Nansen had reached Vardø on 13 August. Sverdrup immediately set sail for Tromsø. On 21 August, Nansen and Johansen came on board, and the original crew was once again complete. The voyage had been completed and its accomplishments were viewed by everyone as remarkable.

Now began a triumphal cruise along the coast, with stops in Trondheim, Bergen, Stavanger, Kristiansand and Larvik. The Greenland Expedition had been viewed as a zenith in the annals of exploration. The *Fram* Expedition, however, was regarded with even greater respect. The *Fram* arrived in Kristiania on 9 September. A grand reception, exceeding any the city had ever experienced, awaited the heroes of the *Fram* Expedition.

King Oscar II invited the crew to a banquet, at which the King stressed that the voyage was Norwegian "to the fullest

The Fram's reception in Trondheim became a national event.

meaning of the word", ending with the following: "My thanks will not fade with the great excitement of the hour. It will survive all of us who are present. It will outlast the generations in centuries after centuries to come, for as long as (Mt.)Dovre stands." His Majesty's homage was concluded with a rousing three times three cheer for Nansen and his men.

Throughout the voyage the political undertones of the day were palpable. For instance, during that year's celebration of Norway's National Day, 17 May 1895, there were slogans on banners which read: "'Fram' 'Fram'! Norwegian Man!", probably an allusion to the ship's name and what it meant, i.e. forwards – to liberty? *"Our Own Flag for This Land!"* On yet another, *"What We Do, We Do for Norway!"* A purely Norwegian flag, one lacking the Swedish colours, was hoisted several times. There can be no doubt that the *Fram's* voyage helped strengthen nationalist feelings in Norway, and the road to 1905, when Norway seceded from the union with Sweden, was not long.

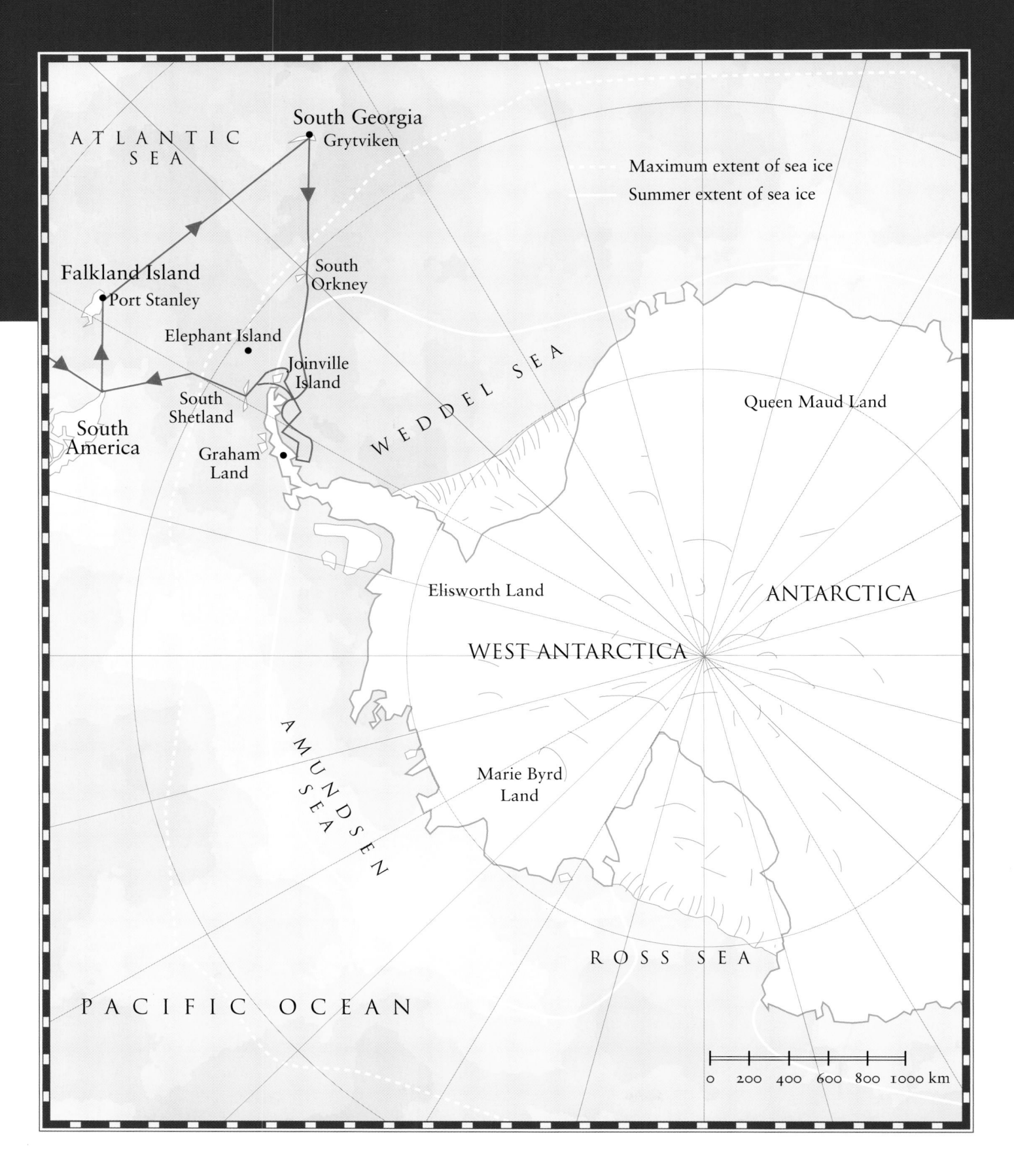

ATLANTIC SEA

South Georgia
• Grytviken

Maximum extent of sea ice
Summer extent of sea ice

Falkland Island
• Port Stanley

South Orkney

Elephant Island •

Joinville Island

South America

South Shetland

WEDDEL SEA

Queen Maud Land

Graham Land

Elisworth Land

ANTARCTICA

WEST ANTARCTICA

AMUNDSEN SEA

Marie Byrd Land

PACIFIC OCEAN

ROSS SEA

0   200 400 600 800 1000 km

C.A. LARSEN 1893

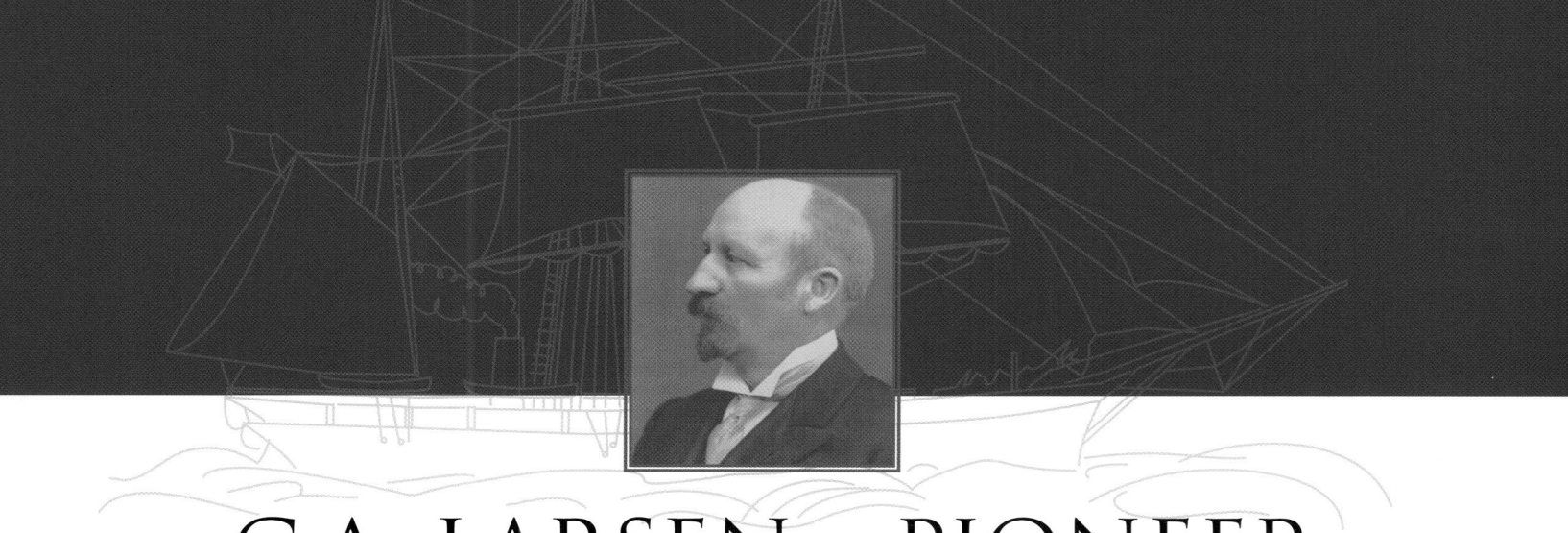

C.A. LARSEN – PIONEER OF THE ANTARCTIC OCEAN

BY THOR N. DEVIG

C. A. Larsen is one of the most important explorers in the history of the Antarctic. His work with the geographical mapping of this south polar region has proved of immense value. He was also the first to show that the Antarctic comprises sedimentary rocks. In addition, he was a bold innovator in the field of commercial whaling and whaling on the open sea. In 1904 he established a land-based whaling station at Grytviken in South Georgia – financed by Argentinean capital.

It is just after dawn. A ship under full sail makes for Paulet Island in the Antarctic Ocean. Her engine and deck pumps work ceaselessly to run off the seawater streaming in through large gashes in the hull. The crew struggles frantically, hoping to run the ship aground and salvage provisions and equipment. Without these they have little chance of survival.

The stiff current works against them, forcing the ship in among gigantic icebergs which threaten to crush her already badly damaged hull. Her timbers groan as the engine is started up in an attempt to make steerage way. Reaching more open waters, it becomes obvious that the engine vibrations actually increase the flow of water through the hull. The

water reaches the fire box flue and the second engineer is up to his waist in icy water.

Every effort is made to hold the ship afloat while the captain manoeuvres the doomed 100-toner as close as possible to the edge of an ice floe. With the ship alongside the ice, frenzied activity begins with the unloading of as much equipment as possible. Provisions, clothing, working boats, sails and canvas, some planking, and a few personal belongings are hastily thrown out onto the ice floe. With that the crew abandon the doomed ship. She drifts away from them, sinking deeper and deeper into the icy polar waters.

At noon the sinking ship keels over and disappears into the deep. Twenty men are left standing on floating ice in a

81

vast and ice-bound wasteland. There are no means of communication, they have no way of contacting the outside world, and no-one knows where they are. It is mid-February and the Antarctic summer is waning. Winter is uncomfortably close at hand, meaning that a possible rescue operation cannot be expected until November.

The men have no way of manoeuvring toward land. They are soon surrounded by sea ice, drifting helplessly at the mercy of wind and weather. The situation appears hopeless but no-one gives way to despair thanks to their captain, whose indomitable optimism steadies his men. During that first day on the ice floe, the captain notes in his diary: " Nothing will be gained by whining and complaining, what we need is courage and strength. We will have to defy the elements even though they use their worst efforts to strike us down. It remains to be seen who will win – the ice or we."

After 16 days the ice unexpectedly breaks up and the boats are launched, loaded with the most essentials items. Most of the clothing and provisions have to be left behind. The exhausted crew then rows continuously for six hours, finally reaching the desolate beaches of Paulet Island. That very night

the wind blows up to hurricane strength and the crew, who would have faced certain death, give thanks that they no longer are on the ice floe. The captain's brief entry in his diary undoubtedly expresses the feelings of them all:

"Praise be to the Lord for allowing us to reach this place. We will manage, one way or another, to survive this year. We have not reached shore only to be left to our own devices. The same hand which led us here will surely protect us from now on and ensure that all ends well."

The situation may be under control for the moment but the outlook for the future is bleak. No doubt some among the crew regret having set out on this exploit, this daring adventure which had begun some 15 months earlier on the other side of the world.

THE ANTARCTIC EXPEDITION

The story began on 16 October 1901 when the former sealer *Antarctic* left Gothenburg in Sweden for Sandefjord in Norway.

The sealer Antarctic in the Antarctic Ocean prior to capsizing.

Here the last pieces of equipment, including gear for whaling and sealing, were loaded on board,. After a short stay the voyage continued southwards towards the final destination, the vast ocean areas of the Antarctic.

On board were a number of Swedish scientists including Senior Lecturer N.O.G. Nordenskiöld, a geologist and geographer. Planning for the expedition had begun in 1899 and Nordenskiöld had procured the *Antarctic* as the expedition's ship. She had already proven herself to be a robust and highly suitable polar vessel. Built in 1871, the ship had a long tradition as a whaler under the name *Cap Nord*. Under the new name, *Antarctic*, she had already been used on expeditions, among them one led by H.J. Bull to the Ross Sea in 1893.

The ship had been partly rebuilt and reinforced to withstand the pressures of the extreme conditions in the Antarctic. Just as important as a good ship, however, was the right captain, one with knowledge of – and previous experience from – arctic conditions. The plan was for the scientists to be landed and set up in a separate summer base camp in order to carry out their studies while the ship would investigate both the adjacent waters and the ocean between the Antarctic peninsula and South Georgia. With this program of activity, the captain's qualifications would have an important effect on the expedition's overall scientific results.

Nordenskiöld was, in other words, looking for a person with personal characteristics not easily found in one and the same individual. And he had to leave Sweden in order to find his man. He quite clearly had a specific person in mind when he wrote, "As soon as the purchase of the ship was settled, I immediately contacted the one man whom I above all wanted to sign as captain of the ship for the voyage."

This man was Carl Anton Larsen, or simply C.A. Larsen as he became known. During his two expeditions to the Antarctic on the *Jason* and his work in the Arctic Ocean, Larsen had gained a reputation as a daring and resolute captain, "one whose total experience gave him the greatest knowledge of those regions of the Antarctic Ocean which I intended to visit".

Due to meagre funding, the expedition was to hunt seal and right whale in addition to carrying out scientific work. In this capacity too Larsen had many years of experience both in hunting seals and bottlenose dolphins, and as a whaling station manager on the coast of Finnmark in northern

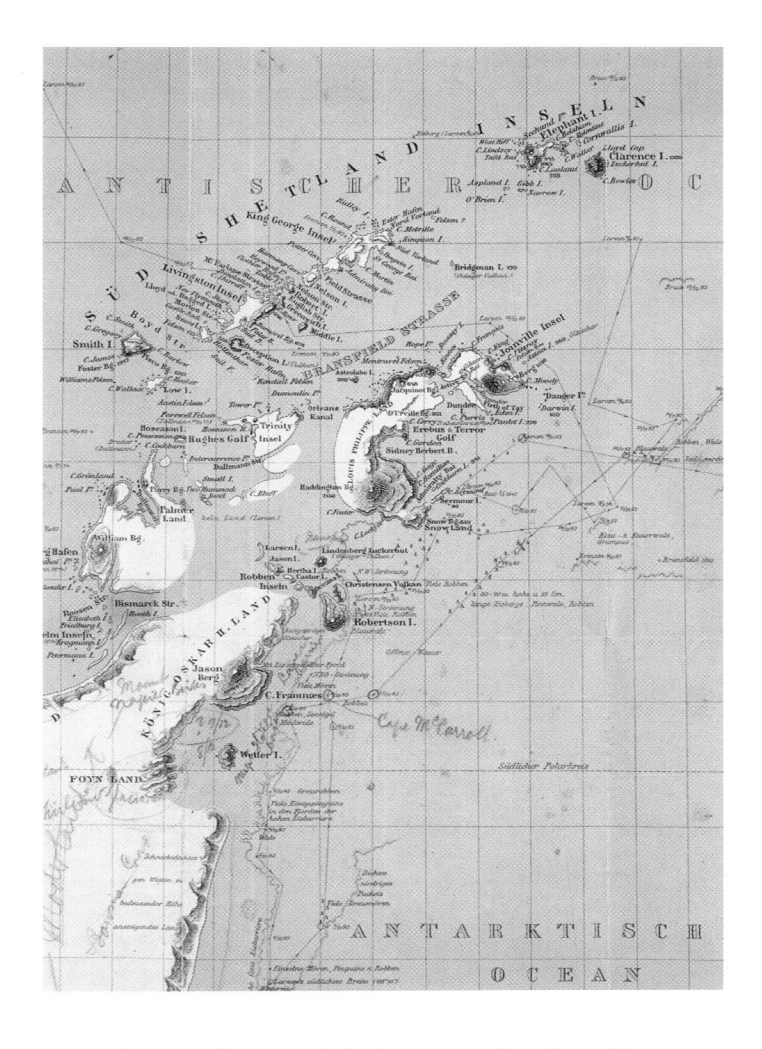

Map showing the area C.A. Larsen explored on his voyage with the Jason in 1893.

Norway. C.A. Larsen agreed to command the *Antarctic* on the proposed expedition and resigned his position as whaling station manager.

After leaving Sandefjord the voyage continued on to Buenos Aires and then to Port Stanley on the Falkland Islands. From here the expedition departed on New Year's Day 1902, and by 10 January had its first encounter with pack ice off the coast of South Shetland Islands. It was later learned that ice conditions in the Antarctic Ocean were exceptionally severe in the summer of 1901/1902.

The *Antarctic* pressed on further south, passing Astrolabe Island and the coast of Louis-Philippe Land. Off Cape Seymour the expedition ran into massive ice to the south and

south-east and had to abandon all hopes of continuing. It was decided that the scientists who were to winter on shore would be landed immediately. By 12 February, winter quarters were set up in the interior of Snow Hill Island off the eastern shore of Graham Land.

The plans called for Nordenskiöld's party of scientists to be picked up in October or November at the beginning of the polar summer. The *Antarctic* would proceed to Ushuaia on the coast of Tierra del Fuego to bunker coal and continue on to South Georgia to conduct scientific studies and collect specimens. The ice forced Larsen, however, to sail into the sound between Louis-Philippe Land and Joinville Island. In a full storm with poor visibility, the vessel sailed north into unknown waters, struggling against strong currents and drifting ice floes in order to clear the South Shetlands. The normally optimistic Larsen writes in his diary, "I have now told everyone that they must be ready to give account of their past lives to their Maker, because I cannot tell whether we will be alive or dead by evening."

After two days' nerve-wracking sailing they managed to come out between South Shetland and the Elephant Islands and finally reached Tierra del Fuego. After bunkering, the voyage continued on southward to South Georgia by way of Port Stanley on the Falklands. It was now April. The expedition would have enough time until mid-June for observations on South Georgia. A party led by J. Gunnar Andersson, and including cartographer S.A. Duse, were put ashore.

Grytviken on South Georgia, anno 1999.

Meanwhile C.A. Larsen was determining the population of whale along the coast of the island. He observed large numbers of humpback and fin whales but right whales were nowhere to be seen. This affirmed earlier observations made by Larsen in other regions of the Antarctic Ocean.

Later the ship anchored up at Grytviken where Andersson's party waited. C.A. Larsen was impressed by the harbour which was calm and sheltered. Streams flowing down from the surrounding mountains provided a surplus of fresh water. Taking Larsen's whaling experience from northern Norway into consideration, he must have been struck by Grytviken's pronounced suitability as a land-based station. In addition, he observed enormous numbers of blue, fin and humpback whales in the immediate vicinity.

Summer was approaching and C.A. Larsen and his men caught large numbers of seals and sea elephants. Skins and blubber were delivered to the Falklands before the ship bunkered coal and prepared to pick up the men who had wintered at Snow Hill.

In early November the *Antarctic* and her crew head toward Graham Land but because ice conditions are even worse than the previous year, they are soon forced to a complete halt. The vast masses of ice worry Larsen. He is

The Jason on a voyage in the Antarctic Ocean.

afraid that they will have "a tough time reaching the winter station if conditions do not improve".

They fight their way through the ice belt, experiencing both storm and calm weather, and by 23 November are finally off Deception Island. During the following days the expedition maps a sizeable region stretching westward from Astrolabe Island towards the Belgica Strait. One result, among many others, is that Larsen is able to eliminate Middle Island from existing charts. He arrives at the island's supposed position and begins taking soundings. "The results were 785 fathoms of seawater and a clay bottom. It is hereby determined that the island does not exist."

Time is beginning to run short if the winter party is to be picked up and C.A. Larsen sets course for Snow Hill. The plan is to approach Erebus and the Gulf of Terror by way of the Antarctic Sound. Once again the ice proves impenetrable and the *Antarctic* swings north of Joinville Island and proceeds eastward. The ship is soon in the midst of ice masses which hinder further progress to the south. Conditions become extremely difficult with the ship now helplessly drifting in the grip of the ice.

C.A. Larsen now abandons the plan to reach the expedition's winter party even though he is so close that he can see Cockburn Island which is also visible from the Winter

Station. On 29 December, three men are set ashore at the Bay of Hope on the eastern side of Trinity Peninsula. The plan is for them to go on by foot and alert the expedition members who are now completely isolated at their summer base camp.

It proves, moreover, impossible for C.A. Larsen to get clear of the ice. The ship now drifts about with the crew unable to do anything one way or the other. On 10 January a full storm sets in. The ship is also racked with even more difficulties with the ice soon having "pressed the ship about 4 feet upwards at the stern while the old hull creaks and groans so as to make one think it will split".

During the following night the ice pack crushes the solid hull of the ship. All pumps are manned and preparations for abandoning ship are completed. She remains firmly in the grip of the ice, however. The ship drifts about on the ice floe for some three weeks until she finally slides off and the crew is able to set sail for Paulet Island.

As we learned from the opening lines of this chapter, the *Antarctic* gained Paulet Island under full sail. We know what happened to the ship and that the crew did manage to reach land. Here they built a primitive hut, measuring 5.5 x 6 metres, of stone and guano with a canvas roof. There was, of course, no means of communication with the outside world at this time. Contact with the three men at the Bay of Hope or with the party at Snow Hill was also impossible. It was now a case of depending on one's own strength and concentrating on one's

The colourful emperor penguins are native to Antarctica.

own survival.

During that long winter the crew subsisted on a monotonous diet of penguin and seal meat. The provisions salvaged from the *Antarctic* were severely rationed. Despite all privations, it appears that the men's morale was high and that they managed quite well through the long polar night. C.A. Larsen writes in his diary, for example, that he is "fit and in good health as well as being in the best of sprits".

On 31 October 1903, the ice finally yields and Larsen makes an incredible decision: a boat will be launched and he and five men will head for the Bay of Hope. After four days of hard rowing, the six finally reach the bay. There they find a message that the three men set ashore there have gone on to Snow Hill on 28. September.

Larsen and his men have no alternative but to head south toward Snow Hill. If Nordenskiöld and his party have already been found and have left the winter quarters, Larsen and his crew will have few chances of being rescued. Their only hope lies in re-joining the rest of the Nordenskiöld expedition.

C.A. Larsen's little group finally reaches the Snow Hill base on 8 November and their joy is immeasurable when they see the corvette *Uruguay* anchored up in the bay. The Argentinean naval vessel had arrived that very day to rescue Nordenskiöld and his men. It was pure coincidence that Larsen himself had arrived in time.

This dramatic shipwreck ended well for everyone concerned, but margins are close in these areas of the world. The balance often rests with the crew itself, with the courage and experience of their leader and with his intimate knowledge of the extreme conditions found in polar regions. C.A. Larsen was such a leader and such a man.

CARL ANTON LARSEN – THE MAN AND HIS ENVIRONMENT

Carl Anton Larsen is far less well known than Roald Amundsen, Fridtjof Nansen and the other pioneering polar explorers and adventurers. His exploits did not get the same headlines and he never was acclaimed a national hero. His activities in his field were, nevertheless, a significant contribution to Norway's position as an important maritime and polar hunting nation.

C.A. Larsen was born in Larvik, in Vestfold county on the Oslofjord, on 7 August 1860, as the third son of Ellen Andrea and Ole Christian Larsen. He grew up in Østre Halsen, a typically seafaring neighbourhood whose shipyard played a significant part in the town's economy. Here were sailing ships laid up for the winter, here were deep-sea sailors and their stories of adventure, here were tall tales told and the lust for the sea wakened in many a young boy's heart.

In keeping with tradition, Carl Anton went to sea as soon as he had been confirmed. At the age of 14 he went off with his father, a captain who for many years had commanded ships for the P.J. & P. Berg shipping company. His older brother was also on board as first mate. Carl Anton rose rapidly in the ranks and at the age of 18 had taken his Mate's Certificate. He was captain of his own ship 22 years of age.

C.A. Larsen was born into surroundings in which going to sea, seamanship and the urge expand to one's potential were vital elements. This was especially evident in the founding and further development of sealing and whaling activities, in which Vestfold county would play a leading part. In fact, when it came to whaling, Vestfold was a world leader for several generations. C.A. Larsen came to have a vital role in this development.

Sealing had been run from Vestfold as early as in the 1840s. Sealers had also noted the large numbers of bottlenose whales in areas they passed through on their way to and from the northern sealing grounds. They recognised a commercial opportunity with many of them later combining sealing with whaling. Developments led to further specialisation, however, and in 1883 the first specially-equipped ship steamed north with the sole aim of hunting bottlenose.

In 1884-85 C.A. Larsen makes contact with this whaling activity. He is signed on as captain of the schooner and bottlenose-hunter *Freden* ("Peace") owned by Johan Bryde. In

1886 he commands the *Fortuna* ("Fortune"), a larger steam-powered, specially-built bottlenose hunter owned by shipowner Chr. Christensen from Sandefjord. Then he becomes captain of the sealer *Jason*. This is owned by the Oceana Company, whose owner was the same Chr. Christensen, together with the German firm Woltereck & Robertson whose Norwegian agent was Carl Lindeberg.

One curious coincidence in this connection is that C.A. Larsen brought Fridtjof Nansen to Greenland with the *Jason* in 1888. That same year Nansen crossed the Greenland ice cap.

C.A. Larsen was engaged in sealing and whaling in the following years. Populations slowly but surely became decimated, however. C.A. Larsen was undoubtedly one of the first who realised what this meant, and he was most certainly one the first men who also had a solution to the problem:

"We'd better get moving, boys – from the North Pole to the South Pole, or thereabouts." This is an oft-quoted remark made by Larsen in conversations with whaling colleagues in the far North. It shows the vision which C.A. Larsen held for the future. And his words would become reality before he realised it.

THE JASON EXPEDITIONS

On 26 July 1892 C.A. Larsen returned from the Arctic Ocean with a fully-loaded *Jason*. Before the 6000 skins were even unloaded a new destination had been decided upon: the *Jason* was to head south. Those responsible for this decision were probably Chr. Christensen and Carl Lindeberg. It can appear impulsive but was not taken on mere chance. One main reason may well have been that Scotsman Robert Kinnes had equipped four ships which were to sail for the Antarctic. Here they were to hunt for whale in the area between Paulet and Seymour Islands east of Graham Island.

Larsen's principle assignment was the hunting seal and whale. Another objective was to determine the population of seal and whale in Antarctic waters with the intention of future commercial exploitation. In this context "whale" meant the right whale. This was strange, in that it had been the huge fin

---

The Jason heading for the Antarctic Ocean.

whales which had given the greatest profit from the northern grounds. However, since the whale populations of the North were greatly reduced because of intensive hunting, it was necessary to find new areas to exploit. One explanation can be that the value of one right whale at that time was a staggering 40.000 crowns. In addition, far different and more complicated equipment was necessary for hunting the massive and strong fin whales.

On 1 September the *Jason* left on the long journey south. The first stop was made at South Shields where she bunkered. The voyage went well for C.A. Larsen and his crew who reached South Orkney by way of South Georgia on 16 November. Seal-hunting began immediately but the results were disappointing. Larsen therefore decided to proceed to the real goal of the voyage, Graham Land and the surrounding islands.

Jason was now moving into partly unknown waters with incomplete and often quite misleading charts. Groups of islands had been drawn as adjoining land areas, sounds and waterways were left out, non-existent islands had been plotted in while existing islands had not. C.A. Larsen carried out important correction work on the charts he had available. Later whaling expeditions regarded navigation in these waters as being extremely difficult. Misleading charts and the ship's weak

engines made the job even worse for C.A. Larsen. The *Jason*-expedition is therefore considered to be an extraordinary piece of seamanship. Not the least when the strong currents and massive pack ice are taken into consideration.

The *Jason* finally reached Erebus and the Gulf of Terror's outermost regions between Seymour and Paulet Islands. Expectations of great numbers of right whale were high, and the disappointment when none were sighted was correspondingly deep. "The right whale ought to be here in colossal numbers, so many that ships can go right in and start loading whalebone. Feed is carried right to this bank by the currents, – this is where they ought to be. We have storms and snow and a terrible number of icebergs which we can't see until we're right on them because of the driving snow. We keep our steam up, ready to clear ship. The pack ice drifts by at good speed while small ice floes move at a speed of several miles. But we have not yet sighted a right whale."

In early December C.A. Larsen sighted Graham Land. A couple of days later he was the first man to go ashore at Cape Seymour. This volcanic island fascinated Larsen who brought back a number of finds, including fossils, to the *Jason*.

The *Jason* cruised these waters for weeks, first westward and then eastward again. No right whales were sighted. It is difficult to accept James Clark Ross' observations in his account, *A Voyage of Discovery and Research in the Southern and Antarctic Regions during the Years 1839–43*, where he tells of enormous numbers of right whale on the banks east of Graham Land. It is possible that Ross can have mistaken the larger fin whales for the right whale. C.A. Larsen assumed this to be the case after having searched the area thoroughly. We now know that the fin whale is dominant in Antarctic waters.

For the remainder of the polar summer the crew of the *Jason* toiled at securing a full load. Since no right whale were sighted they had to make do with seal. By 20 February the ship was fully loaded and able to set a northbound course. Although the expedition was a financial disappointment, the scientific results were far better. In his book *Sydpolforskning (South Polar Research)*, Dr. O.J. Skattum maintains that on this voyage C.A. Larsen made several important scientific

The sperm whale is readied for processing.

Whaling on South Georgia in the early 1900s.

discoveries, not the least of which was the collection of the first Antarctic fossils on Seymour Island and Louis-Philippe Land. These provided evidence of sedimentary strata in Antarctica.

The owners were not prepared to give up despite the meagre financial return. The next autumn, in 1893, the company sent three sealing vessels to the south: the *Jason*, the *Hertha* and the *Castor*. C.A. Larsen, captain of the *Jason*, was leader of the expedition. The plan this time was to concentrate on hunting seal since the company had more or less given up on the right whale. Each ship was to get two full loads which would then be delivered and processed on board a special freighter at the Falklands.

A MAJOR ACHIEVEMENT IN MAPPING

Cape Seymour was reached on 16 November and the search for seal began immediately. The result, however, was poor leading the *Jason* to search farther and farther south. Whereas C.A. Larsen and his crew had reached the then known limits and beheld unknown areas on their first expedition, they now sailed straight in towards regions where no-one had ever been before – virginal, unexplored territories. In the following period C.A. Larsen achieved

important results in the field of geographical research. This established his reputation as one of the most significant explorers in the history of the Antarctic.

From Cape Seymour Larsen proceeded as far south as to 68°10' S. On this voyage he discovered and named important land areas and islands. Without going into too much detail concerning Larsens voyage in this unknown territory it should be mentioned that he named and mapped the following important new areas: King Oscar II Land, Mount Jason, Cape Framnæs, Veier Island, Foyn Land, Robertson Island, Christensen Volcano, Lindberg Sugar Loaf and the Seal Islands. Larsen calculated the position of all new territories he discovered "as accurately as possible with the navigational instruments at my disposal".

In the aftermath of the expedition there was some discussion as to the accuracy of Larsen's calculations in positioning his discoveries. Taking the instruments he had access to into consideration, there is no doubt that his geographical registrations are impressive. He has also received recognition for this on a par with Palmer, Biscoe and

Weddell. Dr. O.J. Skattum goes so far as to say that this was "the first geographical triumph since Ross and the greatest until Scott".

One more point should be mentioned. C.A. Larsen and his first mate used skis while searching for seal in the area. They are thus considered to be the first skiers on the Antarctic continent.

The expedition was unusually fortunate in the weather and ice conditions during this season. This has clearly contributed to the success of the expedition. Seen from another angle, if Larsen had not been on a sealing expedition, and had been able to concentrate his efforts on pure exploration, his results might have been even more sensational. Instead he was forced to hunt seal all along the north-south ice barrier, often with little success. One important reason for this was that the seal remained too far in on the ice barrier.

An outbreak of scurvy among the crew led to the loading of the ship being speeded up. On 8 March the ship was finally ready to set course for the Falklands. Here the seal was unloaded onto the freighter, the sick crewmen received medical attention and the long voyage home could finally begin.

After two seasons in the Antarctic one right whale was finally harpooned in April right off South Georgia. Despite high seas, the men were able to put the huge animal to death but because they were unable to tow it to land for further processing, it was lost.

The *Jason* arrived in her home port on 5 July. The ship's main objective had been to hunt seal and whale which the owners anticipated would be profitable. Viewed in this light, C.A. Larsen's work in mapping and collection of scientific material is nothing less than astounding. The observations he made concerning the huge fin whale population were certainly of vital importance. These, together with his stay at Grytviken on the *Antarctic*, have undoubtedly been the basis for C.A. Larsen's later important contributions to the development of the whaling industry.

THE WHALING PIONEER

C.A. Larsen's pioneering work is mostly linked to the mapping of new lands and territories on the enormous Antarctic continent. His greatest achievement was, however, in another field. This was the investigation and evaluation of

the prospects for commercial exploitation of these new territories, especially as regards the hunting of large sea mammals. Focus was gradually trained on whale hunting and the possibilities lying in the enormous populations of blue whale, fin whale, sei whale and humpback whale which arrived every spring on their annual migrations from the north.

During the *Antarctic*-expedition C.A. Larsen began to understand in earnest the resources lying in these populations. On the voyage south in January of 1902, he notes in his diary that the entire channel "is full of spouting whales, – no matter where one looks. All of them are humpback whale and in such numbers as to be beyond comprehension." He notes further that those north of South Shetland are mostly fin whale and that "they are also present in colossal numbers".

C.A. Larsen had experience in hunting both seal, bottlenose whale and the huge fin whale. This was not at all odd, since he came from Vestfold county. As early as in 1864, Svend Foyn, who was also from Vestfold, had developed the technology necessary for hunting the great fin whale. When Foyn's patent-rights and consequent hunting monopoly expired in 1883, a number of new whaling stations were established along the coast of Finnmark. One of these, "Skjold & Værge", was managed by Larsen from 1895 to 1901.

But it was in the Antarctic that C.A. Larsen would make his mark as a whaling pioneer. On the *Antarctic*-expedition he had become very familiar with South Georgia and he grasped the enormous potential which lay in whaling in these waters. It was difficult to raise Norwegian capital for the establishment of a land-based station. The idea did not capture the imagination of Norwegian shipowners. Leading men among them expressed misgivings about the venture and these misgivings spread throughout the industry.

C.A. Larsen's faith in his project remained unshaken. During the return voyage of the *Antarctic*-expedition a reception was held in Buenos Aires, in honour of the participants. Larsen was introduced to local businessmen, among them an emigrant Norwegian named Pedro Christophersen and a Swedish-born banker named Ernesto Tornquist. They became interested in both the man and his project. This led to the unusual situation of Argentinean capitalists advocating C.A. Larsen's optimistic belief in the future of Antarctic whaling while Norwegian shipowners

wavered.

As a result, the firm Compania Argentina de Pesca S.A. was established with Argentinean capital and with C.A. Larsen as general manager. The crews for both land-based stations and whaleboat were recruited in Norway. The first group, led by C.A. Larsen arrived at Grytviken on 16 November 1904 while the first extraction of whale oil took place on Christmas Eve. Larsen participated in every phase of the work. Always active, he was harpoonist on the whaleboat and supervisor on land.

All construction materials and all the production and hunting equipment were shipped from Norway. Two ships were purchased for transporting and C.A. Larsen had the whaleboat *Fortuna* built at the Framnæs Yards in Sandefjord. The boat, much larger than was usual for this type of vessel, was regarded with unconcealed disdain by the know-it-alls of the whaling industry. Larsen had the right idea, however, and Grytviken was an immediate success. The first year's yield was 5,300 barrels of whale oil, a result which could not pass unnoticed in Norwegian whaling circles. The entrepreneur had shown the way and others were not slow in following him. Over the next five years, until 1909, the number of expeditions

Flensing of a whale at shipside.

(both land-based stations and factory-ships) rose from one to 13 and the number of whaleboats from one to 37. Prompted by C.A. Larsen's pioneering enterprise, the great whaling venture of the South Polar seas had started up in earnest.

In 1914 C.A. Larsen left Grytviken for good, apparently due to a lengthy conflict with the Argentinean owners who in Larsen's opinion took out too much profit at the expense of necessary reinvestments in the works, equipment and crew facilities. By then Larsen had, largely on his own, financed the building of a church and together with the crews built up a well-stocked library.

After an interlude during which Larsen unsuccessfully tried to farm in Ringerike county, the challenges of the Antarctic once again lured him. This time he wanted to test a new idea. Up to now whaling had been based on use of a land-based station or of a factory-ship permanently stationed right offshore, in a sheltered inlet etc. The technology for bringing a whale carcass on board ship for processing was not yet available. That meant that the whale was flensed shipside

Grytviken on South Georgia at the end of the 1920s.

which was dependent on calm waters. C.A. Larsen's bold plan was to force a way through the belt of pack ice in order to gain the open waters of the Ross Sea. The sea here was, as a rule, calm enough for flensing and partitioning could take place without complications. It would no longer be necessary to tow the whale carcass to land. This gave the industry new and improved potential.

The idea was revolutionary but not entirely new. H.J. Bull had taken the expedition ship *Antarctic* through the ice belt out into the Ross Sea, observing there "blue whale and fin whale in huge numbers". "It should be possible to replace, at least partly, the customary shore station with a freighter equipped for storing the catch and, using a modern whaleboat, I have no doubt but that skilful men can get any quantities of blubber they might desire during the short summer months."

This was written in 1895! But it was not until 1923 that these ideas would be implemented. Nor surprisingly, indeed almost obviously, it was C.A. Larsen who once again proved the pioneer. Commanding what was then the largest ship ever used in whaling, the *Sir James Clark Ross,* with a gross tonnage of 8,223, Larsen left Sandefjord on 22 September 1923 and set his course for the Antarctic. After rendezvousing with the five whaleboats at Hobart, Tasmania, the expedition left for the Ross Sea on 30 November.

As had been the case with the *Antarctic*-expedition, the weather and ice conditions were terrible and Larsen barely managed to break through the sense belt of pack ice. But by 20 December, all the boats had pushed through only to meet new difficulties: "The temperature is minus 20° and the whale are hard as blocks of wood. It is a great pity that these colossal resources cannot be utilised. We have more than 300,000 crowns worth of blubber lying alongside the ship. What little time we have is running out and it will get worse. The outlook is bleak indeed." On 7 March C.A. Larsen had to abandon all hopes of further whaling in order to avoid being frozen fast. The year's result was 17,299 barrels of whale oil, giving a net profit of 44,776 crowns. Against a share capital of 3,500,000 crowns this was less than nothing.

Looking toward the next season, Larsen was preoccupied with the idea of profit. Improvements were carried out on both ship and equipment. Departure for the field was speeded up by one month and by 3 December the *Sir James Clark Ross* was busy whaling. The results for this year were 31,460 barrels, giving a profit of almost 2 million crowns with a dividend of 15% to the company's shareholders.

Larsen had once more showed the way. The whaling company Rosshavet with its factory ship *Sir James Clark Ross* represents the beginning of pelagic whaling and the start of a new golden age for the whaling industry. Seven years later, and six years after C.A. Larsen's death, the industry climaxed. In the late summer of 1930, a fleet of 41 factory ships and 200 whaleboats headed for the Antarctic. During this season more than 28,000 blue whale were caught. Today we realise that

this activity almost decimated the whale population. The whaling industry is a lesson in how man should not exploit renewable resources.

Developments of this nature were something that C.A. Larsen could not have foreseen. It was extraordinary that at the age of 63 Larsen had been able to assume responsibility for raising capital, hiring crews and equipping what was until then the greatest whaling expedition ever, for a completely new kind of whaling – whaling on the open sea, completely independent of land. But the venture took its toll. He had for some time been troubled by chest pains, angina pectoris, which had increased in intensity. As time passed the attacks became so painful that he handed over the command of the expedition to his first mate, Oscar Nilsen. That same day he wrote movingly: "I no longer expect a long life, but I wish with all my heart I could see my wife and children once more, but God's will be done, if only my soul might rest with God, I have worked so hard down here."

On Monday, 8 December 1924, Carl Anton Larsen died

Grytviken anno 1999. The church and whaling manager's house have been restored. The house has been turned into a museum which is under British supervision.

without seeing the fantastic success of that year's expedition. According to his wish, his body was embalmed and carried home. On 15 May 1925 he was buried in the churchyard at Sandefjord.

An adventuresome and active life had come to an end. C.A. Larsen had made a lasting impression. His achievements in finding and mapping new territories in the Antarctic regions have given him a lasting position among Norway's great polar explorers. And he is responsible for two lasting milestones in the history of whaling: commercial hunting of the great fin whale and whaling on the open sea (pelagic whaling). These are both innovations which make C.A. Larsen a gigantic figure in the history of the industry.

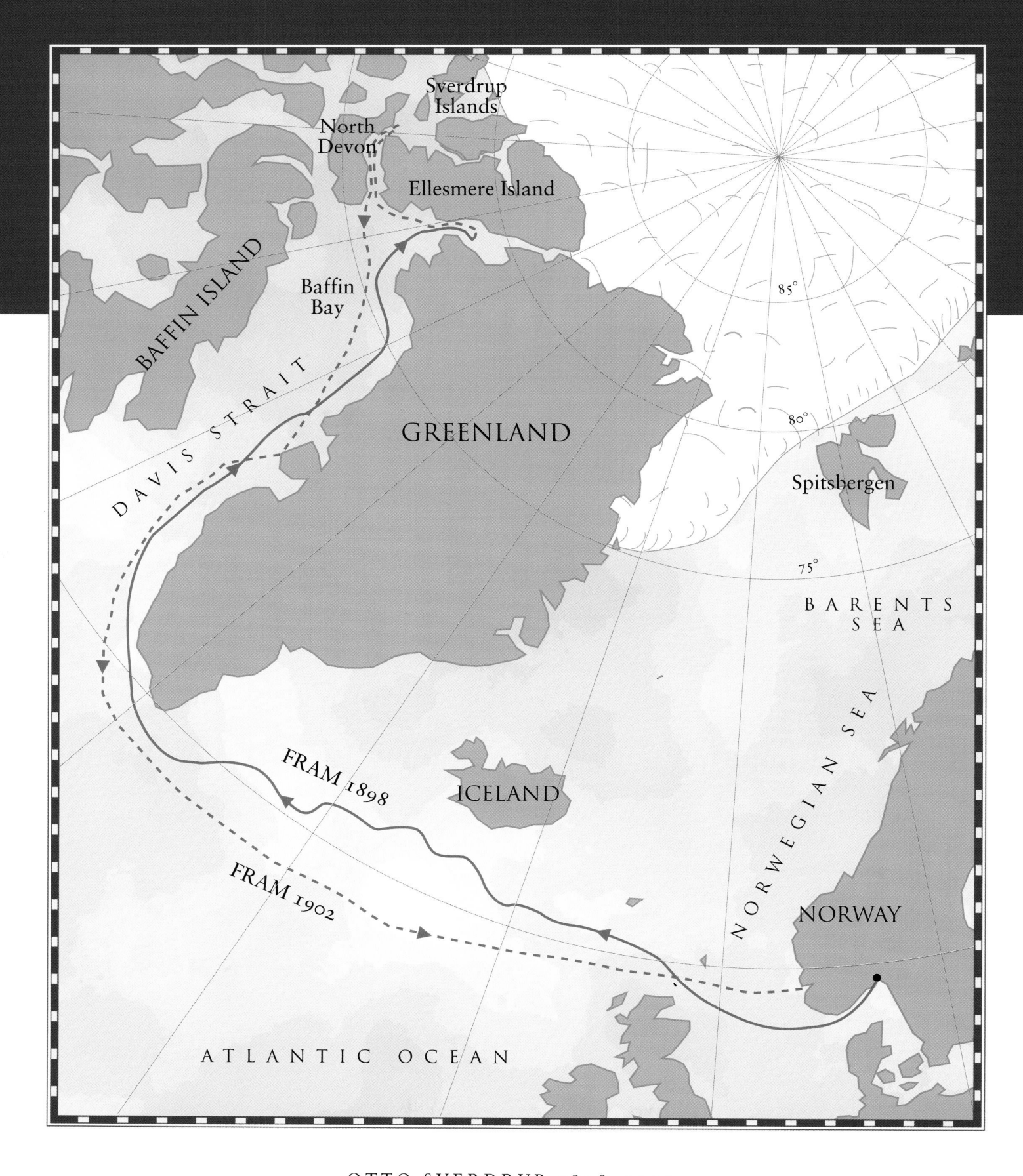

OTTO SVERDRUP 1898–1902.

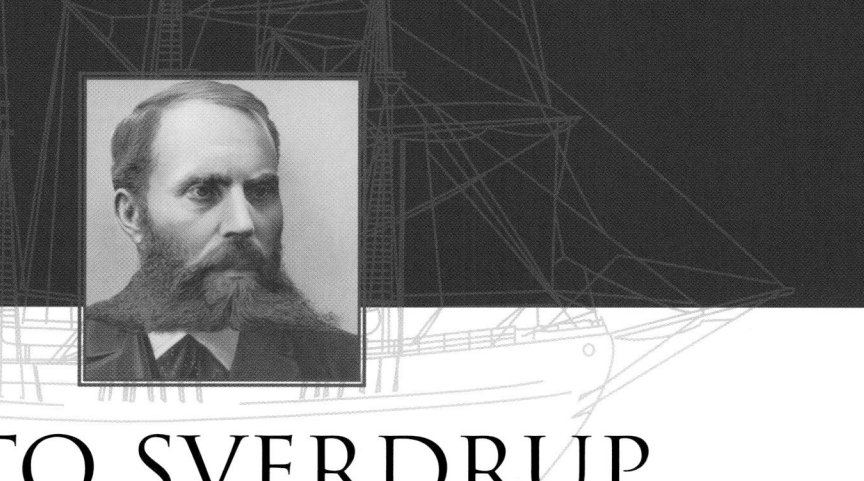

OTTO SVERDRUP
– DISCOVERY OF NEW
TERRITORIES IN THE NORTH

BY KÅRE BERG

No polar expedition charted such vast tracts of territory, and yielded so much scientific information as Otto Sverdrups's Second Fram Expedition to North Canada. The dazzling amount of material he brought back took 30 researchers 20 years to process. There are still a number of Norwegian names on Ellesmere Land and Axel Heiberg Land. Sverdrup claimed the lands he discovered in the name of King Haakon VII, but the Norwegian government failed to follow up on his claim to sovereignty...

Otto Neumann Knoph Sverdrup was born on 31 October 1854. His grandfather and tutor put great emphasis on toughening the young boy through sports and participation in undertakings which required resiliency, courage and a good portion of quick thinking. The "swimming lesson" he subscribed to consisted of rowing Otto and his brother, Peter Jacob, out on the fjord where he threw them both over board, saying, as he rowed away, that it was now up to them to make their way to shore.

Sverdrup went to sea at an early age, and passed his Mate's examination at the age of 23. A couple of years later, he obtained his Master's certificate. For a while he sailed on American merchant schooners freighting goods between the American East Coast and the West Indies.

In 1888–1889 Sverdrup participated in Fridtjof Nansen's crossing of the Greenland Ice Cap. When applying for participation in the expedition, Sverdrup attached a letter which attested to his stamina and expert skiing abilities. His application was accepted and during the voyage to Greenland

The crew of the Second Fram Expedition just before their departure.
From the left: Adolf Henrik Lindstrøm, Per Schei, Karl Olsen, Gunerius I. Isachsen, Rudolf Stoltz, Victor Baumann, Otto Sverdrup, Oluf Raanes, Herman G. Simmons (eye glasses), Peder Henriksen, Edvard Bay, Ove Braskerud (white hat), Johan Svendsen and Sverre Hassel. Svendsen and Braskerud died in 1899.

a mutual respect and friendship developed between Nansen and Sverdrup. When the *Fram* was under construction, Nansen gave the position of Ship's Inspector to Sverdrup, who moved to Larvik for the period from 1891 to 1892 while the ship was being built. It was Sverdrup who suggested how the *Fram* should be rigged. He skippered the vessel across the Arctic Ocean and headed the expedition from 14 March 1893 to 1896, after Nansen and Hjalmar Johansen left the *Fram* to go to the North Pole on skis. Johansen, too, had the greatest respect for Sverdrup, declaring, "This man who went on board silently and calmly – saw everything, said little, but accomplished all the more." Sverdrup was regarded by many as Norway's most silent man.

As early as September 1896 while the *Fram* was anchored at Lysaker, just outside Oslo, unloading equipment which remained from the First *Fram* Expedition, Nansen came on board to ask Sverdrup whether he wanted to set out on yet another northward-bound voyage. Sverdrup replied, "Of course I want to go if only I am given the opportunity."

The First *Fram* Expedition had been an overwhelming success, its fame reverberating well beyond Norway's borders.

Consul Axel Heiberg and the two founders of the Ringnes Brewery, Amund and Ellef Ringnes, were therefore willing to equip the *Fram* for a new voyage of discovery. Heiberg and the Ringnes brothers formed the *Fram* Shipping Company, leasing the vessel from the government. Since the First *Fram* Expedition had yielded a prodigious quantity of scientific material which needed to be processed and evaluated, Nansen was unable to participate in the journey. However, a plan for the expedition began to evolve, calling for the vessel to penetrate as far north as possible, in order to investigate the "white spots" on the map of Greenland's northern and

western coasts. If this could not be done, Sverdrup was given the authority to explore the region according to his own discretion. The Second *Fram* Expedition lasted for four years and ran into formidable hurdles of a magnitude which put both the crew and ship in harm's way.

On the First *Fram* voyage, the freeboard was found to be too low, causing the vessel to take in unacceptably large amounts of water. Sverdrup consequently had the freeboard raised by an additional six feet, building a new deck which extended forward from the engine-room and thereby adding six new cabins in the foreword segment of the ship. In addition to the cabins, a new saloon was built as well as two relatively spacious work rooms. These and other modifications were carried out in Larvik by Colin Archer, who had designed and built the *Fram*.

Since the First *Fram* Expedition brought back two years' worth of provisions, the vessel was stocked with stores to last for five years. The nutritional composition remained the same as for the maiden voyage.

Of the *Fram*'s crew of 16, only 14 would return. There was a large number of scientists on board:

- First Lt. Gunerius Ingvald Isachsen, cartographer.
- Scientific Assistant Herman Georg Simmons, Swedish, trained at the University of Lund, botanist.
- Scientific Assistant Edvard Bay, Danish, trained at the University of Copenhagen, zoologist.
- Scientific Assistant Per Schei, trained at the University of Kristiania, geologist.
- Medical Doctor Johan Svendsen, trained at the University of Kristiania.

The second-in-command was First Lt. Victor Baumann who had been trained at the Royal Naval College, in addition to studying electrotechnology for two years.

THE FRAM SETS OUT TOWARD ITS GOAL

On Midsummer's Day, 24 June 1898, five years to the day the *Fram* first set out toward the Arctic Ocean, she left Kristiania once again. Her first stop was Kristiansand, from where she headed for Egedesminde, Greenland. During the crossing the weather was foul, with one storm following closely after the other. Her famous inclinations to lurch and reel were not affected to the better by the modifications to the keel. The least

experienced hands began to visit the doctor, complaining of headaches, stomach pains and many other kinds of discomfort, in sum, everyone was sea sick, "and for that there is only one, very simple remedy – dry land, but we had forgotten to bring that along on our otherwise extremely well-equipped expedition..." In a letter to his parents, Ivar Fosheim, one of the hunters on board, described seasickness as follows: "The nature of seasickness is such that for the first hour one is afraid of dying. The rest of the time one is afraid that one will not die quickly enough."

The *Fram* arrived at Egedesminde where she loaded 31 dogs. At her next port-of-call she took on board an additional 35 dogs, bringing the dog population to 56, and bunkered coal supplies. The last harbour to be visited on Greenland was Upernivik, where another 30 dogs were ready to be loaded, but were rejected due to an infectious disease which had spread among them.

The *Fram* then entered Smith Sound, running into such thick pack ice that the ship was unable to proceed to Kane Basin from where she was to sail to the Kennedy and Robeson Canals in order to reach northern Greenland. On 21 August, Sverdrup realised that he had no choice but to find a suitable harbour where the *Fram* would spend her first winter. He sought refuge in Rice Strait and in its northern section found a small, well-sheltered inlet which was christened Frams Havn (Fram's Harbour).

WINTER LIFE AND THE FIRST STIRRINGS OF SPRING

Life on board went into high gear. The preparations for winter had to be completed before its onset. With more than 50 dogs on board a large supply of dog food would be needed, and walrus meat and blubber were just the thing. The men were excellent, avid hunters and the mountain of meat grew with each passing day.

Polar "Chef" Adolf H. Lindstrøm. "Steak à la Lindstrøm" made out of musk-ox meat.

Early in 1899 work on mapping and investigating the area in the vicinity of Frams Havn commenced, keeping the expedition's scientists more than busy. Many areas which had previously been unknown were now named and added to the map. The zoologist collected animals, insects and other organisms, and the botanist was fascinated by the diversity of plant life. A vital part of preparing for the coming of winter was the establishment of an advance base consisting of a tent measuring 16 ft long, 8 ft wide and 6 ft high. As soon as it was ready, a caravan of 11 men and 60 dogs set out. Two days later they reached Hayes Sound, where they erected a tent. Here they hunted, especially after finding musk-ox tracks. Sverdrup shot two oxen, returning to the tent with some of the meat out of which a superb meal was cooked. Some of the sites which were given Norwegian names at about this time are a mountain, Køla-Paalssen, near the base, after a benefactor of the expedition who had provided coal free of charge. The men continue to hunt musk oxen, preserving the meat for consumption during the winter.

The 6th of October was a memorable occasion. A sledge carrying two men came into the fjord; one of them was the renowned American polar explorer, Robert Peary, whose base was located further north. The visit was extremely brief, leading Sverdrup to comment, "Peary's visit became the event of the day in our tent. We didn't talk about anything else... The visit was so short one hardly had time to take off one's mittens."

When winter finally arrived the number of outdoor activities were reduced, but did not cease. Essential chores continued to be carried out. Before the winter, Sverdrup summarised the situation as follows: "Franklin came here with 138 men. The Polar Night stopped him – not one returned. Greely came here himself with 26 men, and only six returned. In the same year when Nordenskiöld spent the winter at Hvide Bay, 17 Arctic explorers died of scurvy in the midst of plenty; the last man was found dead in a sitting position, dressed in his fur garments with mittens on his fingers and a piece of blubber in his hand. Tinned food lay strewn all about the place, unopened, while the barrels of salted food were half-eaten.

And nevertheless, despite what has happened here, despite the terror which has been experienced here, we basically feel safe. For science has triumphed, freezing temperatures and scurvy will no longer tyrannise us, nor hunger. Yes, I say such imposing words, because such things *should* not and need not

be repeated any longer, if it happens, then it is the fault of the leadership and they should be held responsible for it." However, not much time would elapse before tragedy struck the Sverdrup expedition.

The walrus meat which had been collected at the advance base was a frozen mound which had to be loaded onto the ship. To break up this frozen block, the men used wedges, crowbars and sledgehammers. When Christmas arrived, dinner was served at 1700 hrs, consisting of enough food to merit the description a "grand" meal, with coffee, liqueur, tarts and fried, sugared crullers as well as champagne or a toddy later on in the evening. In general, however, meals on the Second *Fram* Expedition were not as sumptuous as on the First *Fram* voyage. Dr. Svendsen, a constant source of new ideas, was also one of the writers of the ship's newsletter which was issued in connection with Christmas and New Year's.

Signs of early spring meant that the beginning of the sledging season was near at hand. Around this time, the expedition was visited by Inuits who wanted to get a better look at the rich *Kablunakker* (white men) who had such fascinating objects as sewing needles, pocket knives, bullets, gunpowder and weapons. In time the visits were seen as a nuisance since the Inuits came in large groups and rather frequently.

A sledging expedition crossed Ellesmere Land, gaining a fleeting view of its western side which looked enticing. On

Program

17. MAY 1899

7 a.m.	Choral music in the Forward Saloon (R. Stols)
8 a.m.	Breakfast à la Lindstrøm ("Long Live the 17th of May!" Cheer led by Simmons)
11 a.m.	Parade to Sælhullet at Rice Strait
12 noon	Salute. The Speech of the Day (by a dilettante) Unveiling of the Fosheimsæter (literally, the Fosheim summer dairy farm) to the accompaniment of brass(kerud)*
1 p.m.	Diner à la "3 crowns" Coffee and cognac, etc.
6 p.m.	Souper followed by a libation. In the evening celebrations in the Fore and Aft Saloons, Dancing, Music, Fireworks and the Midnight Sun.

Norway's National Day, 17 May 1899, the expedition took time to celebrate with all the pomp and circumstance of a parade and events to fill an entire day's programme:

The men carried banners in the parade, one bearing the slogan, "Down with Oatmeal, Up with Cheese." Dr. Svendsen was the day's keynote speaker. The party became more boisterous as the day progressed, and 18 May was a day most wanted to forget. In his diary, Sverdrup noted: "[The Oslo paper]*Verdens Gang* at one time suggested moving the great Day of Atonement to the 18th of May; I agree with *Verdens Gang*'s suggestion."

THE DOCTOR'S DRAMATIC DEATH

On 6 June 1899, after one of the many sledging expeditions, the men were at the advance base. Dr. Svendsen, who had participated in another sledging excursion, arrived at the tent accompanied by Schei; he had become snow-blind. Complaining of indisposition, he remained behind while the crew went on a four-day hunt. Upon their return, Sverdrup writes in his diary, "To our great sorrow we found the doctor dead." Further details in Sverdrup's diary relate that as the men were returning to the camp, Sverdrup saw Dr. Svendsen come out of the tent. "He stopped at the bottom of a hill outside the tent, what is he doing, he is flailing with his arms. Suddenly he keels over, what could it be, he took a very bad spill as though he were..." It turned out that the doctor had shot himself.

His corpse was brought on board the ship and preserved in the cable locker until a burial at sea could take place. The body was covered with the Norwegian flag, and the ship sailed to Rice Strait where a hole was drilled in the ice. After the funeral service was read, a hymn was sung and then all eyes followed the body sliding slowly into the deep. Sverdrup wrote, "We will never forget it." The service was concluded with a hymn and recitation of the Lord's Prayer. The men raised a monument in Svendsen's honour, which still stands today, and a peninsula was named in his memory.

The doctor's death made an overwhelming impression on the crew, who looked with trepidation on a future of several

The old wooden cross erected in memory of Johan Svendsen still stands, more than 100 years after his tragic death.

years without the benefit of a doctor's ministrations. After Svendsen's death, it turned out that he had been addicted to morphine. Bitterly disillusioned, Sverdrup commented in his diary that the doctor was the only member of the crew who had not been carefully screened. It was his firm advice to future expeditions to be especially careful when selecting medical personnel.

Summer arrived and in August Sverdrup attempted to make his way into Kane Basin. Unsuccessful, he decided to sail down to Jones Sound on the southern coast of Ellesmere Land. This area had never been mapped, and one of the many fjords in the region was christened Fram Fjord. At Havne Fjord they found an excellent winter harbour, in lee of Skreia, a large island, and a headland now known as Spannæset. The region

* Translator's note: A play on words, Braskerud was a member of the expedition. D.P.

was unusually rich in game and since winter was nearing, provisions had to be stocked on board.

In the course of the autumn there had been several sledging expeditions and upon his return from one, on 7 October, Sverdrup found Ove Braskerud dead. He had been unwell for three days when he suddenly died, probably from pneumonia. Sverdrup commented that in many ways Braskerud's death had an even greater impact on the members of the expedition than the doctor's passing. The burial ritual was repeated and a memorial raised on a nearby ridge. A large area around the memorial was now marked on the map as Braskerud Plateau. The doctor's demise made the men feel vulnerable and anxious about their health. Peder Hendriksen was ill and bed-ridden, Nødtvedt was ailing and Lindstrøm took to his bed for a period of three months. The comment, "soon there were very few of us who did not imagine that something was wrong with him", generally described the prevailing mood.

It seemed as though Sverdrup had also become depressed, and about Peder Henriksen Sverdrup observed, "Peder had a bath and changed clothes... hasn't washed his body since he left Tromsø. He hasn't changed his underwear since July. He is very worried about his illness and as a result his mood is as black as it can possibly get, I believe. This damned fool of a doctor who went ahead and shot himself... I am furious with myself for allowing him to deceive me as he did." A bath and change of clothes, however, seemed to revive and lift Peder's spirits somewhat.

The winter season was spent preparing a major assault on new territories. A tent was sewn, and sledges and new equipment were made. An advance base named Bjørneborg, or Fort Bear, was also made ready. A depot containing 610 kg of provisions for the men and 1525 kg for the dogs was left there, and additional equipment for the sledging expeditions was made and deposited. This equipment consisted of fur clothing, Lapp slippers of reindeer skin, dog or wolf fur mittens, knitted oversocks, socks, goggles, veils, ammunition and the like. All were made ready for what Sverdrup labelled the "Great Expedition".

THE SLEDGING EXPEDITIONS, HUNTING AND FOOD

There were numerous sledging expeditions which lasted for long periods of time; they also had different objectives. Some were for hunting in order to secure food, some were for the purpose of geographical surveys, others dealt with the registration of plant and animal life, while still others concentrated on geological investigations and the mapping of new territories. Frequently, an expedition had several objectives and the distances covered were considerable, totalling 18,000 km and entailing 751 nights spent in tents.

Sverdrup relied on a two-layered tent in which the air-filled space between the two layers insulated and kept the tent warm. Nevertheless, tent life could be extremely harsh. On 10 March 1899 three of Schei's toes froze and had to be amputated. During the same night, Robert Peary, who was based somewhat to the north of Bjørnborg, measured temperatures of -67° C. He too had to amputate several toes. The sledging expeditions were frequently bitterly cold, and a lack of food was not a rare occurrence; on two occasions, two dogs froze to death. Under such extreme conditions, even the inner eyelid with which nature has equipped the eyes of the Greenland dogs, drawing over and thus shielding the eyeballs, was not sufficient protection There were times therefore when the men had to scrape snow from the animals' eyes. Dogs were indispensable to the Norwegian polar expeditions. Sverdrup relied on his Greenland dogs for their robustness and consequently enormous tractive power.

On 20 May 1899, two sledging expeditions were slated to travel in opposite directions. They had taken along a bottle of cognac to share a farewell drink where their ways parted, and Sverdrup writes as follows: "[The bottle)was brought out and we each brought a mug to receive our allorted portion of the spirits. The mate, who was now our bartender, pulled up the cork and was about to pour our fine, three-star cognac, but what was this? Had someone emptied our bottle? No, it was too heavy for that... The cognac had frozen. Simply frozen solid!...We had intended to have a farewell swig, for one reason to warm ourselves a bit, it was -42.5°, but all we got was a cold tot. Yes, indeed, we ate our tot, then ceremoniously said farewell to one another, and departed, each going in our separate direction."

On 20 March 1900, Sverdrup set out on one of the major expeditions. Divided into four groups, each group was given a specific assignment. On this journey Sverdrup arrived at the northernmost point on Heiberg Land, i.e. 80°55'N, having covered a distance of 635 km from the *Fram*. Here the men raised a cairn and planted the Norwegian flag. A report was

A churned pileup of ice sheets and blocks in the Arctic summer.

inserted into a cognac bottle and the bottle was left inside the cairn, which is marked on the map as Sluttvarden, or Final Cairn. Sverdrup claimed the land in the name of the Norwegian king.

On his return to the *Fram*, he learned that there had been a fire on board. On 27 May, Simmons was walking on deck when he suddenly noticed that the canvas awning covering the deck had caught fire; a spark from the galley had probably set the canvas ablaze. The fire spread rapidly and suddenly the mainsail resembled a bright torch. The fire developed downwards, heading for a pile of bone-dry planks and 15 or 16 kayaks which had been impregnated with paraffin. Right next to the scorching hot deck there were several gunpowder crates, which were removed. The situation, however, was extremely precarious since in the midst of the conflagration there was a

tank filled with 200 litres of alcohol, which could not be removed. Fortunately, there was plenty of water alongside the ship and after 30 minutes, the fire was put out. The damage was relatively minor, and neither the hull nor the mast was damaged, but a good deal of the rigging and sails had been destroyed. Since there were ample supplies of rope and canvas on board, the ship was soon restored to its original condition.

The hunting on which the expedition relied focused mainly on bear and musk oxen. Dubbed by the men "polar oxen", they were not much of a challenge for a genuine hunter. Once the dogs got the scent, they became excited and difficult to control. The only way to stop them from racing off was to turn the sledge on its side. The barking and baying of the dogs caused the male oxen to form a protective ring around the cows and their calves, and then it was an easy matter to go into the flock and simply shoot as many animals as they wanted to bring down. During one such hunt, a total of 21 were shot in one fell swoop. Later, the frozen carcasses were hung in the

Musk oxen forming a square to defend the cows and calves.

---

forward saloon where they were thawed, trimmed, dressed and sorted according to the cut of meat. Lindstrøm had the job of preserving and handling the sides of ox meat, tongues and lungs. Sverdrup decided to bring the shipowners a barrel of salted musk-ox meat, to give them a taste of this delicacy. In general, however, he was rather unhappy about the number of musk oxen that were killed, regarding the exercise more as wholesale butchering than a hunt.

The polar hare, a large animal, was a very popular quarry among the men because being very tame, it too was easy to hunt. Reindeer hunting, on the other hand, was more of a challenge, but few were shot. Ptarmigan were plentiful as were other types of birds. Wolf hunting required the greatest skill, as the arctic wolf is a shy animal, and difficult to approach. Nonetheless, many curious wolves dared to approach the *Fram*.

During the expeditions, food was the highlight after a day's work. Once the tent was erected, the Primus lit and the dogs fed and secured, a sense of calm enveloped the camp and the preparation of dinner began. It either consisted of food which had been brought from the ship or, preferably, meat from the day's hunt. The job of cook was rotated and therefore the results were uneven, at best. Sverdrup wrote in his diary, "One day at the end of our exile we wanted to treat ourselves to some seal meat we had left. It had already turned quite rancid, and therefore we decided to cook it and add oatmeal to the soup, to make it easier to swallow. We were half-starved and filled the pot to the rim. Unluckily for me, I was the cook that day, and the burden of my responsibility [weighed so heavily on my shoulders that] I allowed the soup to burn! Rancid soup is bad, and burnt soup is worse, but [when it is] both rancid and burnt, [it] is awful. And the soup I served that day, I must confess with genuine remorse and contrition, was the worst ever. But that isn't all. The next time it was to be heated, it was burnt once again, and its taste is simply indescribable. I proposed that it be thrown out, but Fosheim and Isachsen were so hungry that the proposal was rejected, and the soup went down."

CONFLICT AND STRAITJACKET

Life on board could be rather monotonous during winter nights. A piano had replaced the organ which held such a

prominent place during the First *Fram* voyage. Stoltz, whom Sverdrup did not respect, was a pianist, but a moody sort who often refused to play for the men. Otherwise the time was passed by playing various types of card games, but the most important form of entertainment was food.

Sverdrup was bitterly disappointed by the ship doctor's suicide. He also felt disdain for one of the crew members, regarding him as too incompetent to bring along on sledging expeditions. No one else wanted him along either. The man in question took this badly and wrote a letter to Sverdrup complaining about the treatment he was receiving. Sverdrup commented in his diary, "I attempted to make him understand that it was necessary for everyone to exercise a degree of self-criticism, and when no one wanted to take him along, then I cannot assume that the fault lies with all of them, but that he must look within himself for the cause...When I spoke with him, he cried like a child, even though I spoke as gently as possible and chose my words as carefully as I could. I don't know what the hell one should do with this type of fellow who is more akin to a woman than a man." He nevertheless allowed him to join a sledging expedition, which ended in total disaster, and Sverdrup noted, "...he doesn't have enough insight to understand that he is the biggest fool on whom the sun has ever shone, and that he is the biggest louse of a man to have worn breeches…" A harsh judgement!

The scientists were placed under the supervision of the second-in-command, Victor Baumann, a situation which resulted in a number of problems. Baumann was more preoccupied with making sailors out of the scientists than in providing support for their work. The botanist Simmons complained frequently in his diary about the fact that Baumann was extremely uncooperative and assigned him all sorts of tasks which interfered with his botanical work. "How were we, the scientific delegation of the expedition, come to be put under the authority of such an uncouth and ignorant individual as Baumann…", was Simmons' perplexed question. The crew, on the other hand, found it difficult to respect a man who picked flowers for a living. Simmons was not alone in his criticism of Baumann. The scientists did not find the courage to take the matter up with Sverdrup, who in fact began to realise that Baumann was going too far, and gave him a reprimand. In the contract the men signed prior to departure, they swore to faithfully, and always, follow orders and carry out any work assignment given by the skipper, or his representatives. Not until the moment of departure did Simmons become aware of this paragraph in the contract, commenting wryly, "It was an unpleasant surprise." Similar clauses were included in the contracts written by Nansen and Amundsen.

Among the extraordinary incidents which took place during the expedition was the injury First Engineer Karl B. Olsen suffered in October 1900 when he fell on the ice, dislocating his shoulder. The doctor was dead by this time and Simmons was told to read up on the subject in the doctor's many books. Since they did not dare to use chloroform for fear that it would kill Olsen, Sverdrup decided to give him enough alcohol to make him pass out. He first drank 12 tot glasses of naphtha – the principal chemical used today in dry cleaning – mixed with water, a potion nicknamed "ugly drink". After that, a bottle of cognac was put on the table; when Olsen had drunk half a bottle, he was both drunk and splitting his sides with laughter. He was placed on a crate, and Simmons and Fosheim had the first go at setting his shoulder in place, but to no avail. The men were aghast at the thought that Olsen's shoulder might remain out of joint for months, even years, on end. To everyone's great relief, the second attempt was effective. Sverdrup, the far-sighted skipper that he was, organised a watch to ensure that Olsen did not kick up a row while drunk. Three weeks later Sverdrup wrote in his diary that the straitjacket in which Olsen had been restrained had been removed.

FROZEN IN THE FJORD FOR TWO YEARS

On 6 August the *Fram* left the Havne Fjord and Sverdrup attempted to sail westwards in Jones Sound. First he tried to sail through Cardigan Strait, and later Hell's Port, with the result that the ship was immobilised by pack ice. The question was whether they would drift out in the autumn or remain there for the entire duration of the winter. Since winter supplies had to be accumulated for such an eventuality, a hunting party was sent ashore. On 3 September the boilers were extinguished and preparations were made to spend the winter in the pack ice. However, on 13 September they noticed a stirring in the ice: a storm was approaching from the south-west, with gale-force gusts of wind. All the equipment and dogs were brought on board again, the boilers were relit and the *Fram* managed to free herself from the ice. They attempted to force their way to Hell's Port but without success. The ship and crew found shelter

almost at the head of the Gaase Fjord where they cast anchor. This decision had major consequences for the expedition, prolonging their stay in the fjord for an additional year.

The expedition was now in a region which was extraordinarily rich in wild life. Before long winter supplies were stored and they made ready for another winter season. Christmas preparations began early that year. Lindstrøm salted at least two barrels of savoury, pressed sausage, lungs, tongue and other delicacies for the Christmas and New Year's breakfasts, in addition to sliced ham. He also started work on making a Christmas tree.

In the spring the scientists intensified their efforts to survey the new land. Several expeditions were organised and enormous stretches of land were visited, during which time parts of North Devon were surveyed and the territories further to the north were explored. The scientific studies continued as before even though spring was late and the summer was a miserable one. By the end of the summer season, all the scientific work was concluded and steps were already being taken for making the return journey. In the beginning of August, Sverdrup went on a reconnaissance trip to study the ice conditions in the Gaase Fjord and what he saw was

Gaase Fjord where the expedition was forced to spend the winter, remaining there from August 1900 until August 1901.

disheartening. The water was open in the *Fram*'s immediate vicinity but further down the fjord, the ice barred the way out. The *Fram* was now ready to depart, tugging at her ropes, the boiler was lit on 12 August, and the ship left its winter harbour. The crew rammed, sawed and dynamited the ice, but their progress was insignificant, ranging from 900 m to two ship lengths per day. In September, the attempt had to be abandoned as futile; a second winter would be spent in the pack ice. The mood among the men was dismal, but worst of all, according to Sverdrup, was "that we had been expected home this year, and that perhaps in the summer an expedition would be sent out to find us. The matter, however, had yet another aspect. Who could guarantee that we would be able to get out the year after this one."

A new, if familiar, major task lay ahead of the expedition, that of securing enough food for the approaching winter season. Sverdrup now took the precaution of rationing coffee, butter and paraffin. As they now entered their fourth polar

night, Stoltz, Simmons and Bay were manifesting clear symptoms of depression. The two scientists spent most of their time sitting on the sofa, refusing to either exercise or go out for fresh air. Baumann, who had already clashed with the scientists on many occasions, became even more aggressive and quarrelsome, and finally Sverdrup felt the need to put Baumann in his place once again.

In order to get ready for next year's departure, Sverdrup began bringing up sand which was strewn on the ice right up to the mouth of Jones Sound. This tactic proved effective when summer 1902 finally came around. During the spring more scientific work was accomplished, including the surveying of more uncharted land. In the spring of 1902 the expedition reached its northernmost point, 81°40'N, where a small cairn was erected and christened Land's Lokk (Land's Lid).

A party was sent to Cone Island in order to build cairns and leave reports on the *Fram*'s position to assist any rescue expeditions which may have been sent to search for them. Another party was later sent to Beechey Island, which was the Franklin Expedition's last known camp. As part of the search for the Franklin expedition, a large depot had been established and a cutter named *Mary* left behind on Beechey Island. Sverdrup had hoped that the cutter would still prove serviceable, in which case it would be possible to reach Greenland and send reports from there. However, the depot and cutter were found to be completely destroyed.

In the summer of 1902, the men charted North Devon. It turned out that Grinnell Island which was marked on the map, was a peninsula and not an island at all. Like Ellesmere Land, the Ringnes Islands and Heiberg Land, North Devon also bears Norwegian names.

Finally, on Tuesday, 15 July, the *Fram* managed to free herself from the grip of the ice and on the 16th the boiler was filled with water from a stream. The lifeboats, which had been in the water for a long time so that their wooden planking would swell and become watertight, were brought on board and the ship was readied for the longed-for departure. However, it would be several days before she was finally out of the fjord. The *Fram*'s stern struck a shoal, but after considerable effort they succeeded in freeing her and on 6 August they finally bade farewell to the Gaase Fjord. The journey home took them first to Godhavn, Greenland. Many on board had expected mail from home, and were disappointed to find none because it had been forwarded north to Upernivik. In the afternoon of 18 September, the *Fram* arrived at Utsira. Here they remained until the next day, leaving at 0800 sharp. "If anyone can be questioned to death, then it would have to be the first man to come on board a ship which had been away like ours had...", one of the ship's crew commented. In Stavanger the *Fram* expedition was met with great jubilation, and in Kristiansand the crew was treated to an official banquet and ball. The Norwegian government came to meet them on the royal yacht *Heimdal*, skippered for the occasion by Captain Scott Hansen, who had been Sverdrup's first mate during the First *Fram* Expedition. The victory procession continued to the naval base at Horten, where an entire flotilla of vessels sailed out to meet and escort the *Fram* and her crew. Finally, they arrived in Kristiania where thousands of people came out to welcome home the polar explorers. Unfortunately, two men never made it home to enjoy the warmth and pride which flowed toward the men of the Second *Fram* Expedition.

THE SECOND FRAM EXPEDITION LEFT NOTHING UNDONE

The Second *Fram* Expedition was a complete success, if less spectacular than the First and Third Expeditions, charting and discovering somewhere between 150,000 and 200,000 sq km of land (by way of comparison, Norway's total area is 324,000 sq km). The maps drawn by Lt. Gunnar Isachsen show 250 sites in the Canadian Arctic bearing Norwegian names, some of which are both descriptive and most likely reflect the men's state of mind at the time the sites were christened. Among these are Møkka (Dung) Fjord, Hatten (the Hat), Nore Sound; Ekskrement (Excrement) Point, Hoved (Main) Island, and Smørgrautsberget (Butter Porridge Mountain). The western part of Ellesmere Land was named King Oscar Land and one sea was registered on the map as Crown Prince Gustav Sea. Most of the names have been retained on Canadian maps, although Smørgrautsberget was renamed Butter Porridge Point because it was unpronounceable for Anglo-Saxon tongues. No polar expedition, either before the Sverdrup expedition or after it, came close to discovering and charting as much land as the Second *Fram* Expedition. Sverdrup claimed the land in the name of Norway's monarch but the Norwegian government never followed up on the claim. Even after the 1905 dissolution of the union between Sweden and Norway, the Norwegian

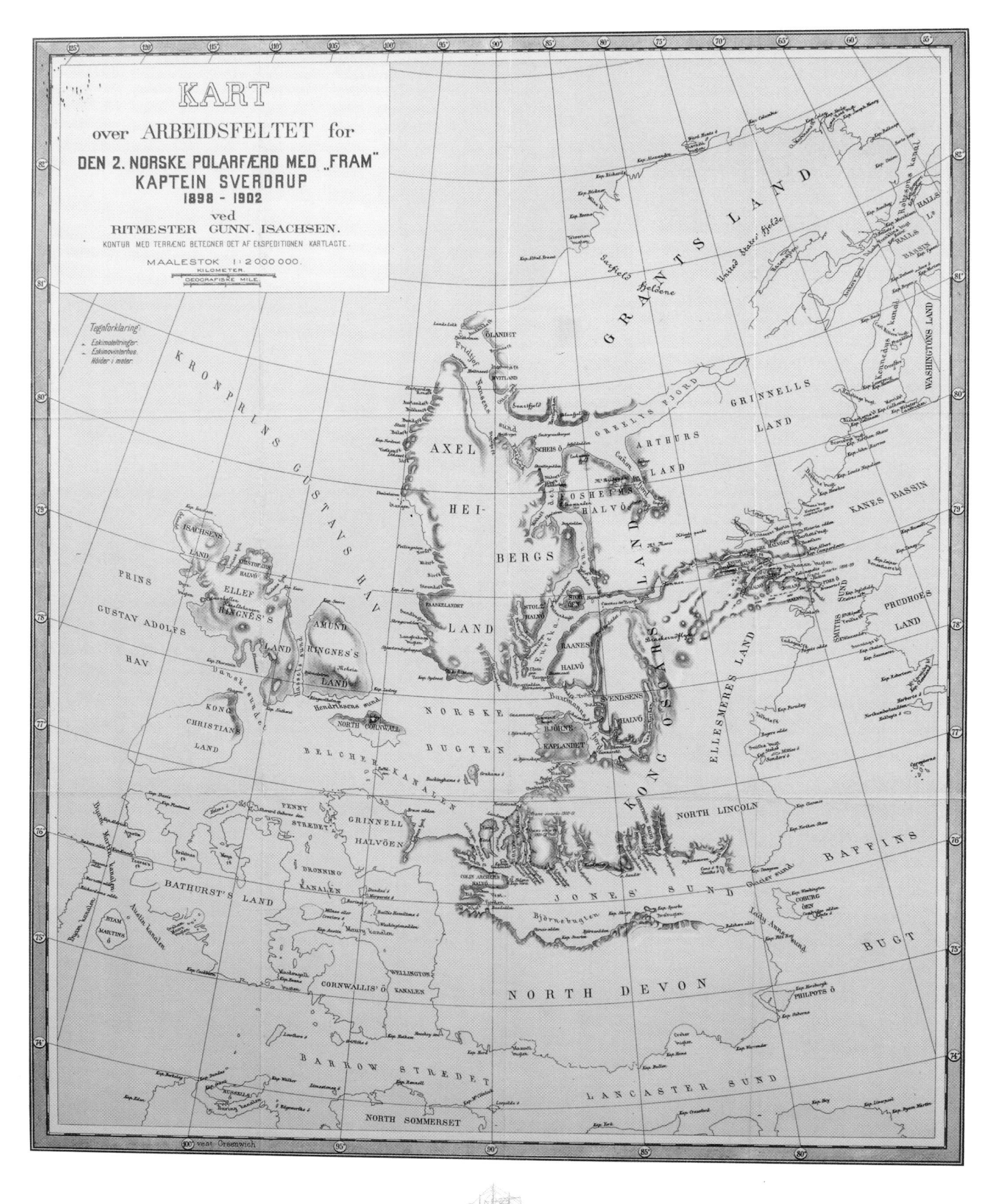

Sverdrup charted a vast territory corresponding in size to southern Norway.

---

authorities did nothing to take possession of Sverdrup's claim, despite his many memoranda reminding the authorities that he had annexed land and followed the procedures practised for hundreds of years to establish a land claim. Applying the sector principle of international law, Canada laid claim to the land in question. Canada's sovereignty over the territories was approved by Norway by Royal Decree of 19 December 1931. Canada awarded Sverdrup 67,000 dollars in 1930, the year he died, in recognition of his research and original maps, diaries and private journals.

The scientific material which the expedition brought back comprised 50,000 samples of higher and lower botanical plants, 2000 laboratory vials with lower animal life, a large collection of plankton and sediments from various sections of the Arctic Ocean, a wide range of geological material, fossils and animals. Moreover, the expedition carried out astronomical observations, meteorological measurements and surveys related to the earth's magnetism. The expedition proved that Ellesmere Land had once been inhabited by Inuits, finding traces of Inuit habitation. The scientists also found traces showing that Norwegians living in Greenland had visited Ellesmere Island. The sheer enormity of the scientific material brought back by the Sverdrup expedition would take 30 researchers 20 years to study and process. In the period between 1907 and 1919, a four-volume work was published by the Scientific Society, followed by a supplementary volume in1930. These five illustrated volumes were entitled *Report of the Second Norwegian Arctic Expedition in the Fram,* with the additional information that the volumes were published *At the expense of the Fridtjof Nansen Fund for the Advancement of Science.* The work contained 39 dissertations.

It is safe to say that the expedition led by Captain Otto Sverdrup, known as the Second *Fram* Expedition, was the one voyage of exploration which yielded the most significant scientific information and lasted the longest, i.e.four years.

EPILOGUE

Upon Otto Sverdrup's return, he was 48 years old. His subsequent life was marked by many fluctuations, including financial difficulties. He spent two years in Cuba, where he tried his hand as a plantation owner, albeit without much luck. His stays in Alaska and Seattle, from 1910 to 1913, were no more successful. In 1914–1915 he led a Russian rescue expedition in the Arctic, saving two Russian polar cutters, *Taymir* and *Vaygatch.* He was now the master of the *Eclipse,* and later wrote a book, *Under the Russian Flag.* The Czar invited him to Petrograd where he was given a hero's welcome. In 1919 he captained the Russian icebreaker *Svyatogor* (the world's largest, later renamed *Krassin*), rescuing the crew of the Russian vessel *Solovey Busimirovitch* which had been drifting helplessly in the Kara Sea with its crew of 85 men. Later he was master of the icebreaker *Lenin,* which led a fleet of steam freighters to Ob and Yenisei.

Otto Sverdrup became the first chairman of the Committee to Preserve the Polar Ship *Fram.* It is mainly thanks to him that the *Fram* was saved from condemnation and break-up. He took the matter up with the authorities and led the way in the effort to restore her. He spent the winter of 1929 and spring 1930 in Larvik to supervise the *Fram*'s restoration, despite the fact that he was suffering from terminal cancer. Sverdrup died in the same year, on 26 November. His polar career was remarkable: he skied across Greenland, was ship's inspector during the construction of the *Fram,* shipmaster during the First Expedition and leader of the expedition after Nansen and Johansen left, and shipmaster and expedition leader, once again, during the Second *Fram* Expedition, rounding off with his heroic exploits under the Russian flag. Finally, and certainly not least in importance for future generations, he rescued the *Fram* from an ignoble demise.

Fossil from Gaase Fjord. It took 30 researchers 20 years to process the scientific material brought back by the expedition.

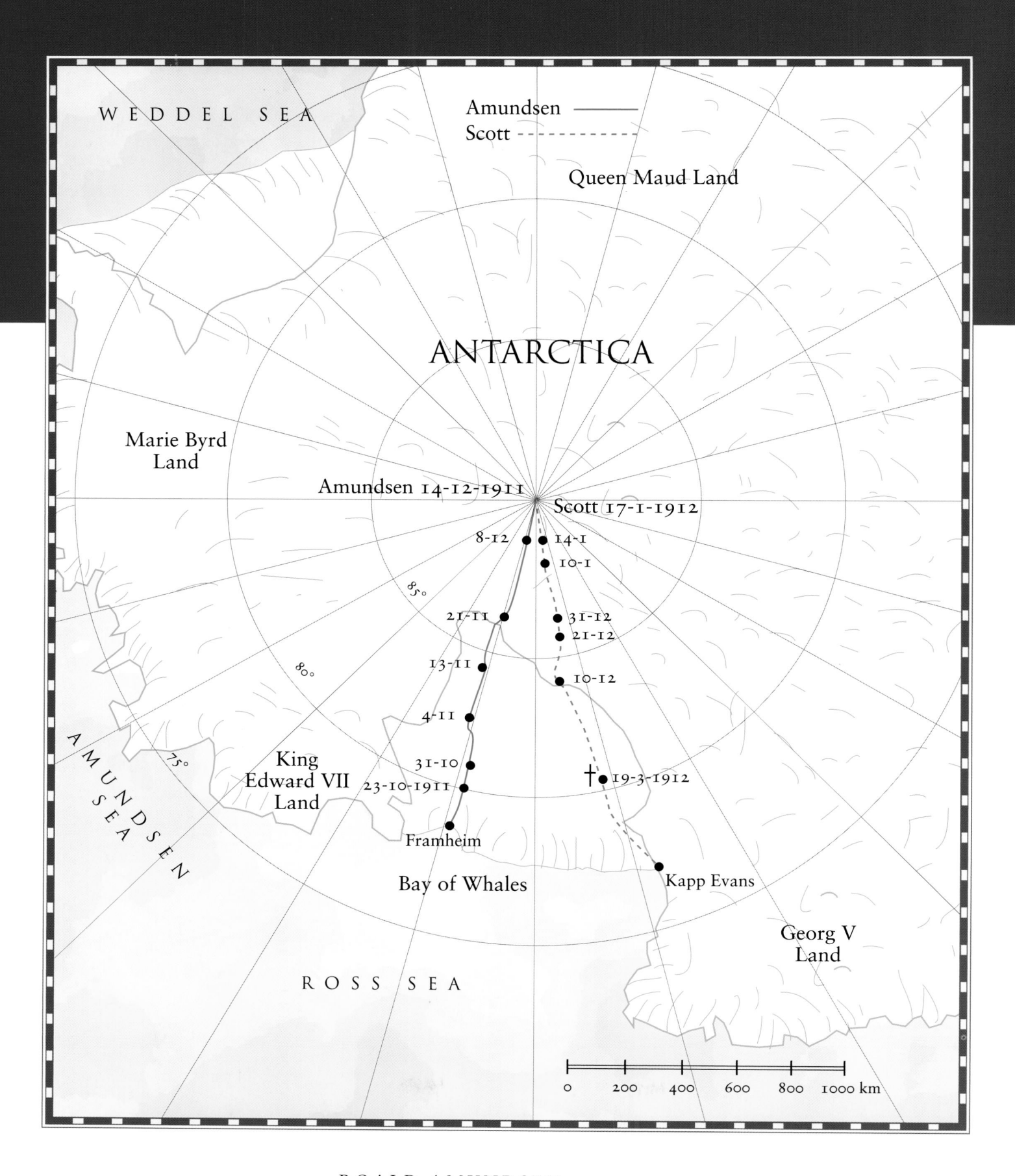

ROALD AMUNDSEN 1910-12.

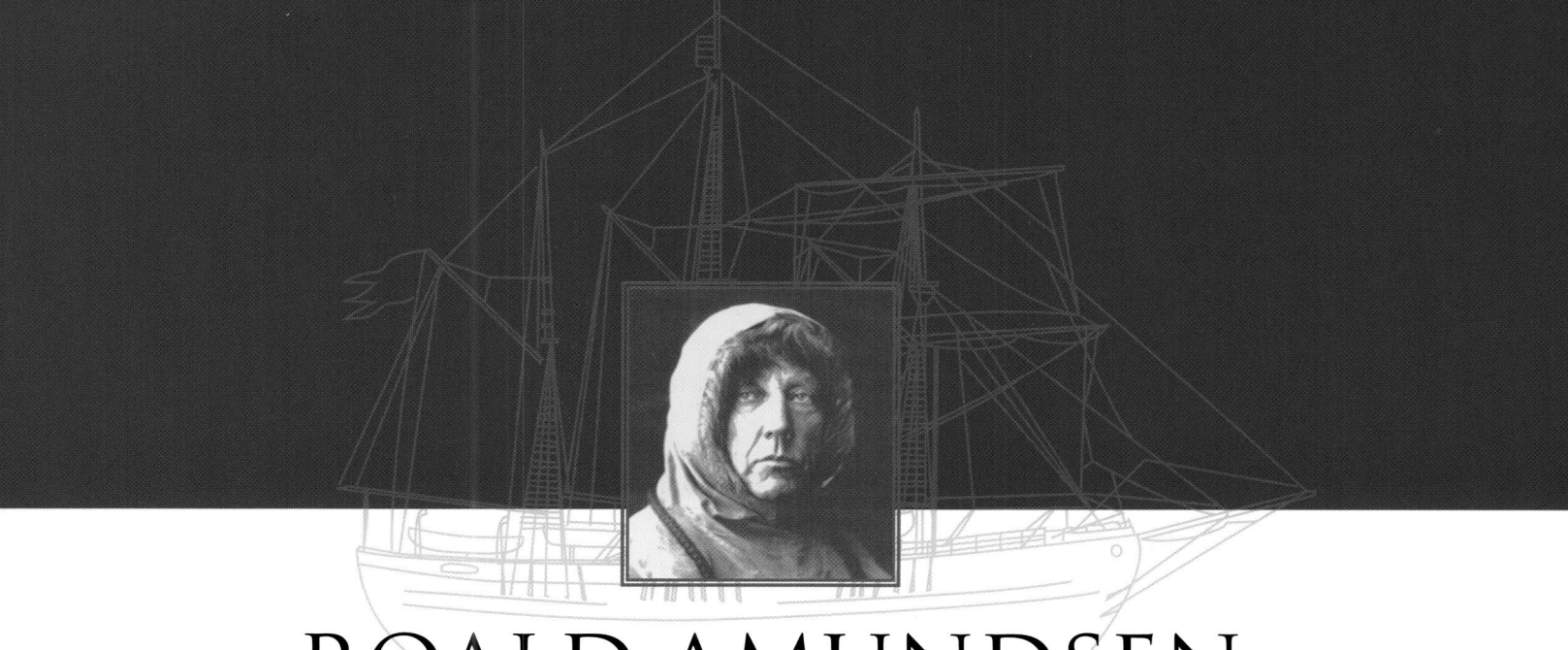

ROALD AMUNDSEN CONQUERS THE SOUTH POLE

BY KÅRE BERG

Roald Amundsen had scarcely returned home from his universally acclaimed navigation of the North-West Passage on the Gjøa before he began to plan an expedition to the North Pole. He had a different idea from Fridtjof Nansen, who in 1893 had deliberately allowed the Fram to be frozen into the pack ice near the New Siberian Islands, on the theory that it would slowly drift on the Arctic current towards the Pole. Amundsen was convinced that sailing the Bering Strait would be a more effective way of attaining the same goal – arriving at or near the Magnetic North Pole. Nansen agreed to lend Amundsen the Fram, though not before giving the matter considerable thought. From 1909 to 1910, the Fram was refitted at the Horten Naval Yard, where the steam engine was removed and a 180 hp diesel engine was mounted instead. The preparations for a second expedition to the North Pole progressed steadily, but caused bewilderment among the crew on more than one occasion.

One source of perplexity was the hut being constructed in Amundsen's garden at Svartskog, which was to be brought along on the expedition. Scratching their heads, the men remained puzzled by the explanation that the hut was to serve as an observation point on the ice. It was almost luxuriously appointed, its floor even covered with linoleum, and Helmer Hanssen commented in his diary, "But what do we need a wax cloth for? I really don't get it." The explanation set no minds at ease because these seasoned mariners knew that once the structure was positioned on the ice, huge, churning ice blocks were bound to crush it.

Prior to the expedition's departure from Kristiania (Oslo), the King and Queen came on board to wish Amundsen a good journey to the North Pole. In the morning hours of 3 June 1910, the *Fram* departed from Kristiania,

King Haakon wishes Amundsen a good journey to the North Pole prior to the departure on 3 June 1910.

arriving at the small town of Svartskog, Amundsen's home in the inner Oslo Fjord, three days later. Before setting out for the Pole, *Fram* sailed for the North Sea where oceanographic studies were carried out. During the cruise, the diesel engine proved to need a thorough overhaul and a different type of fuel. Subsequently, the *Fram* proceeded to Kristiansand where it took on new provisions and, to the surprise and bewilderment of the crew, loaded a pack of 97 Greenland dogs which were to make the long journey across the Equator and round South America and to the Bering Strait, where the voyage to the Pole would finally commence in earnest. Why, the men wanted to know, weren't the dogs boarded in Seattle or another American port? Again, the explanation would be forthcoming later.

On 2 September 1909, while the *Fram* had been undergoing modifications, an extraordinary news story had broken: Frederick Cook claimed to have reached the North Pole on 21 April 1908. Only four days later, on 6 September, a second sensational story had made the headlines: Admiral

Peary had reached the North Pole on 6 April 1909, just a year after Dr. Cook. The time had now arrived for some tough decisions. A voyage to the North Pole was no longer of burning interest, making the work of raising funds still more difficult. Additionally, Amundsen was already deeply in debt in the aftermath of the *Gjøa* expedition. It was at this point that he decided on a radical change of plans and chose a new destination: the South Pole.

He confided in his brother, Leon, who also acted as his secretary, and the ship's officers about the *Fram*'s new destination. The ship departed from Kristiania on 9 August 1910, with Funchal on Madeira's southern coast as the first port of call. From there, it would ultimately head for the Bay of Whales near the South Pole, 16,000 nautical miles away.

THE POLAR RESEARCHER

Roald Engelbregt Gravning Amundsen was born in Borge in Østfold county on 17 July 1872. He descended from a long line of mariners, and his mother's greatest wish was for one of her children to acquire an academic education. Unfortunately for her, Roald had from a tender age been fascinated by Polar research and researchers. 30 May 1889 was a day to remember for the impressionable young Roald Amundsen, because Fridtjof Nansen returned from his astonishing feat of skiing across the Greenland Ice Cap. Amundsen writes: "And for the first time I heard a tentative voice whispering in my innermost thoughts: if only you could get through the North-West Passage." Nevertheless, loyalty to his mother meant that he completed a rather mediocre *examen artium*, the secondary school leaving exam, the prerequisite for entering and studying at university. But when his mother died shortly after he had begun his medical studies, Roald wasted no time in abandoning them and starting on the long training needed to become a polar researcher.

In 1894, at the age of 22, Amundsen signed on the Tønsberg-registered *Magdalena* as an ordinary seaman to take part in a sealing expedition to the Arctic Ocean to seal. This was his first encounter with the ice, and he loved it. After receiving his Mate's Certificate, the young Merchant Marine officer shipped out on the *Belgica* under the command of Captain Adrian de Gerlache. The *Belgica,* which was commissioned to make a scientific survey of the Southern Ocean, was beset by ice and forced to spend an entire winter in the pack ice, the first ship to do so in the Southern Ocean. But the expedition was dogged by hardship, including an outbreak of scurvy and other calamities. Thanks to Dr. Frederick Cook, and in part to Amundsen, the expedition was saved. In the course of this voyage the idea of an expedition to the North-West Passage began to germinate in Roald Amundsen's mind. The venture would have a clear scientific objective, to determine the geographic location of the Magnetic North Pole at the time.

On the night of 16 June 1903, *Gjøa* weighed anchor and set out for what Amundsen believed would be a navigable channel through the North-West Passage, expecting to spend a winter at a sheltered harbour near the Magnetic North Pole. What was intended to be one winter turned into two at Gjøahavn on King William Land. Here, Amundsen met the first Inuits, from whom he learned invaluable lessons about living off the land. An acute observer, Amundsen learned about the way the Eskimos dressed and the technique of building igloos which could be used as an alternative to tents, and gained an insight into the strength and tenacity of Eskimo dogs. This knowledge became supremely important later when Amundsen led his South Pole expedition. During the stay at Gjøahavn, Amundsen did in fact locate the Magnetic North Pole and proceeded to navigate through the unknown part of the North-West Passage in 1905. As the ship headed toward the Bering Strait, it was beset by ice at King Point on Herschel Island and it took a third year before the entire voyage was completed.

The transit of the North-West Passage was an extraordinary achievement which placed Amundsen among the elite in the world of exploration. For 400 years, explorers were fired by the idea of finding a North-West Passage. Roald Amundsen was similarly inspired but, unlike the countless men whose lost their lives in the dismal wastelands of the Arctic, he returned to tell the tale, as well as make a contribution to Polar science.

THE RACE TO THE SOUTH POLE IS ON

On Tuesday 13 September 1909, the London *Times* wrote, "Captain Scott informs us that another expedition ought to be arranged at once…(It) will, it is hoped, start in August next." The expedition was to sail to the Ross Sea, to which the British claimed sovereignty. Amundsen's own plans also envisioned the establishment of a base camp on the Ross Sea Barrier.

On 24 March 1910, Scott received a report that Shackleton had come close to conquering the South Pole, failing to reach it by a mere 180 km. In fact this meant that a passable route to the South Pole had been located via the Beardmore Glacier. When the news reached Scott, he was in Lillehammer testing his motorised sledges on Fefor Lake. The sledges were regarded as a great sensation, indeed everyone felt they were an outstanding innovation. The pilot Tryggve Gran was acting as ski instructor, and convinced Scott, who had many reservations, that skis were an effective form of transport in polar regions. The outcome was that Scott signed on Tryggve Gran as a ski instructor.

In September 1910, *Fram* had reached port at Madeira; the time of departure for the South Pole would soon be at hand. On 9 September 1910, the entire crew – 19 men, since one had been dismissed due to incompetence – were assembled on deck. Thorvald Nilsen, the *Fram's* second in command, unrolled a map tacked onto the foremast which to everyone's astonishment was of the southern hemisphere. There followed

The Fram prior to her departure for the South Pole.

a short briefing on the expedition's expanded plans: before conquering the North Pole, it was first to head for the South Pole. It was made clear that anyone who wished to sign off would have to do so now: the next stop was the Ross Sea Barrier. To a man, the crew expressed a wish to continue on the *Fram*. Finally, the crew had an explanation for everything that had caused bewilderment during the preparations for the expedition – the hut, the boarding of the dogs at Kristiansand and sundry other perplexing details.

The expedition's changed objectives required skilful handling of the information which would have to be communicated first to His Majesty the King, and then to

Fridtjof Nansen. Subsequently, a telegram was also sent to Scott telling him of on the expedition's revised plans. The telegram, dated 10 November 1910, reads, "To Captain Robert Falcon Scott, S/S *Terra Nova*, Melbourne. Beg leave to inform you *Fram* proceeding Antarctic. Amundsen."

Now the press was informed. In England the reaction to Amundsen's expanded plans ranged from condescension about his chances of success to pure outrage in some circles. On Sunday 2 October the Norwegian newspaper *Aftenposten* wrote, "The *Fram* Heading for the South Pole: A Sensational Announcement by Roald Amundsen." Fridtjof Nansen's opinion was, "A terrific plan." In the article, Amundsen is quoted as saying, "I have made this decision alone, and alone I will bear responsibility for it." Nansen was in fact disappointed by Amundsen's deception. His reaction was that, "the fool could have informed me, and then he would have received the plans I had made when I wintered on Frans Josef Land."

The *Fram* departed from Madeira on 9 September and was expected to arrive at the Barrier on 15 January 1911. An adequate water supply posed a problem, so all available tanks and the large lifeboats were filled to the rim with fresh water. On the day of *Fram*'s departure, *Terra Nova* had a 9,000 km lead. The *Fram*, a three-masted schooner of 440 g.r.tons, 38.5 m long, 10.70 m wide, was manned by a crew of 19 men. The S/S *Terra Nova* was a 747 g.r.tons barque, 57 m long, 9.50 m wide. The *Fram* had a diesel engine which could very easily be operated by one man. The *Terra Nova* was equipped with a steam engine.

The choice of heading for the Bay of Whales was based on two factors: firstly, it is the closest one can get to the South Pole by sea. Secondly, it was a suitable place to make landfall on the Barrier. The Barrier, also called the Shelf, is a nearly permanently frozen sea some two million km² in area.

When the *Fram* crossed the Equator, the event was celebrated with a meticulous observance of the traditional rituals. On Christmas Eve, the holiday was celebrated with a Christmas dinner prepared by the polarcook Lindstrøm. During the crossing, the crew worked assiduously to make preparations for the arrival at the Barrier and for the push to the Pole. During a stormy passage through the "Roaring Forties", the *Fram* proved itself to be a highly seaworthy vessel in the roughest of conditions. On 14 January 1911, the Barrier was reached one day ahead of schedule. The original dog population of 97 had increased to 116.

The Fram and Terra Nova (background) meet at the Barrier, Bay of Whales.

The Framheim base and its 16 tents forming a small village at the Barrier.

FRAMHEIM IS ERECTED

It was necessary to find a good site for the hut. Originally Amundsen considered placing it some 18 km into the Barrier, to avoid the danger of it drifting into the Pacific in the event the Barrier calved. However, after a careful study of the terrain, he decided on a spot roughly 4 km from the landing site. Work was begun immediately, with initial excavations for the foundation beginning on 17 January. The following day the plot was ready and all the necessary equipment was in place by 20 January. On 28 January, 900 crates containing a total of 45 tons of provisions were unloaded, and the hut was ready for occupancy. Around *Framheim* they pitched 16-man tents, 14 in all, eight of which were for the dogs and six for storage. Three of the latter were to hold stockfish, one was for fresh meat, one for provisions and one for coal. A small village had taken shape.

On 4 February, two vessels were anchored at the Barrier, making this a day to remember. Scott's *S/S Terra Nova* lay close to the *Fram*. *Terra Nova*, under the command of Lt. Campbell, was to explore King Edward VII Land. The crew had not been able to go ashore and were now getting ready to return to McMurdo Sound. After an exchange of courtesy calls, the crew of the *Terra Nova* expressed its admiration for the quality of the living conditions on the *Fram* and in *Framheim* and, not least, for the dogs' capacity to pull. But Amundsen could not refrain from casting a worried glance toward *Terra Nova*. Weighing heavily on his mind was the question: did she have a telegraph on board? Happily, he quickly registered that this was not the case. His anxiety with regard to the telegraph was based on his conviction that the first to report to the world that the South Pole had been reached would also end up having the greatest impact on public opinion. Also preoccupying Amundsen's mind was the matter of Scott's motorised sledges and, cautiously, he inquired about their condition after the long journey. The reply, again, was pure music to Amundsen's ears, "One of them is already on *terra firma*", i.e. had been lost to the bottom of the sea during unloading.

Fram left the Barrier on 15 February 1911, to sail as far south as is possible, thus becoming the ship that had reached both farthest south and farthest north. She and her crew, now reduced to 10 men, then headed for Buenos Aires.

The landing party installed at *Framheim* comprised eight men in addition to Amundsen. They were: Adolf Henrik Lindstrøm, steward, and a member of the *Gjøa* expedition and the second *Fram* expedition; Helmer Hanssen, also a member of the *Gjøa* expedition; Hjalmar Fredrik Johansen, who had sailed on the *Fram*'s first voyage; Sverre Hassel, who was on the second *Fram* journey; ski champion Olav Bjaaland who hailed from Telemark; Naval Chief Gunnar Oscar Wisting; Lt. Kristian Prestrud and Jørgen Stubberud. At *Framheim* the men lived under Spartan conditions, co-existing in a livingroom/bedroom area which measured 24 m², with a small kitchen measuring 8 m².

PREPARING FOR THE ONSLAUGHT ON THE SOUTH POLE

The time for making the necessary preparations had arrived. On 10 February, four men driving three sledges pulled by 18 dogs and carrying a total load of 750 kg, plus provisions and equipment needed for this first trip, left in a southerly direction. Their job was to lay depots at 80° S and to explore the surrounding area. *Framheim* was located at roughly 78° 35' S, and the distance to 80° S is about 170 km. Every 500 m, they marked their route with tall bamboo staves to which were attached black flags. On 14 February they reached their destination, establishing the first depot 4 m above the ground. On the return journey, the route was marked with stockfish planted into the snow at 500 m intervals. In his diary Amundsen notes that, "The dogs pull extremely well and snow conditions on the Barrier are ideal. Don't understand why the English believe that it is impossible to utilise dogs here."

There were to be more depot-laying trips. The next depot was laid at 81° S, and the depot at 80° S was marked even more clearly with 20 black-flagged staves, 10 on each side of the depot at 900 m intervals, i.e., markings for 9 km on either side of the depot. The longest trip was to 82 °S, a distance of 390 km from *Framheim*, where a depot was laid on 8 March.

From 14 January to 11 April the expedition had achieved the following:

- *Framheim* was established and equipped for occupancy by nine men for a period of several years.
- Fresh food was provided for nine men and 115 dogs for six months. Seals weighing 60,000 kg had been slaughtered.
- a total of 3000 kg provisions had been divided between three depots at 80, 81 and 82° S.

The depot at 80° S contained seal meat, canine pemmican, biscuits, butter, milk powder, chocolate, matches, kerosene and a considerable amount of equipment, weighing a total of 1900 kg. The depot at 81° S held 500 kg canine pemmican, and the one at 82° S held 620 kg human pemmican, canine pemmican, biscuits, milk powder, chocolate, kerosene and some equipment. Amundsen improved the pemmican, which is dried, finely ground meat or fish saturated with fat, by mixing oatmeal and vegetables in both varieties.

During the winter months, life in *Framheim* was busy. The hut was improved with the addition of a porch and three new subterranean rooms built into the ice under *Framheim*. These became the sewing room, the storeroom, pendulum observatory, laundry room, a WC, carpentry workshop and bathroom. Work on the sledges, for instance, was done here. Bjaaland planed the original sledges to make them lighter. In addition he produced four new ones, each weighing 24 kg, a saving of 50 kg per sledge. The boots, which were too small, were remade. The packing crates were also planed to make them lighter. To make it easier to reach into the crates without dismantling the straps which held them in place, an opening was made on top. Johansen had packed more than 40,000 biscuits in the crates, filling the empty spaces with powdered milk. By spring, the sledges were packed and could be hoisted from their subterranean storage room onto the ice above. In every aspect of his behaviour, Amundsen displayed a clear grasp of what were the essential details and ensured that they were not neglected. All was now ready for the arrival of spring and the assault on the South Pole.

Life in *Framheim* was simple. Breakfast was served at 0800 hrs, consisting of hotcakes with jam expertly prepared by

Sewing room at Framheim. Intrepid men in deep concentration.

Amundsen had learned a great deal about cold-weather clothing from the Inuits. This had a decisive impact on the outcome of the expedition.

Lindstrøm. Lunch nearly always included seal meat, and tinned fruit, pies or tinned puddings for dessert. The main course at dinner was seal steak with cranberry sauce, cheese, bread, butter and coffee. There were special menus for important days, such as Easter, which fell on 12 April. Johansen noted in his diary, "We are now leading a luxurious existence with respect to food and drink. Today we were served a wonderful dinner of chicken soup and grilled breast of veal, asparagus, a pudding, a drink, port, fruit syrup and water, and coffee and Benedictine." On 7 June, Hassel's diary records that a wonderful four-course dinner was served: soup based on a type of eel, a meat stew with asparagus and a caramel flan for dessert. The dinner was followed by coffee and Munk liqueur. Every Saturday the crew were treated to a toddy and a cigar. On special occasions, the gramophone was brought out and raised spirits, filling the room with merriment.

SCOTT ESTABLISHES THE CAPE EVANS BASE

Terra Nova was finally free of the pack ice on 30 December 1909 and entered the Ross Sea. On 2 January the volcano Mt. Erebus came into view. However, ice blocked the entrance to the *Discovery*'s base camp which Shackleton had used. Scott therefore decided to establish his camp at Cape Evans, named "in honour of our excellent second in command". Disembarkation began on 4 January.

The push to the Pole was now to be carried out with three motorised sledges (the fourth having been lost during unloading, as mentioned earlier), 17 ponies and a few dogs. Scott remained unconvinced about the efficacy of dogs. He believed that they could not run against the wind because snow would get into their eyes and block their vision. Tryggve Gran was dismayed by Scott's attitude to dogs, commenting in his diary, "I rather doubt whether the dogs are as useless as they are presumed to be. In this matter of the dogs, could there possibly be a certain attempt at self-consolation vis à vis Amundsen and his hundred dogs". The ponies were to be utilised on the Barrier until the time arrived to ascend the Beardmore Glacier, when they would be slaughtered. The rest

of the way, the men, in accordance with good British Royal Navy tradition, were to do the hauling for a distance of 1800 km while climbing 3000 m. In his diary, Bowers wrote, "I, for one, am delighted at the decision. After all, it will be a fine thing to do that plateau with man-haulage in these days of the supposed decadence of the British race". The clothes they wore was made of woollen cloth, about which Scott had some misgivings, as he confided to his diary, "One continues to wonder as to the possibilities of fur clothing as made by the Esquimaux, with the sneaking feeling that it may outclass our more civilised garb… "

The departure was scheduled for 3 November, which meant that it was doubtful whether the expedition could return home from the South Pole and return with *Terra Nova* the following year.

As the "ski expert", Tryggve Gran's first task was to do away with the widespread bias against skis which all earlier British expeditions to the South Pole had shown. The best way to do this was to demonstrate personally the superiority

of a man on skis to one on foot in a snow-bound landscape such as Antarctica. Gran was convinced that he succeeded, and had proved the great advantages of "wooden planks" on the snow and ice of the South Pole. It is nevertheless unlikely that Scott ever fully appreciated the possibilities inherent in the use of skis.

A SUMMARY OF THE STATUS QUO

Now the two expeditions were almost ready to begin their assault on the South Pole, and the situation may be summarised as follows:

• Amundsen had his base at *Framheim*, at roughly 78° 40' S, i.e. some 1250 km from the Pole. Scott's base was at McMurdo Sound, situated at roughly 77° 30' S, i.e. about 1400 km from the Pole. Thus, Scott was 190 km further from the Pole and had to cover 380 km more to complete the return journey. Scott was to follow a track which had already been laid out by Shackleton, while Amundsen expected to meet obstacles in the Transantarctic Alps.

• Amundsen's strategy was based the use of dogs and light-weight sledges. Scott based his plans on ponies, motorised sledges, dogs and man-haulage.

• Amundsen outfitted his crew with fur clothing modelled on the traditional dress of the Inuit people. Scott provided his men with clothes made of ordinary wool cloth.

• Amundsen planned his provisions on the basis of experience gained during the first and second *Fram* expeditions, with modifications suggested by Professor Torup who had assessed the results of these voyages. Scott first began to think about the sledging rations two months before setting off, in spite of the fact that scurvy had ravaged the *Discovery* crew. He instructed one of his crew to read up on sledging rations in the books available on board.

• Lifestyles were different in the living quarters of the two expeditions. At *Framheim* nine men shared the same room, at Cape Evans 25 men were quartered in two rooms, and the officers and men were separated.

Amundsen feared Scott's motorised sledges, which were something modern and perhaps effective. For that reason he was eager to set out as fast as possible. The sun had barely returned to the Antarctic latitudes when he set 23 August as the date of departure, and disappointingly the temperatures

were unusually low. By 16 August, four sledges had already been packed in what came to be known as the "Crystal Palace" and the storeroom. It was a great advantage that it was possible to pack the sledges indoors, given the fact that outside temperatures hovered at around minus 50 – 60 °C, accompanied by a fresh breeze at 6 m/s. Because of the appallingly low temperatures, the departure was postponed several times. However, on 8 September, all was ready for setting forth to the South Pole and the temperature had already reached an agreeable minus 22 °C on 6 September.

Eight men and 90 dogs pulling seven sledges set out confidently in spite of Lindstrøm's warning that departure on a Friday was very unlucky. On their first day, they covered 19 km in three hours, finding that the temperature was not a problem and the snow conditions were good. On the next two days, they covered 25 and 30 km respectively, which was satisfactory as far as they were concerned. On Monday 11 September, they woke to minus 55 °C, tough skiing conditions and crevasses in the ice. The following day the temperature was minus 52 °C, and the choice was clear: the time had come to return to base. Amundsen decided to drive to 80° S, unload and return to *Framheim*.

TEMPERATURES PLUMMET
AS TEMPERS BOIL

On 14 September they arrived at the depot. For the past two days the temperature had fluctuated between minus 52.5 °C and 56.5 °C. Amundsen laconically observed that there is a great difference between minus 40 and minus 50 °C. They now built igloos since these were warmer than tents, but returned to the tent on the evening of 15 September. Suddenly Hanssen said, "Good Lord, I believe my heel has gone." Stubberud's voice followed, "Believe it or not, I think the same has happened to mine too; yes it has." It was still about 75 km to *Framheim* and the freezing temperature had not eased. Amundsen wrote the following entry in his diary, "To risk men and animals just in order to continue is too hazardous, even though I have already set out – wouldn't even occur to me. If we are to win the game, then we must move carefully – one mistake and all may be lost."

Amundsen, who had been the front runner, had no sledge. He therefore jumped onto Wisting's sledge, and with Helmer Hanssen they began their return journey. Their two sledges

Bjaaland planes a sledge in the workshop at Framheim

quickly outpaced the others. Bjaaland notes that their speed was so great, "that we saw them as a white dot far away." The three arrived at *Framheim* at 16.00 hrs. Amundsen first considered waiting at the 160 km flag, 30 km from *Framheim*, but in his opinion the weather was very good and he saw no reason to wait. The others began returning, one after the other. The last to arrive at the base were Johansen and Prestrud, who got there on the following day, 16 September, at 0030 hrs. Amundsen wrote, "God only knows what they were dawdling about". The fact is that Johansen and Prestrud were left on the Barrier without food or fuel. Presterud's dogs were so weak that they hardly had the energy to pull even the empty sledge. With frost-bitten heels, and in terrible shape, Presterud was clearly in danger. Johansen's team was also close to exhaustion, but he managed to overtake Hassel who had no food or fuel either, and gave him a tent. Johansen waited for Presterud and thereby probably saved his life.

At breakfast next morning Amundsen asked why Johansen and Prestrud had arrived so late. Johansen became agitated and berated Amundsen for his actions on the previous day. "I don't call this an expedition. This is panic." There followed a torrent of bitter criticisms of Amundsen's leadership. It has never been clear exactly what Johansen said, but Bjaaland noted, "Johansen said things that would have been best left unsaid". Amundsen's reaction was that this was not only a case of Johansen using unsuitable language, but that he had challenged Amundsen's position as the leader of the expedition. Amundsen wrote in his diary, "The crass and unforgivable (aspect of Johansen's) statements, is that they were said in everyone's hearing. Here we must take the bull by its horns and immediately make an example (of him)".

The confrontation ended with Amundsen ordering Johansen to take part in an expedition to King Edward VII Land, under Presterud's leadership. Stubberud was also selected to participate in the expedition. Johansen refused, submitting a formal, written protest. Thus Johansen was considered to be in breach of contract and Amundsen regarded him as a mutineer. Morale at *Framheim* was now coloured by these events, and the sense of camaraderie disappeared, to be replaced by low morale and tension.

DEPARTURE AT LAST

It took time to heal the frost-bitten heels. Stubberud, Hanssen and Presterud were bedridden for several days. Amundsen used the time to review his plans and make a number of changes.

His decision to organise an expedition to explore King Edward VII Land was probably taken because it was in no way certain that the South Pole would be conquered. By sending a party to King Edward VII Land, he could be sure that the expedition would achieve some results. As mentioned, three men had been chosen to make up the survey party, leaving five to head for the South Pole. Some suspected that having reached the Plateau, Amundsen would dispatch two or three men to the base camp and make the final assault with a party of two or three men. However, a new tent was sewn for five men. The party also took a reserve tent for three men and two Primuses as cooking equipment. Amundsen decided to use four sledges and a total of 52 carefully selected dogs. This rearrangement made for a lighter expedition while the depots, which had already been laid, were intended for eight men and 90 dogs.

Finally the day arrived, Friday 20 October. Lindstrøm was as unhappy about the choice of day as he had been the previous time, again predicting that they would soon be back. The sledges were now very light since quantities of equipment

had already been taken to 80° S during the first unsuccessful assault, and the depots at 81 and 82° S were amply stocked.

The trip to 80° S began in bad weather. They lost their course and found themselves in a dangerous, highly crevassed area which Amundsen called "the pig's hole". On several occasions they only just avoided falls into bottomless chasms in the ice. After four arduous days, they reached 80° S. Here the 48 remaining dogs – two had been set loose because they were useless – were well fed. Amundsen considered this the real beginning of the push for the Pole.

At 0900 hrs on 26 October, they left the depot at 80° S, with roughly 1100 km ahead of them before the South Pole. The plan was to cover 28 km per day, something they managed with ease. To make the return journey safer, they started to erect landmarks, snow cairns two metres high, from 80° 23' S. Each cairn contained a piece of paper indicating the direction to the next snowy landmark. A total of 150 cairns were erected using 9000 blocks of snow. At first they were erected at 13-14 km intervals, but later this was reduced to 5 km. The voyage to 82° S was dramatic, and both dogs and humans were on the verge of plunging into treacherous crevasses in the ice on several occasions. Amundsen wrote about them, "These crevasses are impressive when one lies at the edge and gazes down into them. A bottomless abyss from light blue going into the deepest darkness…". A lunch routine was established and at mid-day, the members of the party

The Norwegian flag planted at the South Pole.

consumed 3-4 dry oatmeal biscuits. If they were thirsty, snow was mixed with the biscuits.

On 7 November the group set out on the main push. Until then, the terrain had been relatively well known. The sledges were now loaded and a decision was made to lay a depot at every whole degree of latitude. This lightened the sledge loads quickly. Supplies for 100 days were taken from the depot at 82° S. At 83 ° S they laid provisions for five men and 12 dogs intended to last four days. The depot was two metres square and constructed of hard blocks of snow. Flying from the top of the structure was a large black flag. The other depots followed the same pattern, but also contained matches and kerosene. The dogs which had to be slaughtered were placed in the depot as reserve provisions. Gradually in the clear air they saw 5,000 m high mountain formations.

With nothing untoward obstructing their progress, they reached 85° S on 16 November. They had now reached the foothills of the Transantarctic Mountain Range, and the next question was how best to ascend to the polar plateau. The return journey to the Pole was now 1100 km as the crow flies, and the climb to the plateau would be exhausting for man and beast. Furthermore, as they climbed they expected to suffer from altitude sickness caused by a lack of oxygen. Amundsen decided to bring provisions for 60 days and leave behind provisions for 30 days at a main depot located at 85° 10' S. There were now 42 dogs left, most of which would be slaughtered on the plateau. Of the 18 remaining dogs, six would be slaughtered before leaving the Pole, making 12 dogs available for the return trip.

After four days, on 21 November, they had ascended from to the plateau. They had expected to use 10 days for the climb. Amundsen made the following entry in his diary, "It's a wonder to see what the dogs achieved today, 17 km and a 5,000 foot climb. Don't try and tell me that dogs aren't any good here." In the course of the climb up the Heiberg Glacier, they sighted mountains which loomed as high as 5,000 m. They named a number of them, and names such as Don Pedro, Wilhelm Christoffersen, Fridtjof Nansen and Ole Engelstad Mountains can still be seen on the map today.

In the month since they had left *Framheim*, they had covered 800 km. The members of the party now took a well-deserved five-day rest. Yet another depot was built and the superfluous dogs were slaughtered. One sledge was left in the

depot, while six dogs were harnessed to each of the three sledges.

On 2 December the men arrived at 86° 47' S, where they decided to discard their leather clothing, keeping on the reindeer skins and gabardine clothing. Describing the usual way Hanssen, the chef, prepared the food, Amundsen wrote, "The spoon never stopped stirring the contents of the pot. There was vegetable soup in mugs, scalding hot, as you could see on people's faces. Later the mugs were filled with pemmican and then water and bread (biscuits)." They struck camp the following day and arrived at the area which they gave the ominous name the Devil's Dance Floor. Here the icy surface was everywhere slashed by merciless crevasses. Amundsen reported that every time he asked what the crevasses were like, he received the reply, "Oh, the usual ones, the kind which have no bottom. Time and again the dogs fell through, humans also stepped into crevasses, but all went well."

On 8 December they were close to the point Shackleton called "Furthest South", at 88° 23' S. On Hanssen's sledge preparations were being made to raise the Norwegian flag. Amundsen had issued an order to stop when they reached the right position, where the flag would be hoisted. Amundsen was the forerunner on this day. Suddenly, he heard a chorus of loud cheering behind him: Shackleton's Furthest South had been reached and passed. Amundsen wrote, "It is impossible to recreate the feelings which welled up in me when facing this situation. All the sledges had come to a halt, and from the first (sledge), the Norwegian flag waved…No moment in the entire voyage gripped (me) as this one(did). Tears pressed their way out one after the other…" They now moved forward to 88° 25' S and established camp. Here they laid their last depot, totalling 100 kg. They took with them enough provisions for one month, sufficient to reach the depot at 86° 21' S. From now they built cairns every 3.7 km. One of the difficulties they encountered was snow which did not lend itself to the construction of cairns.

On 13 December they arrived at 89° 30' S. Skiing conditions were fine, the weather excellent, all was quiet and the sun shone.

THE FLAG IS PLANTED ON THE SOUTH POLE

On the morning of 15 December, or rather 14 December since they had passed the dateline, the weather was as good as the day before, as though orchestrated for an arrival at the South

Amundsen and his men bid farewell to the South Pole.

Pole. At noon they were at 89° 53' S, with only about 13 km left to go. Snow conditions were variable. At 1500 hrs there was a unanimous cry of "Halt!". The sledgemeter now registered that the goal had been reached and the voyage was at an end. They were well aware of the fact that they were not standing exactly at the Pole. They gathered around and congratulated one another on their achievement, and there was an exchange of firm handshakes.

And then they proceeded to plant the Norwegian flag at the South Pole. The only manner in which Amundsen could demonstrate his gratitude to his colleagues was to let them all hold on to the pole, and together they planted the flag on the Geographical South Pole. "So we plant you, dear flag, on the South Pole and give the plateau on which it lies the name King Haakon VII's Plateau." It was 67 days since their departure from *Framheim*. The next task was for three men to travel 20 km in three different directions, since observations indicated that the Pole would definitely be located within the area of the triangle. Each man was equipped with a small bag containing a report on the location of the camp site, and a large flag made of windproof material to be planted at the point he reached.

Repeated, accurate observations showed that their camp was located at 89° 54' S, or 10 km from the actual Pole. Their measurements had proved accurate. They now prepared their

return. The provisions were checked, and they found there was enough food for humans and dogs for 18 days. One sledge that was to be left behind was raised on end at the camp site. On 17 December (really 16 December), the party headed for the actual Pole Point. The job of forerunner was assigned to Bjaaland, which everyone saw as a mark of honour, a way of recognising the extraordinary contribution made by the people of Telemark to the promotion of skiing as a sport. In a line as straight as an arrow, Bjaaland headed toward the Pole followed by Hassel, Hanssen, Wisting and Amundsen. That is how it came about that Bjaaland was first to arrive at the South Pole.

At noon on 18 December (really 17 December), all the observations at the Pole itself had been completed. Now they began to prepare their return. First, however, they had to erect a small, grey-brown canvas tent, easily visible against the white snow, that had been sewn by sailmaker Rønne. When they opened the tent they found messages of congratulation on their success. On yellow leather patches sewn onto the tent there was the message: Good luck on your voyage – and welcome to 90 degrees. Fastened to the tent pole was a Norwegian flag and under it an ensign on which was painted the name *Fram*. A bag was deposited in the tent containing a letter for HM King Haakon VII detailing their achievements and a short letter to Scott, who Amundsen supposed would be the first to find the site. The objects left in the tent were a glass horizon, a hypsometer, three reindeer skin foot-warmers, and a number of kamikks (sealskin, waterproofed boots) and mittens. The place was christened *Polheim*. They started back to base on 18 (17) December, with 18 dogs and two sledges.

The return journey was uneventful, and they arrived at *Framheim* on 26 January 1912 at 0400 hrs, after an absence of 99 days. Amundsen's calculations put the distance covered at roughly 3000 km. There were now 11 dogs left. *Fram* had arrived at the Ross Sea Barrier on 9 January. Presterud's expedition to King Edward VII Land was also a success. On 30 January *Fram* was ready to sail, and arrived in Hobart in Tasmania on 6 March 1912. From here the world was informed that the South Pole had been conquered. There had been no word from Scott.

SCOTT'S EXPEDITION BEGINS TO MOVE OUT

Four days after Amundsen and his men set out, on 24 October, two motorised sledges began to move on the sea ice, each carrying a load of 1.5 tons. On 1 November the main party left Cape Evans, a line of eight ponies, each pulling a sledge and one man. A few hours later a bell rang at Cape Evans: in the general confusion, Scott had forgotten the British flag which Queen Alexandra the Queen Mother had given him to hoist at the South Pole. Someone had to go back and retrieve it. Tryggve Gran, who was excluded from the expedition because of Roald Amundsen, wrapped the flag around himself and in three hours skied the 28 km to Hut Point, in spite of a howling blizzard. "An irony of fate," said Scott. A Norwegian had carried the British flag on the first leg of the journey to the South Pole. By now, Amundsen had a headstart of 370 km.

Five days later Scott's party found the motorised sledges abandoned and immobilised. The sledges had pulled 1.5 tons each for a distance of 80 km. Scott commented, "The dream of obtaining great help from machines is over." On 21 November the main party picked up Teddy Evans and the others who had started with the motorised sledges, and who had had to man-haul the provisions for the last part of the trek. The caravan had a relatively complex structure, with 16 men and three types of sledges pulled by men, ponies and dogs. Each morning, a complicated departure schedule was followed, with the man-hauled sledges first to leave, followed by the pony-hauled sledges divided into three groups, with the weakest going first, and finally the dog-sledges. Scott planned for some of the party to turn back after laying depots. The first party returned on 24 November after laying a depot at 81° 15' S. The depots, however, proved to be

Captain Scott dressed for skiing.

Scott's team headed for the South Pole. (l-r): Bowers, Scott and Evans, seated Wilson and Oates.

---

inadequately stocked, and before 1 March food and fuel had to be freighted to One Ton Depot and even further.

Part of Scott's plan was to slaughter the ponies when they no longer served their purpose. The first were shot on 24 November. On 4 December the Barrier was nearly ascended, and they were close to the inland plateau. They had had a number of layovers due to bad weather, weather which would not have stopped Amundsen and his dogs. Scott's tent was unsuitable, there was no fur clothing, the ponies needed special fodder and found it difficult to make their way in the snow. The party's skiing abilities were poor, and there was only one set of snowshoes for the ponies, all of which impeded their progress. In addition, there were considerable distances between the depots. Amundsen had laid seven depots on the Barrier, Scott only two. Amundsen also marked the depots with great care, whereas Scott's were poorly marked.

On 9 December the expedition moved out again. This was to be the ponies' last day. Starved, exhausted and cold, they used 12 hours to cover 11 km. At the foot of the glacier, the ponies were shot. Now there was only manpower left and the distance to the Pole was some 730 km.

The 12 men could now start the conquest of the Pole plateau. Every man was expected to haul 90 kg up the 220 km long Beardmore Glacier, a climb of more than 3000 m. Beginning in deep, loose snow, Scott wrote, "Skis are the thing, and here my countrymen entertain such bias as to keep them from preparing themselves properly". Bowers commented, "To pull the sledge is the toughest thing I have participated in... Getting started is worse than the pulling, because it requires 10-15 desperate jerks of the harness in order to even get the sledge to move...I have never pulled so heavily, or nearly crushed my insides against my backbone because of an endless pull with all my power against a canvas belt around my poor stomach".

When they reached the top of the glacier on 21 December, four men were selected to return. The eight remaining men and

Defeat. Scott (l), Bowers, Wilson and Edgar Evans at Amundsen's South Pole tent.

---

two sledges formed two teams. One consisted of Scott, Wilson, Edgar Evans (chosen as a representative of the "lower deck") and Oates. The second team consisted of Teddy Evans, Bowers, Lashly and Crean. On New Year's Eve, Scott decided to send back Teddy Evans' team, but realising that this would leave him without a navigator, he retained Bowers. Teddy Evans' team had left their skis behind. Scott's decision meant that from now on the expedition consisted of five men with a tent made for four. There were also just enough provisions, utensils, cooking equipment, fuel, etc. for four men. The depots laid for the return journey were also intended for four men. Moreover there were four pairs of skis for five men. Scott immediately discovered one of the results of taking along five men. The day after Teddy Evans left he wrote, "To make food for five takes much more time than for four, perhaps half an hour. These are things I didn't think about when I reorganised."

NOT FIRST AFTER ALL

On 9 January Scott passed Shackleton's Furthest South, triumphantly writing in his diary, "RECORD". They now had 180 km left. Since they had not seen any traces of Amundsen's expedition on the Beardmore Glacier, they assumed that he had been the victim of an accident. Just before arriving, Scott wrote that he was convinced victory was at hand, nevertheless adding, "The only repugnant possibility is the sight of the Norwegian flag hoisted before ours." The first thing they saw was the black flag Amundsen raised in the track where it crossed the 180° meridian. Dog tracks spoke their own clear language. A rather dispirited Scott went to bed that night. But according to Oates' diary, he kept his emotions under control, "Scott is taking the defeat better than expected…Amundsen – I must say that the fellow has his head screwed on right… The 'Norskis' appear to have had a comfortable journey with their dog teams, quite unlike our dreadful man-hauling." Bowers' reaction was "It is a pity that the Norwegians have forestalled us. But I am glad that we have done it by hauling the sledges ourselves, in a good British manner…If ever a voyage had been completed thanks to honest sweat, then ours is such a voyage."

They left the black flag behind and pulled the sledges to what they believed to be the Pole itself. They arrived there on 17 January 1912, 34 days after Amundsen. Scott wrote in his diary, "The Pole. Yes, but under completely other conditions than expected. We have had a dreadful day. In addition to the disappointment we have had a headwind of force 4-5, the temperature is minus 22 degrees, and my companions have suffered from cold hands and feet...Great God! This is a terrible place and it is terrible that we have exhausted ourselves getting here without getting the reward of being first." Observations showed that they were roughly 5.5 km from the Pole. They hauled the sledges to that point and found the flag and *Fram's* ensign still waving vigorously in the wind. In the tent they found Amundsen's letter, which read:

"Dear Captain Scott,
Since you are probably the first to visit this place after us, I ask you kindly to forward this letter to King Haakon VII. If you can make use of any of the objects which are in the tent, do not hesitate. Best regards, and wishes for a safe return.

Your devoted,
Roald Amundsen."

The message was left in the tent. A cairn was then erected on the site taken to be the exact site of the Pole. Scott wrote that they "... built a cairn, put up our poor, slighted Union Jack, and photographed ourselves – mighty cold work, all of it." The cairn was later moved to a point they believed to lie closer to the Pole. The return commenced, the wind now in their backs, a sail was set on the sledge and the terrain was much easier than on Amundsen's Devil's Glacier, with its high mountains and treacherous crevasses. In the three first weeks, they managed to do 26 km per day. This was about the same as Amundsen's daily stages. Every time they expected to find a depot, problems arose because their route had been marked so badly; indeed, the return route was never marked. They were confident that by following their own tracks, they could find their way back, which proved not to be the case. A great deal of time was wasted finding tracks which had been covered up by snow drifts.

On 7 February they began to descend Beardmore Glacier. Scott ordered a day's stop in order to gather geological samples. Having collected 13-14 kg of rocks, they loaded them on the sledge in spite of the lack of food and their state of near exhaustion. The first person to show clear signs of weakness was Edgar Evans. Oates noticed that Evans had lost all hope and was, "carrying on like an old woman or worse. He is entirely exhausted by the work. How he is to manage the, at least, 740 km remaining, I do not know."

Evans was the largest and heaviest of the party, but had to manage on the same ration as the others. He became more and more starved. A cut on his hand which he incurred while working on shortening the sledge would not heal, and a number of other small scratches became infected. On 13 February, Evans was already so feeble that he could not help to haul the sledge. The food was almost finished and the next depot had to be reached as soon as possible. Evans had problems with his boots and was therefore detached from the sledge. He was left behind and told to catch up as soon as possible, but did not show up. Scott and Oates went back with an empty sledge only to find Evans in the snow, crawling on all fours, unable to walk and in a wretched state. When he was brought into the tent, he had lapsed into a coma and died that same night. He probably suffered from scurvy, and perhaps also beri beri.

On 14 February the party descended the glacier and found themselves at Slaughter Camp, where the ponies had been shot. For their evening meal, the first in a long time, they ate pony meat. Not only did they have the Barrier to surmount, it was still 550 km to Cape Evans.

TIME RUNS OUT

The depots were understocked so that the party was short of food and fuel, and their clothes were unsuitable for the harsh conditions, with temperatures down to minus 30 to 40 °C. They made poor progress when they set out again. Oates had frost-bitten feet and gangrene had begun to set in. He could hardly stagger next to the sledge. At Cape Evans he had made it clear that on a polar expedition no one should become a burden to the others. He wanted all of them to carry pistols, so that, "If one or another breaks down, he should have the privilege to use it". On 9 March they reached the Mt. Hooper depot, which they hoped would be their salvation. Scott wrote, "Poor comfort. Lack of all types of supplies. I don't know if anyone has been negligent – but there hasn't been any surplus of generosity and consideration." During the support party's

return, they had found it necessary to use some of the supplies, leaving the depot considerably understocked.

By 14 – 15 March, Oates was on the verge of a breakdown. The pain in his feet could no longer be borne. Wilson had distributed opium tablets to enable each of them to commit suicide. Oates asked to be left in a sleeping bag in the snow, but they managed to take him to the next stop in the hope that a rescue expedition with dog-sledges would arrive.

In the early morning of 17 March, Oates woke up; it was his 32nd birthday. Crawling out of the sleeping bag and out of the tent, he disappeared into the drifting snow. Oates left the tent with the words, "I'm only going out for a short spell. It may take some time..." The weather improved. Scott, Wilson and Bowers struggled on and on 21 March they were 18 km from One Ton Depot. Their food was nearly gone and there was little fuel, and then a snow storm came at them from the south. Scott's leg was frost-bitten and he could hardly walk. Bowers and Wilson got ready to go to One Ton Depot in order to fetch food and fuel. For some reason this trip did not take place, perhaps because the depot was so badly marked that it could only be found in good weather. However, even had they reached the depot, it is doubtful whether they would have survived. It was still 240 km to Cape Evans and winter was fast approaching.

They lay down in the tent, waiting for the end to come and writing their last letters and a few quick notes. Scott had realised from 16 March that the

The skis used by Scott, now exhibited at the Oslo Ski Museum

end was near. He wrote several letters in which he justified his actions. The last to die was probably Wilson.

From Cape Evans, a sledge party was dispatched on 26 February to meet the Scott and his men. The dog sledge was loaded with enough food for 24 days and provisions for an additional two weeks for the Scott's party. But the rescue attempt was in vain. Those remaining at Cape Evans realised that all hope was lost and that nothing could be done to avert the tragedy.

THE TRAGEDY IS DISCOVERED

Summer came, and on 29 October a search party was sent out. On 11 November it arrived at One Ton Depot. Finding it untouched, the party followed the old route as accurately as possible. At daybreak a pyramid-shaped object was located at about 45 degrees from the course they were following. Tryggve Gran quickly took some poles from the sledge and set off. Ten minutes later he stood in front of a partly buried tent. He reported in his diary, "It has happened, we have found what we've been looking for." Almost 20 km from One Ton Depot, in a half-buried tent, lay the bodies of Scott, Wilson and Bowers. Captain Scott lay in the middle, partly outside his sleeping bag. Bowers and Wilson lay entirely inside their sleeping bags. The freezing temperatures had turned their skin yellowish-coloured and glassy, and there were signs of frostbite. Scott appeared to have struggled in the throes of death, while Wilson and Bowers appeared to fallen peacefully asleep. On 21 March Scott had written in his diary, "There is no longer any hope, and I beg you, God, to protect our dear ones at home."

The rock samples were still on the sledge. The diaries and other personal objects were removed from the tent. And then they buried their friends, with Atkinson officiating. Eleven weather-beaten men stood bare-headed in the whirling snow, and before the last psalm had been sung, a soft, white blanket was spread over the dead. Over the grave they raised a 4 m high cairn, on top of which they planted a cross made of Tryggve Gran's skis. Gran saved Scott's skis so that they at least completed the voyage, and they are now displayed at the Oslo Ski Museum. The expedition then went on to find Oates. They found the sleeping bag, but not Oates. At the site where they found the bag they raised a cross with the inscription, "Here abouts died a gallant

Amundsen's letter to King Haakon, which was found in the tent.
Under: Death's tent, where the bodies of Scott, Wilson and Bowers were found.

Amundsen's letter to King Haakon, which was found in the tent.
Under: Death's tent, where the bodies of Scott, Wilson and Bowers were found.

gentleman, Captain L.E.G. Oates of the Inniskilling Dragoons."

On their trip back, they made a short stop at Scott's, Wilson's and Bower's grave. By chance they found a worn-out Lapplander shoe. This contained a small cloth bag in which they discovered Amundsen's letter to HM King Haakon VII. Here there was yet more evidence fact that both Amundsen and Scott had reached the South Pole.

EPILOGUE

The *Fram* reached Buenos Aires on 25 May 1912, and Don Pedro Christoffersen arranged a reception worthy of the dazzling exploits of the Amundsen expedition to the South Pole.

Amundsen received word that the *Fram* could be one of the first ships to pass through the Panama Canal. The vessel was sailed to Colon, where it was docked from 3 October til 1 December 1913. The exact date for the opening of the canal was still not set, so the *Fram* was ordered to sail southwards and around Cape Horn, then northwards to San Francisco.

When it arrived in Buenos Aires again after its 100-day journey, the *Fram* badly needed an overhauling, as it had sustained damage during its passage through the tropics. Amundsen was probably low on funds by this time as well. Reaching the South Pole was a magnificent achievement but not necessarily one that could fund an expedition to the North Pole. In 1914, Captain Nilsen, who had taken over as skipper again, was ordered to sail *Fram* to Horten, where it arrived on 16 July. And the *Fram*'s day as an active Polar schooner came to an end.

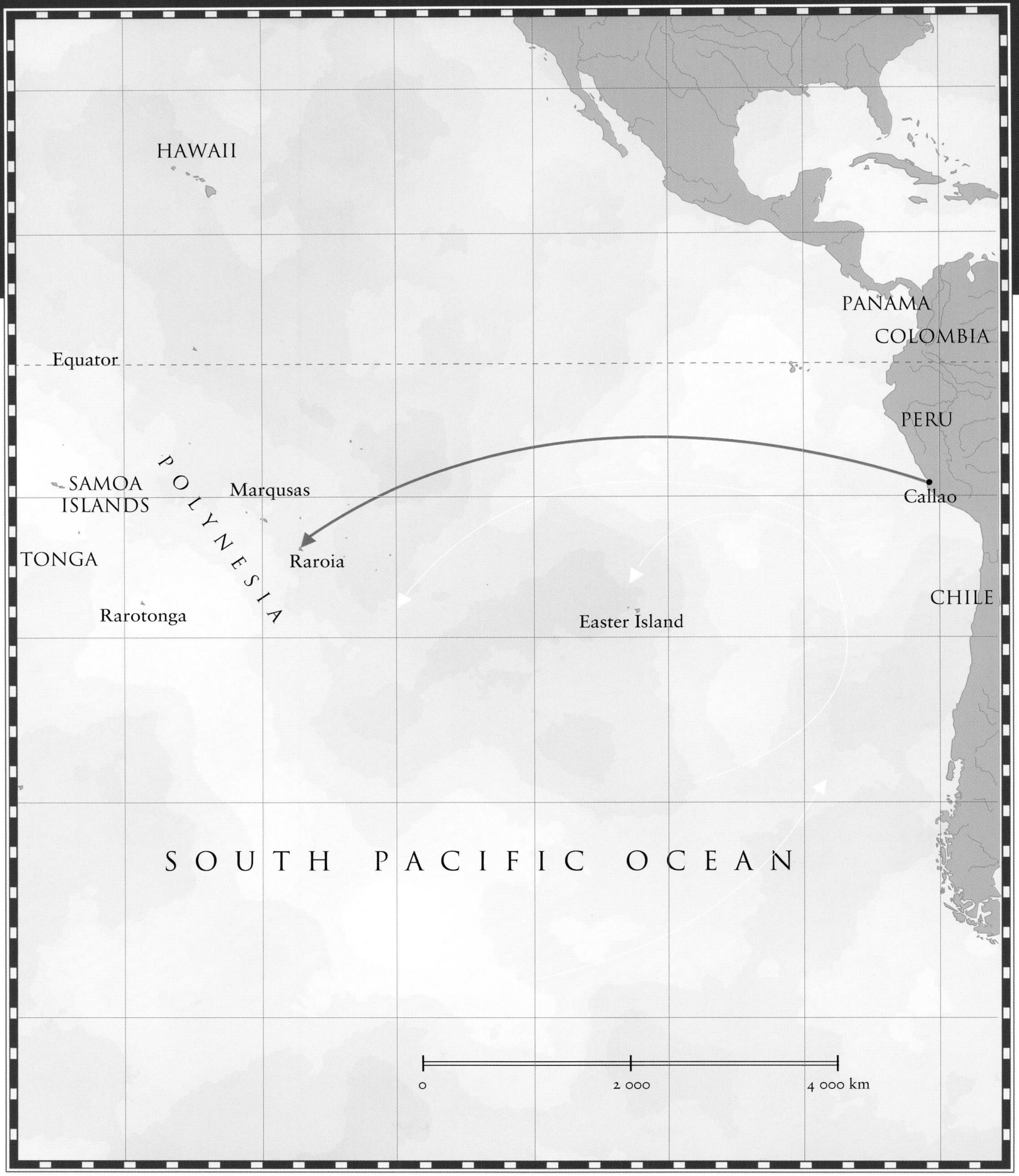

HAWAII

PANAMA

COLOMBIA

Equator

PERU

SAMOA
ISLANDS

P O L Y N E S I A

Marqusas

Callao

TONGA

Raroia

Rarotonga

Easter Island

CHILE

S O U T H   P A C I F I C   O C E A N

0   2 000   4 000 km

THOR HEYERDAHL 1947.

THOR HEYERDAHL
– THE KON-TIKI EXPEDITION

BY ØYSTEIN KOCK JOHANSEN

As onlookers laughed in derision and shook their heads, the Norwegian explorer Thor Heyerdahl and his crew of five set off for Polynesia from the coast of Peru. By making the voyage on a frail balsa-wood raft, they wanted to prove that there had been a connection between South America and the Polynesian islands in prehistoric times – in direct contrast to the views held by contemporary researchers and scientists. For these young people, as for prehistoric Polynesians, the oceans offered no barrier.

It was 1947. For the first time for hundreds of years a balsawood raft was being built in Callao bay in Peru. Nine thick balsa logs had been lashed together with strong ropes. Not a single nail, rivet or wire rope had been used. In the middle of the raft, slightly towards the stern, a small, open cabin had been constructed of bamboo canes, with walls of plaited bamboo reeds and a roof of bamboo slats. Rising in front of the cabin was a straddle-mast, which supported a large, rectangular square-sail hanging from a yard. The stern of the raft was cut straight across, except for the three middle logs which projected and supported a short, thick balsa log holding thole pins for the long steering-oar.

The raft in the harbour at Callao, Peru's largest port, was nearly ready and Thor Heyerdahl and his five companions – four fellow Norwegians and one Swede – intended to sail it across the Pacific Ocean. Heyerdahl was determined to prove that the Polynesian islands could have been populated by people from South America. Researchers and scientists claimed the opposite – that Polynesia was first populated from the west, from Southeast Asia and Indonesia. Heyerdahl was firmly convinced that they are wrong, and he intended to prove it by sailing the primitive balsa raft from Peru to an island in Polynesia – from east to west.

The raft was almost finished. Experts and officials came to have a closer look at the strange vessel. They did not have

much encouragement to offer Thor and his crew, to put it mildly. Everyone, from a Peruvian admiral to three Norwegian seamen, poured scorn and ridicule on the expedition and its crew: "You'll never come out of this alive!". Thor was urged to give up the idea of such a foolhardy voyage while there was still time. When the US ambassador was unsuccessful in his attempts to change Heyerdahl's mind, he gave him a bible!

A total of twelve huge balsa trees were felled in the jungle at the foot of the Andes.

Heyerdahl and his crew felt that many of the criticisms levelled against the expedition were difficult to swallow: the experts claimed that the raft was so small that it would capsize

in heavy seas, then that it was just long enough to be lifted up on the crests of two waves at the same time and that, with its full load of cargo and crew, the frail balsa logs of the raft would break apart under the strain. Peru's largest balsa exporter said that the balsa logs would only float a quarter of the distance across the ocean before they became so completely water-logged that the raft would sink beneath the feet of its crew. The raft was too square and clumsy to be propelled along by means of its sail, the lashings would not hold for long and the crew would be constantly up to their ankles in water on the "deck". They heard that huge bets were being placed on how many days the raft would last. In a rash moment, a marine attaché bet all the whisky the members of the expedition could drink for the rest of their lives if they reached a South Sea island alive.

But it was too late to cancel the project now. The raft had taken two months to build, about twice as long as envisaged. Heyerdahl and his crew wanted to get away to sea as quickly as possible, not least so that they did not have to listen to any more prophecies of doom. Food and supplies for six people for four months were stowed on board the raft, and on the 28 April they were finally ready to go. The Norwegian flag was hoisted and the vessel, which only the day before had been named *Kon-Tiki* after the son of the Sun-god, was towed out of the harbour. The towing rope was cast off and the tug headed back to Callao. The sail was hoisted. Now it was up to the winds and currents to take over and carry them westwards!

The voyage, the expedition, was to bring success, honour and fame to all those on board, and in particular to its leader, Thor Heyerdahl. His name, and not least the name Kon-Tiki, would later become world renowned. The Kon-Tiki expedition became the symbol of daring, success, experimental research, scientific testing and of ingenuity and practical expertise. But let us not jump ahead of the story. The Kon-Tiki expedition – or rather the spark that led to its inception – had been ignited almost ten years earlier.

Thor Heyerdahl was born in Larvik on the southeastern coast of Norway on 6 October 1914, the only child of Alison and Thor Heyerdahl Sr., a brewery owner. He became interested in zoology and anthropology at an early age, and opened his own little "museum" while he was still in primary school. Thor Heyerdahl decided early on that he wanted to be

an explorer. After completing secondary school in Larvik, he went on to study zoology at the University of Oslo. Heyerdahl received a grant to study animal life on an isolated island, and in 1937 and 1938 he and his young wife Liv lived on the Polynesian island of Fatuhiva in the Marquesas Group. With professors Kristine Bonnevie and Hjalmar Brock from the University of Oslo, Heyerdahl had drawn up a project to study how the fauna on Fatuhiva had made their way to such a distant island in the Pacific Ocean. Heyerdahl and his wife lived like the native Polynesians, without the use of technical aids and without any contact with the outside world.

AN IDEA IS BORN

Fatuhiva was the spark that eventually led to the Kon-Tiki voyage. While carrying out his zoological studies there, he noticed how important the winds and the ocean currents were for the island's animal and plant life. He was also becoming more and more interested in how the Marquesas islands and Polynesia as a whole had been populated. He gradually began to doubt the scientists who claimed that the inhabitants of the Polynesian islands had originally come from Asia in the west. Heyerdahl was sceptical to these claims because he observed that winds and currents always came to Polynesia from the east. And on the other side of the ocean – to the east – lay South America, about 8 000 km away. Wouldn't it make sense if the first inhabitants of the Polynesian islands sailed *with* the winds and currents from South America?

The idea caught his imagination more and more. An old native Polynesian who had become a friend of his on Fatuhiva also told him that his forefathers had lived in *a great country* beyond the ocean. The god *Tiki* had led them to the islands they now inhabited. In the mind of the young scientist, these ideas were taking the form of theories.

When he returned to Norway, Heyerdahl left Oslo University to devote himself to studying how people had migrated, how early seafarers had sailed across the seas in primitive vessels. He continued to work on his theory about the Polynesian population. Heyerdahl believed there were a number of cultural similarities between Polynesia and South America. He threw himself into a scientific hornets' nest. Who were Tiki and his people? Who were these people who had come to Polynesia? All the books Heyerdahl had read on the

The crew of the Kon-Tiki: from left, Knut Haugland, Bengt Danielsson, Thor Heyerdahl, Erik Hesselberg, Torstein Raaby and Herman Watzinger.

subject said that the Polynesians had come from the west, from the islands and lands of the sunset. But this did not tally with what he had seen in Polynesia himself, and – not least – in the literature he had studied after his stay in Fatuhiva.

Thor Heyerdahl first published his theory in 1941. In his article, he wrote that although he accepted that there had been a migration from Asia to Polynesia, he believed the *first* settlers in the Polynesian island kingdom had sailed from South America on balsa rafts. Experienced researchers found it hard to accept a theory like this from a young and unknown student. They did not believe that any prehistoric vessel could have brought people from South America to Polynesia. To a non-scholar, Heyerdahl's theory seemed convincing, but it had the opposite effect on contemporary scientists. The article was otherwise overshadowed by the Second World War.

After the war, Heyerdahl went to the United States to resume and continue to develop his migration theories. He produced a large text with the title "Polynesia and America; a Study of Prehistoric Relations" in which the young researcher implicitly criticized conventional thinking and prejudice. He did not expect to have an easy job convincing the experts on the subject of migration to Polynesia. Heyerdahl almost took it for granted that researchers would reject him on academic grounds because he had not studied archaeology, ethnology and other related subjects. Nor had he any other academic qualifications to his name.

A WALL OF RESISTANCE

The manuscript was sent to well-known scientists at a number of universities. The response was vehemently negative. One of the reasons for this was that one of the leading experts on the subject had published a dissertation a few years earlier in which he concluded that a long ocean voyage could not be accomplished by means of a balsa raft. The logs would absorb water and sink. People could therefore not have sailed a balsa

raft from South America to Polynesia. This was the view held by virtually all Polynesia scholars at that time.

Because of the negative response to his manuscript, Heyerdahl summoned up the courage to visit a well-known archaeologist called Herbert Spinden. On Spinden's desk Heyerdahl saw his unopened manuscript. The older, more experienced researcher shrugged his shoulders, "You're wrong, absolutely wrong", he said, shaking his head indignantly. Heyerdahl countered, looking hopefully in the direction of the manuscript lying on the desk, "But you haven't read my arguments yet." "Arguments," said Spinden, "you can't treat ethnographic problems as a sort of detective mystery!" "Why not?", Heyerdahl replied. "I've based all the conclusions on my own observations and the facts that science has recorded." "The task of science is investigation pure and simple," Spinden said quietly. "Not to try to prove this or that. It's quite true that South America was the home of some of the most curious civilizations of antiquity, and that we know neither who they were nor where they vanished to when the Incas came to power. But one thing we *do* know for certain, that none of the peoples of South America got over to the islands of the Pacific. Do you know why? The answer's simple enough. They couldn't get there. They had no boats!" "They had rafts", Heyerdahl said hesitantly, "you know, balsawood rafts." The older man smiled and said quietly, "Well, *you* try a trip from Peru to the Pacific Islands on a balsawood raft."

Heyerdahl had no answer, but in fact Spinden's words that day laid the basis for Heyerdahl's future voyage. He decided to disprove the old postulate that the highly-developed civilizations of South America did not have the ability – or the expertise – to sail across vast stretches of ocean. Heyerdahl wanted to plan an expedition to sail a primitive raft made of balsa logs, based on drawings made by Spanish chroniclers, and then set a course across the Pacific – westwards. He hoped to show that the balsa raft was a good enough vessel for a voyage such as this and that it was in fact possible to reach Polynesia from South America.

In addition to himself as the natural leader of the expedition and skipper, Thor Heyerdahl chose as his crew four Norwegians, *Knut Haugland, Erik Hesselberg, Torstein Raaby*

and *Herman Watzinger,* and one Swede, *Bengt Danielsson.* And these were the men who, in late April 1947, found themselves drifting westwards on a raft.

Kon-Tiki sailed out into the Humboldt Current, which brings cold water up from the Antarctic, running up the coast of Peru before turning westwards just below the Equator. The Incas used to sail out here too, in their great sailing rafts, which used to go out for 50-60 nautical miles, and it was these rafts Pizarro and other conquistadors witnessed in the 16th century.

At first, Heyerdahl and his men felt they were not making any progress. Then southeasterly winds began to blow more and more strongly and by the afternoon the trade wind reached full strength. From now on, they felt, there was only one way to go – westwards. A never-ending ocean lay before them. *Would everything be all right? Would their voyage be a success? Would they all survive?* As darkness fell that night, doubts began to sneak in. The prophecies of doom they had had to listen to before they set sail filled their heads. They had only just begun their voyage and were uncertain whether the ocean would prove to be friend or enemy. As the darkness of the night enveloped them, they heard how the noise of the ocean was drowned out by the hiss of a roller near them and saw white crests as high as the roof of their cabin come rushing

There was plenty of time for reading.

towards them. They clung to their craft and waited in dread to feel the huge masses of water smash down over them and the raft. But to their relief and surprise, they were to find, again and again, that Kon-Tiki calmly swung her stern up on top of the waves and rose up into the air while the masses of water rolled by on either side. Easy!

On the third night, the wind abated and the sea became calmer. Then at four o'clock in the morning, in pitch darkness, a last foaming wave came unexpectedly towards the raft. It threw itself over the frail craft like a wild animal and capsized the raft before the steersmen had time to react. The sail lashed the bamboo cabin, threatening to tear both the cabin and itself to ribbons. All hands had to go on deck to save the food and

supplies. They heaved and hauled on ropes and stays to try and pull the raft back on course. When day broke, they had managed to turn the stern into the wind and were on their way westwards again.

The raft made good speed over the next few days, covering 55-60 nautical miles a day. One day they sailed 71 nautical miles, the equivalent of 130 km. Everything seemed to be going well. As they became more proficient at steering and more confident in performing their tasks aboard the raft, they began to take notice of the sea around them. They enjoyed watching a sea teeming with life and they lead a carefree existence on board. The men were by now so used to having the sea dancing around them unfettered that it did not bother them. What did it matter if they bobbed about on the waves with a thousand fathoms of water beneath them as long as they and the raft were always on top?

Under full sail.

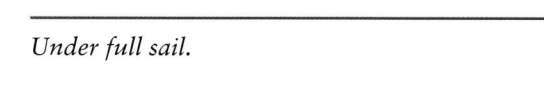

THE RAFT BEGINS TO TAKE IN WATER

But – and it was a big but – how long could they expect to stay on top? *The balsa logs were absorbing water!* One of them had become so sodden that you could press a whole fingertip into the log as though it were a wet sponge. The situation worried Thor, but he did not convey his fears. Secretly, he broke off a piece of the sodden wood and threw it into the sea. He watched as it immediately sank beneath the surface and slowly vanished down into the depths. This was worrying. Later, Thor saw several of his shipmates doing exactly the same thing when they thought no-one was looking. If the logs continued to soak up water, the raft would finally sink. And that meant quite simply that they would drown!

They had marked off the waterline on the raft when they left Callao, but in the rough sea it was impossible to see how deep the raft lay. However, by driving a knife into the timber, they were able to ascertain to their relief that the wood was dry only about 3 cm beneath the surface. They estimated that if the water continued to penetrate the wood as the same pace, the raft would be virtually floating *beneath* the surface of the water by the time they reached dry land. But they hoped that the sap further in would have the effect of waterproofing the wood and would check the process of absorption. And they were right.

Another source of worry was the ropes. The men didn't worry during the day, because they were so busy with their chores that they had no time to think about it. But when darkness fell and they crawled onto their mattresses in the cabin, destructive thoughts accompanied the sounds of ropes creaking and rubbing. How long would the ropes hold? Two weeks, a Norwegian seaman had predicted. They had been at sea longer than that now and the ropes were still holding. They checked all the lashings every morning. Even the underside of the raft was carefully checked. But, strangely, they found no sign of wear. Only after a long time and when they were a long, long way out to sea did they find out why. The structure of the balsa wood was so loose that the ropes were gradually working their way into the wood itself where they were protected, rather than the logs chafing against and wearing the ropes.

Something happened every day. Frequently, they saw fish flying through the air and flapping around the raft. Splash! – something had landed on the deck. The flying fish wriggled and floundered on and between the thick logs of balsa. When the cook got up in the morning, he went out on deck and

Keeping the raft on course in heavy seas was a test of strength.

picked up flying fish that had landed there in the course of the night. One morning, he found 26 large, fat flying fish.

One day, Heyerdahl, heard a snorting sound, like a horse. When he turned around, he saw a large whale right beside the raft. Then a whole flock of toothed whales surfaced alongside it. Porpoises came from all directions and brushed past the small craft. Another day a brown shark more than three metres long followed closely behind the raft. One of the men tied a rope around a small dolphin (dorado). With the fish as bait, he cast the line and drew it on board again. Heyerdahl stood at the stern with a harpoon at the ready, and when the shark was only a metre from him, he threw the harpoon with all his might into the creature's neck. The shark fought back, twisted around, cut the line with one bite and disappeared into the depths.

SWALLOWED BY A WHALE – ALMOST

They saw a great deal of squid, especially young ones. They saw the eyes of the giant squid shining like phosphorus down in the depths. One night, a fish tumbled in between the men

Idyllic conditions on board.

was enormous. Both the head and the body were covered in white spots.

The giant came swimming lazily towards them from behind the raft, its large dorsal fin protruding from the water. Sometimes they could see its tail fin too. The broad back of the creature looked almost like a reef. When it came up to the raft, the creature rubbed its back against the heavy steering oar, pushing it upwards as though it were a match. This was neither animal nor fish – it was a monster. But once they had recovered from the shock, they quickly ascertained that this was a *whale shark*, the largest shark and the largest fish known in the world today. Zoologists say that it can grow to twenty metres in length. It was so large that when it swam around and underneath the raft, the head was visible on the one side while the entire tail section could be seen on the other. It could smash the raft to pieces with one swipe of its tail. After an hour of watching the shark circling around the raft, with all of them feeling the strain on their nerves, Erik Hesselberg's patience ran out and he drove a harpoon deep into the gristly head of the monster. It suddenly transformed itself into a mountain of steely muscle. The creature stood on its head in a cascade of water that sent the three men standing nearest tumbling head over heels across the deck. Then the giant plunged down into the depths of the ocean. Would it resurface to take its revenge? The six men sat on the raft, fearing the worst. But they never saw it again.

asleep in the cabin. One of them pushed it away – "probably just a flying fish". However, it felt more like a snake. They lit the lamp and saw a strange, thin fish about a metre long with the mouth of a carnivore, full of long, sharp teeth. When one of the men squeezed its stomach, fish came gushing out of the huge, gruesome mouth. The Swede, Bengt Danielsson, woken by the commotion, glanced at the strange fish and said: "No, fish like that don't exist". At which he calmly turned over and went back to sleep. And he was right. No-one had ever seen a fish like it alive. Skeletons had been found a couple of times near the Galapagos Islands, and the experts had called it *snake mackerel*, or *Gempylus*.

One day, the others heard a wild war-cry from Knut Haugland who was sitting aft behind the bamboo cabin. "Shark!" he shouted. Haugland had been washing some clothes when he looked up and came face to face with the largest and ugliest face any of them had ever seen. It was the head of a veritable sea monster, so large and ugly that if the Old Man of the Sea himself had jumped up, they would not have been more taken aback. Its head was broad and flat like a frog's, with two small eyes right out at the edges on either side of its face and a mouth that was 1.5 m wide. Long fringes hung drooping from the corners of the frog-like mouth. The body

BY THE SKIN OF THEIR TEETH

In another dramatic episode, they almost lost a man. A sleeping bag left to dry on deck was suddenly caught by the wind. Trying to catch the bag, Herman Watzinger took a rash step and fell overboard. The others heard a faint cry for help and saw Herman's head and an arm flailing in the water. They recalled that anyone falling overboard could quickly disappear for ever because of the forward speed of the raft. Although Watzinger was a good swimmer, this was not much help. Someone threw in a life-buoy, but Herman could not reach it. Knut Haugland threw himself resolutely into the water with a life jacket in his arms and a line around his waist which was attached to the raft. After a struggle, he reached Herman at the last moment and both were hauled back to the raft. They saw the sleeping bag suddenly disappear, drawn brutally down into the sea right behind them. Something had risen from the

depths and pulled it down. The unknown creature had just missed a couple of better prey.

Otherwise, life on board went on as usual. The men had enough to meet their basic needs. The food supply was constantly being supplemented by large amounts of fresh fish that more or less caught itself. Otherwise dried meat and sweet potatoes were the most important ingredients in their simple diet. They also had 56 water jugs on board. By day 45, Kon-Tiki had progressed from 78° to 108° west, which meant they were halfway to the most easterly islands of Polynesia. The ocean stretched endlessly on all sides, with 4 000 kilometres to Peru in one direction and the same distance to the first islands of Polynesia in the other. On 2 August, Knut Haugland made contact with a radio ham in Oslo and they were able to send

birthday greetings direct from the raft to Kong Haakon for his 75th birthday the following day.

At the beginning of August, it was still uncertain where the raft would run ashore. At this point, they were as far from the Marquesas islands as from the Tuamoto islands, and they might easily float between these two groups of islands. If they headed for Marquesas, they would have to be prepared to meet perpendicular cliff walls with tiny coves where mountain valleys joined the sea. The coral atolls on Tuamoto however, were even worse as a landing site because of treacherous submerged reefs and atolls. As early as 3 July, at about 125° west and still a thousand nautical miles from Polynesia, they had observed small flocks of frigate birds – a sure sign that somewhere beyond the infinite expanse of ocean, there was land.

The flocks of birds that appeared and then disappeared in the same direction when night fell were becoming larger. The

A good day's catch of shark.

first land to be sighted was the small island of *Puka-puka*, on the very edges of the Tuamoto group. They could smell the scent of wood, forest, leaves and greenery. But Puka-puka disappeared behind the horizon after only a couple of hours. After three days another island came into view – *Angatau*. They sailed along its coast for a whole day, but were unable to find an opening through the jagged reef. They had reached day 97, which was exactly the minimum number of days the voyage had been estimated to take.

After this, they drifted on the ocean for another three days without sighting land. Then at dawn on day 101, Torstein Raaby came rushing down from the top of the mast shouting "Land ahead!" Ahead of them lay a row of small palm-clad islands. They realized that they only had a few hours left on the raft. But first they had to find a way through reefs that the ocean thundered across, sending plumes of spray high into the air. On board the raft, everything had been made ready for the end of the voyage. Everything of value was taken into the cabin and tied down. Papers and documents were enclosed in watertight bags. A canvas was thrown over the bamboo cabin itself.

When the raft made contact with the reef, they would all have to hold on as best they could. To be thrown onto the reef would mean certain death. The thick balsa logs would have the take the worst of the barrage. An entry in the Kon-Tiki log, made at 9.50 a.m., reads: "Very close now. Drifting along the reef. Only a few hundred yards or so away. ...All clear. Must pack up log now. All in good spirits; it looks bad, but we shall make it!"

A moment later, the stern of the raft swung round into the breakers. The crew tightened their grip. The anchor rope was cut in two. Then the waves lifted them up into the air. They – or rather the raft – rode forward on the back of a wave at breakneck speed. The raft, the logs, the ropes and lashings creaked and wailed under the strain. A green wall of water rose up and Kon-Tiki disappeared in the masses of water. The mast broke and crashed down through the cabin roof. Planks and logs broke up all around them. The reef ripped into the deck. There was chaos everywhere, but the raft held. Heyerdahl clung on and looked for the others. They mustn't die now! "This won't do", a voice beside him says. Thor felt equally discouraged. But after an inferno of water, spray and thunder, the raft came to rest on the reef and they were able to wade ashore.

They had made it. They had survived, every one of them! With dry land under their feet on the white sandy beach of the coral island *Raroia*, they were able to say that they had achieved their – and above all Thor Heyerdahl's – goal: *sailing a balsa raft from South America to Polynesia was possible. They had proved it. The journey had taken them 101 days and they had travelled 8 000 kilometres.*

With the voyage of the Kon-Tiki, a scientific dogma had been shaken to its very foundations. The book about the Kon-Tiki expedition and the film were both worldwide successes. The book has now been published in almost 70 languages and is said to be the second most widely read book after the Bible. The film won an Oscar for Heyerdahl – the first and only one so far won by Norway. The public received the book and the film with great acclaim.

Researchers and scientists, on the other hand, had little other than criticism to offer. With hindsight, it is possible to see that much of this was based on good, old-fashioned envy and prestige. The worst comment came from a well-known Finnish professor who accused Heyerdahl of bluffing and denounced his story as dishonourable nonsense. This was repeated time and time again by the media all over the world.

The goal has been reached. Kon-Tiki approaches Raroia.

Another scientist said, " ... Heyerdahl has proved nothing beyond what we already knew – that Norwegians are good sailors!"

In the midst of all the criticisms, Heyerdahl was encouraged by one voice that spoke out in praise of the expedition, that of the famous Swedish explorer Sven Hedin. He also said: "The doers of great deeds will always be subjected to envy and the grasping vultures of doubt. But it is of no consequence – and is all part of the game".

Today – over 50 years after the Kon-Tiki expedition – non-scientists the world over are on Heyerdahl's side. And research has produced more and more evidence to support the idea that South American people went to Polynesia. In addition, Thor Heyerdahl's own excavations in Peru 1988-94, in which I also took part, have turned up evidence that Peru's advanced civilizations from the centuries following the

After a hundred and one days on board the balsa raft, it was good to stand on dry land again.

birth of Christ up to the 16th century had sea-going vessels. And objects and symbols have been found in Peru that have only been found in one other place in the world, Easter Island in Polynesia. So Heyerdahl was right; *there must have been a connection between Peru and Polynesia in prehistoric times.*

More and more evidence has been found to substantiate Heyerdahl's great belief that in ancient times the oceans offered no barrier to human migration. The Kon-Tiki expedition was the first, and perhaps the most important, link in the chain of evidence. But for Thor Heyerdahl the voyage was not the end, it was just the beginning!

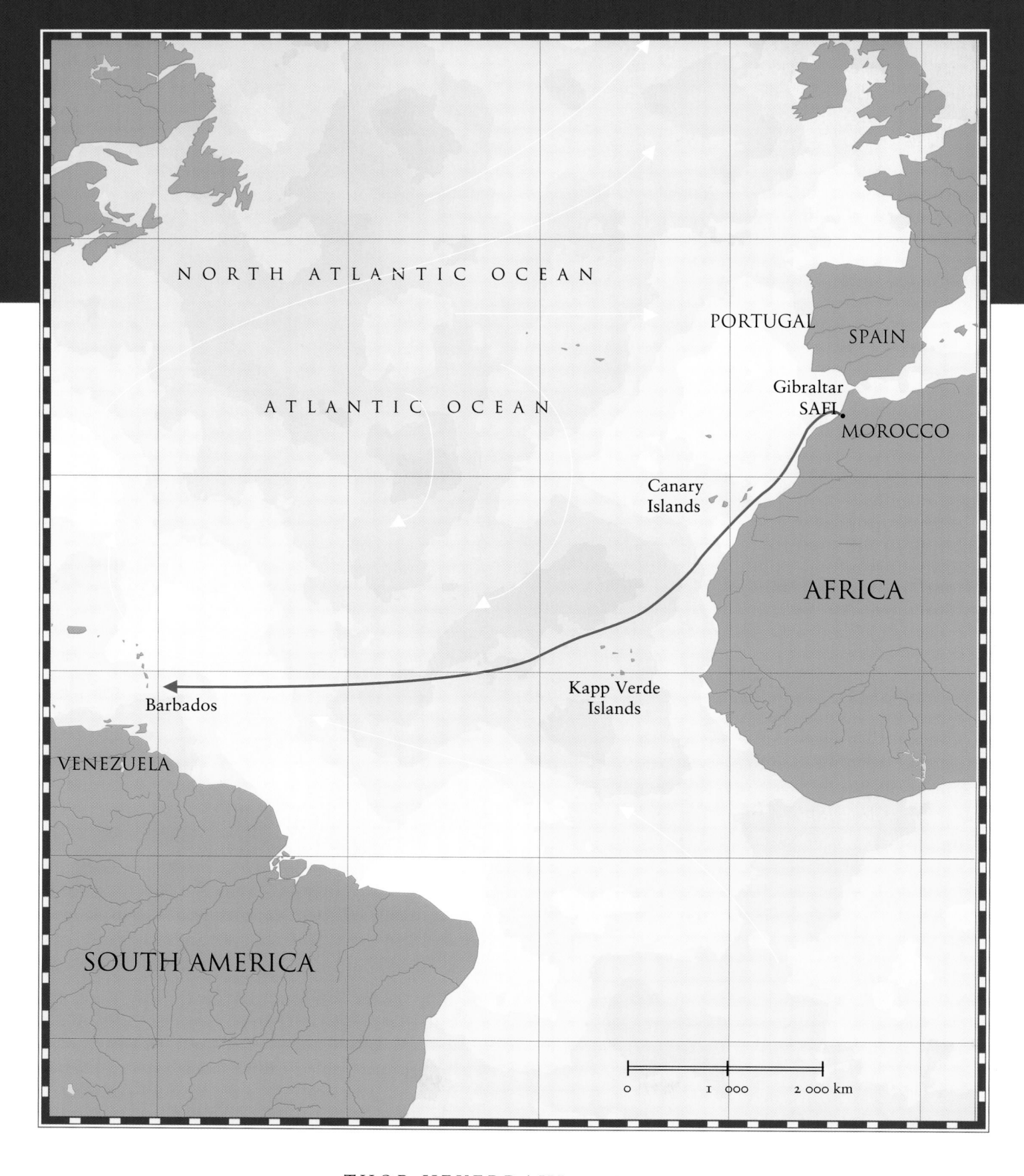

NORTH ATLANTIC OCEAN

ATLANTIC OCEAN

PORTUGAL

SPAIN

Gibraltar
SAFI

MOROCCO

AFRICA

Canary
Islands

Kapp Verde
Islands

Barbados

VENEZUELA

SOUTH AMERICA

0   1 000   2 000 km

THOR HEYERDAHL 1969-70.

THOR HEYERDAHL
– BY PAPYRUS BOAT ACROSS
THE ATLANTIC

BY ØYSTEIN KOCK JOHANSEN

In 1969 Thor Heyerdahl set off on a new expedition. This time he wanted to cross the Atlantic from the west coast of Africa to America on a reproduction of an Egyptian papyrus boat. An international crew was on board. The purpose of the voyage was to prove that ancient civilizations had boats that enabled them to sail to the New World. Contemporary scientists strongly doubted this theory. Due to mistakes in its construction, the Ra 1 began to list and the crew had to be evacuated. A year later, Heyerdahl completed the voyage with a new papyrus boat – the Ra 2.

There can no longer be any doubt. The boat is sinking. It is only a question of time. The boat lies heavy and low in the water, writhing in the throes of death. The crew and the skipper, Thor Heyerdahl, have been fearing the worst for a long time. Now they have to face facts: the ship – and the expedition – is doomed. Nothing in the world can save the vessel. And the lives of the crew are in great danger. "This is the end", says one of the crew. Heyerdahl decides to abandon ship. And only he can give the order to

abandon the ship – and the expedition. It is a difficult decision to make, but to avoid lives being lost, there is no other way.

The year was 1969. The expedition was an experiment. Heyerdahl had had a papyrus boat built that was a copy of the boats the ancient Egyptians used to build thousands of years ago. They had set off from the west coast of Africa to cross the Atlantic to the New World. Now, as they prepared to abandon the vessel, they had travelled almost 5 000 kilometres. That was over 2 000 kilometres more than the shortest distance

The Ra 1 cannot be saved and the attempt must be abandoned.

---

between Africa and South America. A line drawn in a circle around the globe for a distance of 5 000 kilometres from Safi in Morocco, where they had started, would reach past Moscow and the northernmost tip of Norway, cut across Greenland, over Newfoundland, Quebec, Nova Scotia and touch the east coast of Brazil. In other words, they had covered quite a distance. Not bad for a primitive papyrus boat.

Even though the voyage was over, Heyerdahl at least had the satisfaction of knowing that the expedition had proved that a papyrus boat could sail the high seas across an ocean. Even with the few faults in construction that they had discovered during the voyage, they had survived storms with the crew and most of their cargo intact. They had sailed across the open sea for eight weeks and demonstrated the long-forgotten sea-going capabilities of the papyrus boat. But now

they had to give up. The once lofty arch of the stern had collapsed and had lain floating half under the surface of the sea for several days. Now the boat itself was listing badly, the entire starboard side under water. A large amount of papyrus had worked itself loose and been lost. The distinctive straddle-mast was leaning heavily to one side and most of its lashings had come undone. This was indeed a dying vessel, floating helplessly on and below the surface of the water.

Heyerdahl's gnawing doubts had gradually developed into certainty and decisiveness; they would have to call for help and get themselves aboard another boat. It was a difficult decision for him to make, but there were no other alternatives. There was no point in risking human lives, even though the crew wanted to try and keep the wreck going a little longer. Later, Heyerdahl wrote the following: "It might have been all right, but a heavy storm might have washed one or another of us over board. It was not worth it. I had set this experiment in motion because I was looking for an answer. And we had our

answer. A papyrus boat that had set off with landlubbers as its crew, who, with no-one to guide them and no experience, had constructed, loaded and sailed it." In view of this, Thor was satisfied. A primitive papyrus boat had in a way proved its seaworthiness.

On 15 July 1969, the "Shanandoah", a small motorized yacht from Martinique, sailed up and anchored alongside the half-sunken wreck of the papyrus boat. In the two days that followed everything of any value was transferred to the yacht. Finally the crew also came aboard. They watched the remains of the papyrus boat that had housed them for eight weeks sail on alone on the Canary current and the trade wind. That was the last they saw of the boat. A short time later a bunch of papyrus reeds and a steering-oar were washed ashore on the coast of Florida. Two or three years later a few papyrus reeds were found on the west coast of Norway, having completed the round trip on the Gulf Stream.

So the expedition was abandoned. But Thor Heyerdahl was not able to rest knowing that he had in a way – *but only in a way* – reached the goal he had set himself, to make a successful voyage across the Atlantic to the New World. It was true that he and his crew had reached islands in America, but all the same … ! They had had to abandon the vessel before they had completed their journey. So he decided to try again. *He would build a new reed or papyrus boat.*

HOW IT ALL BEGAN

It had all begun long before, many years before, in fact. Heyerdahl's voyage in 1947 from Peru to Polynesia on the balsa raft Kon-Tiki opened his eyes to new horizons and other expeditions. In the years 1955-56, Heyerdahl conducted the first professional archaeological excavations on the famous and mysterious Easter Island in Polynesia. This is where he became interested in reed boats. Heyerdahl found pictures of reed boats carved on gigantic stone statues and stone slabs. In connection with the excavations on the island, he found remains of American *totora* reeds that had been planted here and there on the island. It became clear to Heyerdahl that the earliest inhabitants of the Pacific islands could have arrived not only on balsa rafts, but also in reed boats.

Several researchers had pointed to the similarity between the old reed boats from Mexico and Peru and boats from the Mediterranean area. Many of them asserted that this similarity

had to be a coincidence because reed boats could not cross the oceans. The cultures on either side of the Atlantic would therefore not have had any possibility of influencing each other. They claimed that reed boats had only been used on rivers and along the coast, never on the open sea – these "simple" craft were not suitable for sea voyages. Heyerdahl doubted these postulates. The pictures of large ships that he had seen on Easter Island, *had* to mean that the inhabitants of this island had once had large ocean-going ships. And as far as

---

On the trail of ancestors? Carvings of papyrus boats on the stone statues on Easter Island.

Heyerdahl got important knowledge about the reed boats of ancient times from wall paintings in Egyptian burial chambers.

he could ascertain, they had been built out of nothing but reeds. Some of the oldest Easter Islanders built a small reed boat in order to explain to Heyerdahl the kind of boat their forefathers had depicted on one of the large statues. He saw for the first time how very easily this kind of boat mastered the waves of the Pacific.

ANCESTOR OF THE REED BOAT

Later, on the banks of Lake Titicaca in Bolivia, Heyerdahl's imagination was once again caught by reed boats on a surface of sky-blue water. Heyerdahl himself said of this occasion: "The Aymara Indians manoeuvred their boats back and forth as they fished in the strong breeze. At a distance, only the wind-filled sails could be seen. Most of the boats had tattered canvas sails, but some had kept to tradition and hoisted a large mat of golden *totora* reeds on two straddle-masts joined at the top. Three of the boats came straight towards us at full speed ... Magnificent. They were expertly built. Every single reed had been laid with maximum precision to achieve perfect symmetry and streamlined elegance, while the bundles were so tightly lashed that they looked like inflated pontoons or gilded logs bent into a clog-shaped peak fore and aft ... Boats of this distinctive kind were still being built in their thousands on all sides of this enormous inland sea. Just as they were built by the Indians' parents and grandparents. Just as they looked four hundred years ago when the Spaniards came to South America."

It seemed clear to Heyerdahl that the ancient civilizations that had populated the great land areas from Mexico to Peru and Chile had spread as far as to the nearest islands in the Pacific by means of reed boats. The Easter Island culture was only an offshoot, perhaps the last top shoot on the tree. But where were the roots? Here in America or on the other side of the Atlantic, in the Old World?

If people from ancient civilizations could sail from Peru to Polynesia, they could have made equally impressive voyages across other oceans. In Egypt, Heyerdahl had been fascinated by pictures in the ancient graves of kings and priests in Luxor and Sakkara. These pictures showed reed boats in use in everyday life, being constructed or conveying the dead on their last journey to the kingdom of death. Furthermore, a number of ancient rock carvings from before the time of the Pharaohs depicted reed ships with a mast and sail, one or two cabins on deck and as many as 40-50 pairs of oars protruding from the sides. Cattle and other large domestic animals could be seen on deck on some of the ships. The animals seemed small in relation to the dimensions of the ship. In other words, these must have been large vessels.

CULTURAL FEATURES IN COMMON

Heyerdahl had hoped to see a papyrus boat being built in Egypt, but he was disappointed. It was quite simply impossible because, with a few exceptions, the papyrus reed had disappeared completely from the area. However, he was told that he would find reeds and reed boats in use near the great Lake Chad in inland Africa. And it was on Lake Chad Thor was for the first time to see the latest descendants of reed boats that were once typical of the great civilizations in North Africa and the Middle East. And not only that, they were the same type as the boats Heyerdahl knew from Mexico, Peru and Easter Island.

Heyerdahl had also noticed that the ancient cultures of Egypt, Mexico and South America had several features in common, like sun worship, gigantic stepped pyramids and the cultivation of cotton. Could it be that "emigrants" from the Old World had made their way across the Atlantic to Mexico

and South America in reed boats and brought their skills, traditions and customs with them? After giving the matter much thought, Heyerdahl decided to find out whether such a voyage was possible. How should he go about doing that? *He decided to build a reed boat, a copy of the reed boats he had seen on wall paintings in Egyptian burial chambers.*

So, on 29 January, a Norwegian newspaper published the sensational news: *"Seven to cross Atlantic in papyrus boat. Heyerdahl on new expedition."* Heyerdahl did not waste time once he had made a decision and by autumn 1968 the building had begun. He hired two experienced reed boat builders from Chad to help him build the boat. The building material, papyrus, was brought from the source of the Nile in Lake Tana in Ethiopia. Once upon a time the banks of the Nile had been

covered by papyrus reeds, but now they had to go as far as the source of the river to find them. Heyerdahl contacted the Swedish maritime historian Bjørn Landstrøm, who was an expert on old Egyptian boats. Landstrøm knew nothing of papyrus reeds, but he knew how the boat should look. In partnership with the men from Chad, he set about the exciting work of constructing the boat. As a symbolic gesture, Heyerdahl had the boat built near the three great pyramids at Giza, just outside Cairo.

The boat builders from Chad – two brothers – laughed out loud when they saw that the boat they had been commissioned to build was to be pointed and raised like the prow of a ship at both ends – they had never seen anything like that before. No reed boats they knew of were tapered at each end, and none had a "prow" at the stern either! Nonetheless, they set to work and collected papyrus reeds in larger and larger bundles, just as they were used to doing at home. When a bundle was

The Ra 1 under construction in a historic setting.

The first reed boat since ancient times is ready to be launched.

almost a metre thick, it was stretched out into a "sausage". The work progressed rapidly and the reed cylinders became longer and longer. But on the third day, there was trouble. The brothers from Chad would not under any circumstances make the reed cylinder thinner at one end. The bow was shaped the way they were used to: gradually narrowing and rising to finish in a high elegant curl. But at the stern the reeds were shorn off bluntly like huge shaving brushes – as was the tradition in Chad. Heyerdahl and Landstrøm tried to explain that they were supposed to be building a copy of an *Egyptian* boat. At this, one of the brothers turned his back on them and went to lie down. The other brother remained and tried to explain that a reed cylinder could be made thicker and thicker but not thinner and thinner.

Next day the two boat builders started work before anyone could stop them. They had found an ingenious way to "weave" a new cylinder into the old one, so that they were joined together in one piece. The technique seemed convincing. To Heyerdahl there was no doubt that they knew what they were doing and he felt reassured.

RA GETS ITS ACHILLES HEEL

Work continued and the ship began to take shape. But the narrow end was missing. The conflict between owner and boat builder had not been solved. The two brothers would not budge on the question of the design of the stern. Then they were taken to the biggest store in Cairo and told to choose one gift each. They each picked out a wristwatch and a promise was made to teach them to tell the time. Back at the building site, the two smiling brothers discovered that it would be possible to patch on a very thin pointed extension to the stern which could then be elegantly bent upwards. Now the boat really looked like an ancient Egyptian vessel. At that time, no-one had any idea or could have foreseen what a fatal mistake this solution would prove to be. As Heyerdahl later wrote "… this improvised afterthought of a stern was to prove the papyrus boat's Achilles heel".

Seven men from seven nations, with varying political beliefs and religions, took part in the expedition.

On 28 April 1969, the date of the start of the Kon-Tiki expedition twenty-two years earlier, the boat was finished. The ship was given the name *Ra* after the ancient Egyptian sun god. It was then transported to the port of Safi in Morocco, where it was to set sail across the Atlantic. The crew had been selected by Heyerdahl long ago – seven men from seven countries. All the men had been carefully chosen, each with his own particular skills and tasks on board. Heyerdahl wanted to try out the idea of *One World* in practice on board. All the wars and conflicts that were going on at the time inspired him to try a form of bridge-building between nations. He had also been given permission by United Nations Secretary-General U Thant to fly the UN flag on the reed boat. The members of the crew came from the United States, the Soviet Union, Chad, Mexico, Egypt and Italy, and then there was Thor himself, representing Norway. Heyerdahl wanted to show that people could live and work together regardless of nationality, skin colour, political beliefs or religion.

So there the boat lay, in Safi harbour, waiting for favourable offshore winds. Food supplies had been brought on board, stored in hundreds of woven baskets, goatskin sacks and stoneware jars. The food was either in dried, salted or liquid form. There were no tinned goods on board. They wanted the expedition to be as authentically ancient in form as possible.

DOOMSDAY PROPHECIES FOR A SECOND TIME

As before the Kon-Tiki expedition twenty-two years earlier, Thor Heyerdahl was again told that the expedition would fail. Once again he was met with criticism and his theories were written off by the experts. They said that, although reed boats could be used on quiet rivers and on lakes, at sea they would be broken up by the waves. Others claimed that the salt water would eat away the papyrus. Some said that the reed would not survive more than sixty days in the sea. That may well be, replied Heyerdahl, but voyages by reed boats in the open sea

Even though the Ra 1 was unbelievably buoyant, it slowly began to absorb water.

were in fact mentioned in ancient documents. Naval experts pointed out that in the waters the *Ra* would be sailing through they would have to expect violent storms and hurricanes. The strong and unrelenting motion of the waves would have a disastrously wearing effect on the thin papyrus tubes. Parasites might even rot the reeds from the underside, it was said. And there were many other negative comments. But Thor had an answer for most of them.

Despite all the prophecies of doom, they were determined to go through with the expedition. As a matter of fact, Heyerdahl was not intending to *prove* anything by the voyage; he just wanted to find out if prehistoric people *could* have crossed the Atlantic in reed boats. He wanted an answer to the question: was it possible in *practice*? He himself was convinced that the reed boats were very seaworthy. He was so confident of this that the crew trusted him despite the fact that experts claimed the opposite. The experts had said the same thing twenty-two years ago. But they had been wrong. If Heyerdahl was right this time too, then it might well be true that at some time in ancient history the New World had been populated from the Old World – but it still needed to be demonstrated.

After the *Ra* had been at anchor in Safi harbour for eight days, the papyrus had absorbed a great deal of sea water. "So that was half its lifetime gone already", as the experts said. But then, on 25 May, a promising offshore wind caused all seven national flags and the UN flag on board the *Ra* to point optimistically westward. And at 08.30 hours a broad «shipload of reeds», the *Ra*, began to move away from the quayside. The sail was hoisted and the wind filled the great canvas sail measuring almost 50 square metres. A large red sun had been painted in the middle of the sail – the symbol of the god *Ra*. The strange craft, 15 metres long and five metres wide with a simple cabin on deck, glided out of the harbour. All the fishing boats in the harbour blew their horns and were joined by the factory whistles on shore. Ships' bells rang, people on shore shouted and cheered, and signal rockets soared into the air. The *Ra* glided out to sea to deafening jubilation. And once out on the open sea, the boat rode the waves like a seabird.

Buoyancy was good. Despite tons of equipment on board, the boat was floating high in the water. Even more astonishing was the fact that the hull showed no sign whatsoever of heeling when the wind took a good hold on the large sail. They were on their way. The powerful, dangerous and unpredictable Atlantic lay before them in all its glory. Now they only had themselves to rely on.

SHORT-LIVED HAPPINESS

After a while, the offshore wind disappeared and a northwesterly breeze blew more towards and along the shore, straight towards houses and low cliffs south of Safi. It was now essential to steer their "shipload of reeds". But the crew of the *Ra* had had no-one to teach them and had not been able to test the ancient steering system they had copied from small models and ancient Egyptian wall paintings. Later, Heyerdahl was to write: "The steering system was so ingenious and apparently different from the steering devices used by any living peoples today that we all cheered with joy and relief when for the first time I carefully pushed the cross-bar (on the long steering-oar) to port and *Ra* slowly, but willingly like an amiable horse, obeyed the signal by turning its bow to starboard. I promptly pushed the bar to starboard and *Ra* swung slowly to port." There was no doubt about it. The steering mechanism worked perfectly. There was an almost idyllic atmosphere on board.

But the idyll did not last for long. One of the crew shouted urgently to Thor. It was the Russian. He was so worked up that he could only speak Russian. What on earth was he saying? Thor couldn't understand anything until the Italian shouted in Italian that the steering-oars were broken – and not just one, but both of them. They could no longer steer *Ra*. Would they have to give up? Just at that moment the ship turned so that the sail filled. Now they would really experience what it was like to sail as people of the oldest cultures had done, with no steering-oar. In a way, Thor was excited. Now they would find out how they would get on by just following the wind and the currents.

However, they were able to repair both steering-oars in the course of a few days. For one of them they used a solid square reserve mast of Egyptian wood, for the other they patched together bits of various broken shafts. At full sail, *Ra* now did over a hundred kilometres a day. Nonetheless, there was no lack of drama. The sail was thrown back on itself several times because of sudden gusts of gale-force winds. On several occasions it was close to being ripped in two on the straddle-mast. Sometimes the reed boat drifted sideways or stern first until by rowing and hauling on ropes the crew were able to bring the boat back on course. On another occasion a violent gust of wind took hold of the rigid yard and smashed it against the mast with a splintering sound. The hull itself, however, the bundles of papyrus lashed together, showed their unique qualities. Not a single papyrus stem was broken or had worked loose from the ropes. Even in the worst storm the boat danced safely, riding high on the waves just like a life buoy.

Even so, the crew were not short of problems, but they were able to solve them all. One of the amusing episodes on board was when the man from Chad, who had never seen the sea before, was amazed to discover that the water was salty. And when he saw a spouting whale for the first time, he thought it was a hippopotamus. Apart from that, he had some difficulty finding his bearings when he wanted to kneel down in prayer facing Mecca. But when it came to splicing ropes and repairing damaged woodwork, he was a true master craftsman. The leader of the expedition himself, Thor Heyerdahl, had enough to do studying and making a daily record of everything of interest on the voyage, especially the many observations of the *Ra*'s peculiar capabilities. Otherwise, he of course also took on his fair share of the crew's never-ending struggle against wind and sea.

POLLUTED SEA

When you are as close to the surface of the sea as the men sitting on the deck of the *Ra* were, you are bound to notice anything floating on the water. And the crew did. Heyerdahl later described the days around 10 June in the following way: "Next day we were sailing in slack winds through an ocean where the clear water on the surface was full of drifting black lumps of asphalt, seemingly never-ending. Three days later we awoke to find the sea about us so filthy that we could not put our toothbrushes in it … The Atlantic was no longer blue but grey-green and opaque, covered with clots of oil ranging from pin-head size to the dimensions of the average sandwich. Plastic bottles floated among the waste. We might have been in a squalid city port. I had seen nothing like this when I spent 101 days with my nose at water level on board the *Kon-Tiki*. It

became clear to all of us that mankind really was in the process of polluting its most vital well-spring, our planet's indispensable filtration plant, the ocean…" Heyerdahl's report that the ocean was beginning to be polluted was sent to the United Nations from the *Ra*. This was the first time this problem was recognised.

The entire reed boat had been copied exactly, detail by detail, from prehistoric, Egyptian wall paintings. But they agreed that they had probably not understood everything or done everything correctly. They had not managed to make the rudder correctly, for example. For a long time, Heyerdahl thought that he had made the rudder out of a type of wood that was not strong enough. It was only a long time afterwards that he discovered why the rudder had broken. The rudder, in reality a long steering-oar that reached down into the water, was attached too well. When a large wave came along, the rudder broke, as had happened at the beginning of the voyage. The reason was simple – the rudder was attached to the hull in two places. If it had been attached less tightly in one of these places, the rudder would have been able to break loose. Then at least the oars would not have broken.

MISTAKES ARE REVEALED

But they were gradually to discover that they had made another and far more fundamental mistake. Right from the beginning of the project, they had wondered why the reed boats depicted on the wall-paintings had such a high "curl" at

The crew on board the Ra observed lumps of oil and other forms of marine pollution almost every day.

the stern, a feature the boat builders from Chad were not willing to make at first. Heyerdahl and his men had thought that it had been made so that the boats would look more impressive. But as time went on, they had an unpleasant feeling that this was not the reason after all.

The papyrus was changing – it was swelling up. The change was slow but it was definitely taking place. Consequently, the long bundles or "sausages" the *Ra* was made of were also swelling up. The whole construction was becoming harder. The ship simply seemed more solid. But – on the starboard side aft a pool of seawater had begun to form that grew larger day by day. In addition, the rear section of the boat began to lie low in the water. At the bow, their "proud golden swan still stretched her neck", but at the stern "her tail was beginning to droop". No matter how hard they pulled and hauled on the ropes, they could not pull the stern up again.

The days passed by. More water washed in over the afterdeck every day. The waterlogged stern section must weigh a ton by now! Should they cut off the large curled tail? Maybe that would make the bottom of the boat float up again? But they did not have the heart to cripple their proud craft. It would be like cutting the tail off a swan. Suddenly Heyerdahl remembered something. On the wall paintings they had seen in Egypt, there was a rope running from the top of the high, magnificent stern of the ship and down to the deck. They had not then understood the purpose of the rope, but they did now. The rope that everyone had thought was there just to hold the curled tail in tension had a completely different function. The curled tail kept its shape perfectly well by itself. The rope was not intended to pull the tail-tip down, but the afterdeck up. Yes, that was it! The high, harp-shaped stern was meant to act as a powerful spring, with the rope supporting the free-swinging afterdeck as the stays to the masthead supported the rest of the papyrus boat.

THE HULL BREAKS UP

Heyerdahl was right. The high tail acted as a kind of crane that enabled the craft to float more easily. They promptly attached a rope, a bowstring, from the tip of the tail down to the deck, but it was too late now. The stern had already been under such strain that it proved impossible to repair the damage. The situation was getting worse all the time, but no-one wanted to give in. They sailed on with the stern sinking lower and lower

With no bowstring to hold it up, the stern gradually sank as the sea washed over it. The bow and midship sections showed no sign of sinking.

---

into the water. By 9 July, the water had risen to such a height that much of their food supplies had been ruined. A barrel of 100 kilos of salt meat, for instance, was soaked through. But something much worse was happening: the hull was disintegrating. The raft was beginning to come apart.

Probably, everything would have been all right and the *Ra* would have reached America had it not been for the weather gods. They suddenly decided not to cooperate with the people on board the tiny, damaged reed boat drifting around on the enormous ocean. Perhaps they had upset the gods of the wind and the sea in some way or other? Whatever the reason, a tropical storm was rolling up over the horizon in the east. The *Ra* had passed the degree of longitude that touched Brazil's easternmost point long ago and was about 5 000 nautical miles north-east of French Guyana. This was not the first time they had encountered bad weather, but this time irreparable damage was done. The wind howled around the mast and the stays and threatened to rip the sail in two. The waves crashed into the cabin with such force that the boxes of equipment were shattered and personal possessions, medical equipment and provisions floated in the water.

On 15 July the storm reached a climax. Foaming waves as high as the mast rushed hissing past them. The steering bridge was constantly awash with seething water, making the helmsman's job inhumanly tiring. Steering the *Ra* was virtually impossible. The sail had to be lowered, too. Papyrus reeds on the starboard side worked loose and floated away. The *Ra* was listing badly. The men on board began to suspect how this would end.

The sea was in constant uproar for the next few days. Huge waves sent heavy masses of water weighing several tons crashing over the already badly sunken stern. The bottom of the boat bulged under the strain. The *Ra* writhed as if in agony, twisting in all directions in an effort to follow the chaos made by the waves. It made an eerie, hoarse sound they had never heard before as the pressure and the strain on the bundles of reeds became extreme. The rest of the galley disappeared into the water. The men on board were more

under water than above it. Their lives were in very real danger. Thor decided to abandon the *Ra 1*, to turn it over it to the forces of the sea – which brings us back to where this story began, when the crew were rescued by the motor-yacht *Shanandoah* from Martinique.

The expedition had been an experiment, a test voyage to explore the qualities and capabilities of the reed boat. The fact that they did not quite complete the voyage was not due to a lack of seaworthiness in the papyrus boat, but to a modern

The Titicaca Indians had not lost the ancient skill of reed-boat building.

boat was abandoned, it was capable of keeping itself afloat for weeks or months. None of the seven men on board were in any doubt: the Atlantic would not have offered any real obstacle to proficient and experienced papyrus-boat sailors in ancient times.

ANOTHER TRY

But Thor Heyerdahl could not be content with the thought that he had in a way – but *only* in a way – achieved the goal he had set himself. *He decided to try again.* By 1970 he was already secretly building a new reed boat in Safi in Morocco where the *Ra 1* expedition had started. The papyrus came from the same place as last time, but the boat builders were new. This time, four Aymara Indians from Lake Titicaca built the boat. In the area around the lake, there was a long tradition of building strong reed boats. The new boat was different from the first in both method of construction and size.

The Titicaca Indians used a method of construction which strangely enough was closer to the ancient building technique than the one that had survived in inland Africa. They built the stern as high and as curved as the bow. In addition, and this was important, the hull of the boat was tied together in a different way from the previous time. Two enormous reed cylinders were each bound to a smaller roll in the middle by two independent ropes wound in a continuous spiral. These ropes were so long that there was no need for knots or for the ropes to cross over each other. As the boat builders tightened the ropes as tightly as they could, the small middle roll "disappeared" to make an invisible core. This meant that the visible double-cylinder hull was as rigid as a compact block of wood. Another wise decision was to treat the cut ends of the papyrus with pitch to keep the water out. The new boat was two to three metres shorter than the first and a little narrower. With these fundamental and important changes, the boat was launched.

It was baptized the *Ra* again, but this time the *Ra 2*. Despite being a smaller boat than its predecessor, it carried one crew member more. The crew was the same as before except for the man from Chad, who was not able to take part, and with the addition of two new men from Japan and Morocco.

lack of experience and knowledge of the long-forgotten capabilities of this ancient craft. The *Ra 1* had simply been constructed incorrectly, with elementary mistakes that the reed boat builders of ancient times would never have made. That is why the voyage failed. Nonetheless, Heyerdahl himself was pleased with the result of the expedition, however strange that may sound. He had been able to prove that the papyrus did not sink after two weeks in the water, as the experts had claimed. The *Ra 1* would have been able to bring them safely to America if it had not been for the mistake in construction causing the stern to sink and half of the reeds to work loose in the course of the voyage. The papyrus stems themselves were as fresh and tough as they had been at the start. At the time the

More or less the same provisions were taken along as last time, but were more carefully stowed. Bitter experience had taught them to have less cargo on the starboard side so as to prevent the boat from listing. Because of the prevailing direction of the waves, the boat would absorb most water on that side.

On 17 May 1970, the *Ra 2* left Safi harbour headed out into the Atlantic on the same course as its predecessor. This time, with a better-designed and far stronger reed boat, Heyerdahl was expecting the expedition to more successful than last time. And so it would prove to be. But the boat absorbed a great deal of water this time too. After only one week at sea, the *Ra 2* lay much deeper in the water than Heyerdahl had expected. The boat was sinking at an uncomfortable pace. Could the experts at home be right this time in giving them only two weeks to stay afloat? It was calm for days, and the boat sank by 10 centimetres a day. It got on everyone's nerves. In fact, it was worse than that; a mental

explosion was in the air. To make the boat lighter, they threw anything they could spare overboard. It seemed to have a positive effect. They were no longer sinking, at least for the time being.

The next dramatic episode came when they were halfway across the ocean. On 18 June a storm broke. Waves higher than a 30-foot mast attacked the boat and the men on board. Later that day, a giant wave came from behind and lifted the boat up. The *Ra 2* dipped its nose down and its tail up in a mad rush down into the deep valley of the wave. Later, Heyerdahl was to write: "Just as we tipped over the crest of the wave, I heard the crack of a large piece of timber. When I turned around, I saw that the large blade on the papyrus-covered port steering-oar hung loose in its ropes, broken in

The Ra 2 is halfway. The crew are encouraged.

two… It had snapped like a tooth-pick. The *Ra 2* lay helpless, its starboard side turned towards the raging sea, its sail slamming and thundering against the mast, as huge masses of water engulfed us, just as they did during the last days of the *Ra 1*." Would they be forced to abandon a sinking reed boat again? Would they "fail" again?

When they cut the ropes holding the thick papyrus padding onto the blade of the steering-oar and threw the sodden reed ends into the stormy sea, Heyerdahl watched in despair as all the ends sank. After a week of continuous hard work, they had managed to gain control of the situation again and had repaired the most serious damage. In spite of the fact that the craft was drifting completely flooded by seething water – like the *Ra 1* at its worst – they passed 40° west and were on the American side of the ocean. The crew were all overjoyed.

REPORT TO THE UN

As well as their terrible struggle to survive and the strain they had suffered, mentally and physically, there was another negative factor that Thor Heyerdahl and the other men were

Small craft come out to meet the Ra 2 on its way in to Bridgetown on Barbados.

concerned about, even though it had nothing to do with the boat and was no danger to the crew. They had noticed that the sea was much more polluted than it had been a year earlier. In one year, pollution of the world's oceans had become noticeably worse. Every single day they observed lumps of oil of varying sizes. In heavy seas, they were washed on board the *Ra 2*. A pollution report was delivered to the UN research vessel which was on a research mission in the area around the *Ra* at the beginning of July.

The ocean was not endless, even though it seemed to be. On 7 July they had reached the West Indian shipping lanes and heard on the radio that Barbados would send out a government ship, the *Culpeper*, to meet them and wish them welcome. But it took three days for the two craft to find each other on the unruly seas. Planes came out to them and saluted by rocking their wings, and when they approached Bridgetown they were met by an armada of large and small

boats which escorted the *Ra 2* in to the harbour. On 12 July they berthed at the quay in Bridgetown harbour. They had made it. They had sailed from the Old World to the New on board a papyrus boat, a true copy of the ancient vessel. They had crossed the Atlantic at its widest and sailed 6100 kilometres in 57 days. The expedition was a success. Any doubts about the seaworthiness of the papyrus boat had been swept aside.

THE BOAT THEORY CONFIRMED

Once again, Thor Heyerdahl had shown that something that no-one thought was possible could well have taken place. Ancient peoples could have reached America in prehistoric times – in a reed boat. Heyerdahl had pointed out several times that the *Ra* expedition was only meant to show that people in ancient times could have made their way across the Atlantic in a reed boat, not that they necessarily had done so. Herein lay an essential distinction which was unfortunately often missed – not least by so-called experts. And the critics wasted no time, especially Norwegian ethnographers and Danish Egyptologists. Heyerdahl's *Ra*-expeditions were described as a sort of sports achievement, a daring adventure that had nothing to do with science. It was claimed that the two voyages had proved nothing except that Heyerdahl was an experienced adventurer. One of the Danish Egyptologists went as far as to say that even a clog could have drifted across the ocean to Barbados on the northern equatorial ocean current. Furthermore, she claimed that papyrus ships like the one built by Heyerdahl had never existed. The Egyptian ocean-going ships were wooden, she said. Similarly, she disputed Heyerdahl's claim to have found "drawings", on which the *Ra* was based, in the tombs of ancient Egyptian kings.

Heyerdahl agreed that a clog could well have sailed across the Atlantic. The purpose of the *Ra*-expedition was to show that a *reed boat* could cross an ocean. In spite of the fact that so-called experts said that it would sink after two weeks. If a clog – or for that matter anything that could float – could drift from Africa to America, there was of course even more reason to imagine that organized voyages across the Atlantic, by vessels drifting on the currents, were made before Columbus. As far as the argument about reed boats and pictures of them in Egyptian tombs was concerned, Heyerdahl could produce evidence in the form of a number of colour photos of paintings and reliefs from royal Egyptian graves that even depicted how the papyrus was harvested and bound together to make boats.

Once the *RA*-expedition had been completed, publishers, press agencies, TV stations and film producers became very interested in the story. The book about the *Ra 1* and *Ra 2* voyages was a great success and was translated into 60 languages. The documentary made about the voyages was nominated for an Oscar. While the *Ra 1*, as we know, had a sorry end, the *Ra 2* was transported by ship back to Norway, where it became the main attraction in a newly-built wing of the Kon-Tiki museum in Oslo, where Heyerdahl's balsa raft was already exhibited.

Looking back, we see that the *Ra* voyages were an important test and an impressive demonstration of human imagination, courage, and the will to cooperate, and a shining example to prove that borders, religion and national prejudice are no obstacle to human endeavour and peaceful coexistence. Add to this the triumphant completion of a scientific, practical test of ancient techniques, and it is no exaggeration to say that with his *Ra*-expeditions Thor Heyerdahl once again claimed his rightful page in the history books.

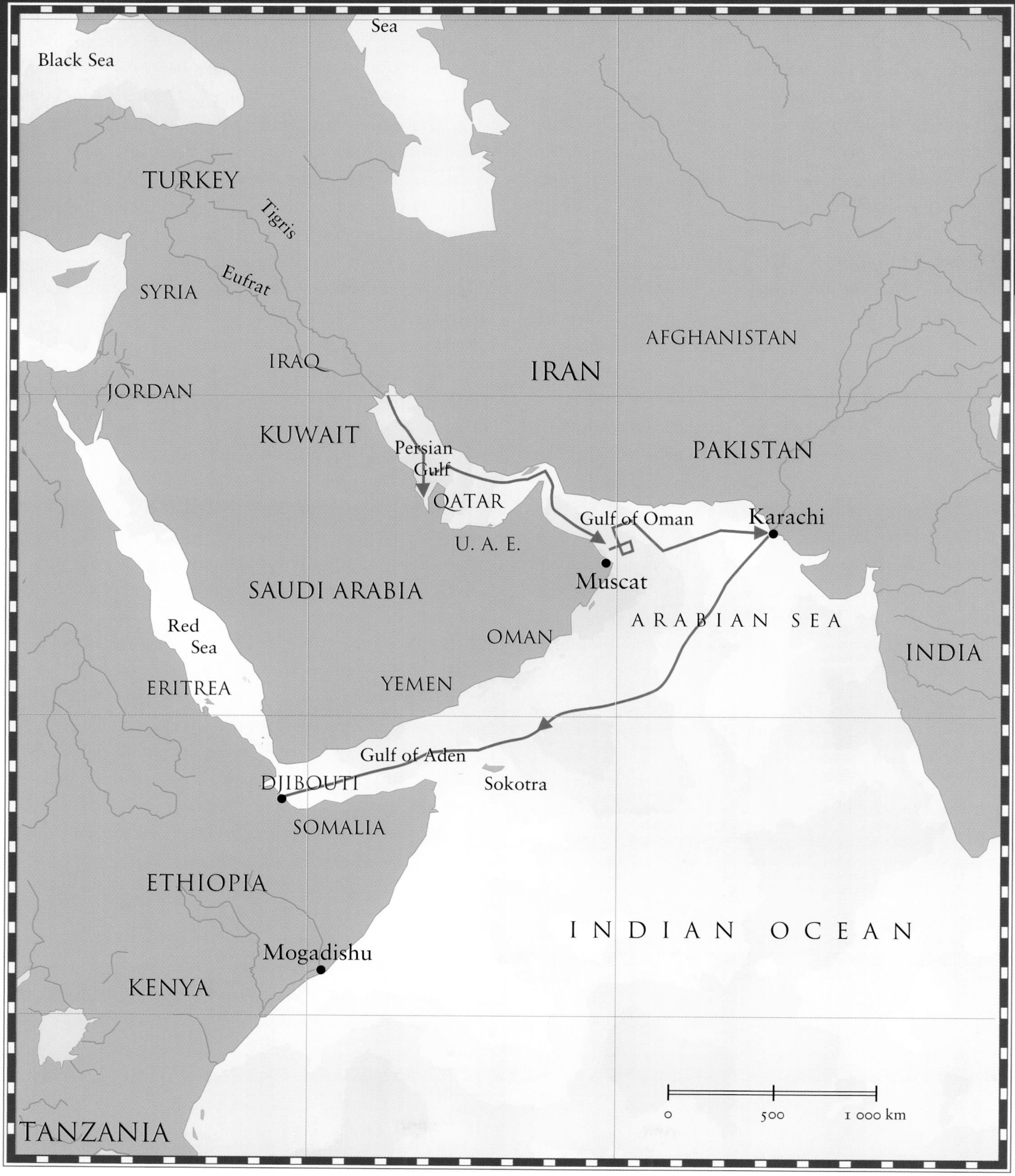

Black Sea

Sea

TURKEY

Tigris

SYRIA

Eufrat

IRAQ

JORDAN

KUWAIT

AFGHANISTAN

IRAN

PAKISTAN

Persian
Gulf

QATAR

U. A. E.

SAUDI ARABIA

Red
Sea

ERITREA

YEMEN

OMAN

Gulf of Oman

Karachi

Muscat

ARABIAN SEA

INDIA

Gulf of Aden

DJIBOUTI

Sokotra

SOMALIA

ETHIOPIA

INDIAN OCEAN

Mogadishu

KENYA

TANZANIA

0   500   1 000 km

THOR HEYERDAHL 1978.

WITH THOR HEYERDAHL AND THE "TIGRIS" IN THE WAKE OF NOAH

BV ØYSTEIN KOCK JOHANSEN

In 1977-78, Thor Heyerdahl carried out another experimental ocean-going expedition. In the Tigris, a copy of an ancient reed boat, and with an international crew, he sailed out of the Persian Gulf and crossed the Indian Ocean and the Red Sea. Heyerdahl wanted to solve the riddle of how the ancient boatbuilders had improved the buoyancy of the reeds. He also wanted to prove that people of ancient civilizations were able to sail from Asia to Africa.

The flames reached high into the air. The wind snatched the heavy, black smoke and carried it up into the evening sky. The once so magnificent reed boat was now ablaze. The crackling of burning reeds could be heard far into the gathering twilight. The sun's great, red disc was slowly sinking behind Africa's deep blue mountains, yet it was still light. The powerful flames from the burning boat made sure of that. The fire licked out of the cabin door and the sail caught fire in a shower of sparks and sputtering flames. Burning pieces of canvas flew into the air like small fireballs.

In a matter of seconds the sail was burnt up, and only the blazing straddle-mast lit up the evening sky. Sharp cracks from the splitting bamboo of the burning cabin filled the air.

On some coral cliffs some distance from the burning boat, eleven men stood gazing at the sea of flames. They were the crew of the reed boat *Tigris*. The captain of the ship and leader of the expedition was Thor Heyerdahl. Yet again, Heyerdahl had built a reed ship and had made an extraordinary voyage. Here, outside Djibouti by the Red Sea, the voyage had ended. The *Tigris* was burned as a protest against the war that raged

The Tigris is burned as a protest against the war that is raging between the countries bordering the Red Sea.

between the countries bordering the Red Sea, the Gulf of Aden and the Horn of Africa. Wherever the expedition wanted to put into harbour they found war and hardship. So, as a desperate protest, the reed ship that had been their home for several months was set alight under full sail.

No-one said much. Each man stood lost in his own thoughts. They all felt a strange emptiness, a longing back to their unique voyage on this remarkable ship. "Take off your hats", was all that Thor Heyerdahl managed to say as the flames licked out of the door of the main cabin. No-one answered. They stood in silence gazing at the crackling fire out at sea. An almost inaudible voice reinforced the gloomy, sorrowful atmosphere and the silence, "It was a fine ship." Heyerdahl could hardly hear his own mumbling, nor did he know whether anyone else registered what he said. It didn't really matter. It was all over now. On 3 April 1978, in keeping with ancient heathen traditions, the *Tigris* was cremated. Thor's inaudible mumbling was the finest epitaph a ship could be given. But then it had certainly been an outstandingly well-crafted and safe vessel. The finest that Thor Heyerdahl had ever built.

As was the case with all Thor Heyerdahl's expeditions, there was a story behind the *Tigris* expedition. And, as always, the impetus for the expedition had occurred several years earlier. In fact, almost immediately after the completion of the *Ra 2* expedition. For something must surely have been wrong with the *Ra 2*. The boat builders of ancient times would never have continued using reeds to build their craft for thousands of years unless it was possible to keep the cargo dry on deck. Nor would they have done so if it had been necessary for the crew to seek refuge on the top of the cabin in order to keep their feet reasonably dry, as they had been obliged to do during the last week on board the *Ra 2*. Reed boats were built and used by

people of a number of ancient cultures in different parts of the world. They would never have been if the reeds had become as waterlogged as those of both the *Ra* boats. In Peru, Mesopotamia, Egypt and China, the reed boat was the preferred form of water transport. But what did the papyrus boatbuilders of ancient times do to prevent the reed bundles they used from becoming so waterlogged that the crew and the provisions or cargo were more under the water than they were above it? This was a question that Heyerdahl wanted to find the answer to, and this is why he decided to build his *third reed ship*. He wanted to carry out a new experiment, a new expedition, *to find out how the ancient boatbuilders improved the buoyancy of the reeds.*

Scientists maintained that Mesopotamian reed boats could never have been used for anything but river traffic since, after two weeks, they would have had to be taken up on the shore to dry out. However, the views of the scholars failed to tally with Heyerdahl's own experience with reed boats and, not the least, with his observations in the countries around the Persian gulf and the Arabian Sea. In a number of these countries archaeological finds pointed to distant connections. For example, Egyptian scarabs and ivory work were known in the countries around the Gulf, and a number of items originating in Mesopotamia were found on the island of Bahrain. Furthermore, some items discovered in Mesopotamia, the land between the Euphrates and the Tigris, clearly originated in the Indus Valley in Pakistan.

In Heyerdahl's view, this could hardly be explained in any other way than that trade and cultural connections between the oldest civilizations known to science were maintained by reed boats. The scholars' assertions regarding the ocean-going properties of reed boats could not possibly be correct. The archaeological finds indicated that extensive communications took place over large stretches of ocean, from Mesopotamia and perhaps all the way to Egypt or, in an easterly direction, to India or even China!

Ancient myths and legends often have a core of truth. A myth found throughout the most ancient civilizations tells of an enormous flood. The myths on this theme are so similar from country to country that they must have a common origin. One of them is the story in the Bible of how Noah built an ark to survive the Flood. The Assyrians had a similar myth, even older than that of the Hebrews. However, the oldest version of the story of the Flood was that of the Sumerians, which is approximately 5000 years old. These Flood myths from different parts of the Middle East appealed strongly to Heyerdahl's imagination.

All three myths tell of *big* ships. They must have been big because all the myths tell of a number of animals being taken on board. And the ships were made of reeds – this is stated explicitly. In the Hebrew version of the Bible, Noah was commanded by God: "Make yourself an ark with ribs of cypress; cover it with reeds, and cover it inside and out with pitch." Noah was the skipper of a reed ship. According to Sumerian clay tablets, he came ashore on the distant island of Dilmun. The location of the mysterious land of Dilmun has preoccupied scholars for many years. Today it is believed to be what is now called Bahrain. In other words, Noah had sailed a long way!

The archaeologist Geoffrey Bibby, who specializes in ancient cultures on the shores of the Indian Ocean and who has conducted major excavations in Bahrain himself, reviewed Heyerdahl's book on the *Ra* expeditions. He concluded his review by recommending that the reed boat be given renewed

The Marsh Arabs still live in Southern Iraq. They knew the secret of how the reed boats should be prevented from becoming waterlogged. The reeds must be cut in August!

consideration in his specialized areas as well. Mesopotamia is a region with a plentiful growth of reeds. Finally, he added, "Perhaps, on his next expedition, Thor Heyerdahl will consider sailing such a craft from Babylon to Mohenjo-Daro in the Indus Valley". These were indeed prophetic words!

During the first half of the 1970s, Heyerdahl concentrated on field research and museum studies in the Middle East. He had turned his gaze from investigations of ancient American and early Egyptian ocean-going vessels to ancient Mesopotamia, which lay between the rivers Euphrates and Tigris in what is now southern Iraq, and was known as "the land between the rivers". It was the home of ancient civilizations such as the Sumerians, Babylonians and Assyrians. Cultures flourished for a time, then perished and new cultures sprang up. The centre of the oldest civilizations was "the land between the rivers", Mesopotamia.

THE EXPERTS IN THE MARSHES

In the course of his studies, Heyerdahl had paid several visits to a people known as the Marsh Arabs, who inhabit an area of southern Iraq that was once part of ancient Mesopotamia. These Marsh Arabs, or *Madans,* to give them their correct name, dwell in the large marsh area by the rivers Euphrates and Tigris. This is an area of reeds and water, with not a single tree, rock or mountain, just marshland. The life of the Madans is entirely centred around reeds. Indeed, they are great experts on reeds. They make floating islands of reeds, build their big houses of bent bundles of reeds, and sail between their islands in reed boats. In short, reeds are the main component of their culture and their most important building material. The local *berdi* reeds are much more branched than the papyrus reeds and the South American *totora* reeds used respectively to build the two *Ra* boats, and are actually more difficult to use as building material. But the Madans succeed in using them to construct architectonic and functional masterpieces. Thor Heyerdahl decided to enlist the help of the Marsh Arabs to build his third reed boat to test his theories.

Once more the question arose as to what must be done to prevent the reeds from becoming waterlogged. The Marsh Arabs had the answer. "The reeds must be cut in August", the most senior of the Madans told Heyerdahl. There were nods from all of the other Marsh Arabs. This was something that

everyone knew! The old man continued, "If it is not done then, the reeds rapidly absorb water and sink." In August, when the moon is full, there is sap in the reeds that prevents water from being sucked up. There was nothing about this in any scholarly books. No wonder they had had problems with *Ra 1* and *Ra 2*. The papyrus reeds were cut in December!

In the searing heat of August 1977, Thor Heyerdahl himself supervised the harvesting of berdi reeds from the marshes. Large quantities of reeds were cut and dried. Several Marsh Arabs were chosen to bind the reeds in cigar-shaped bundles approximately twenty metres long. However, the Arabs were not to build the boat. This was to be done by the same Aymara Indians who had built the *Ra 2*. They had already proved themselves to be extremely accomplished boat builders and were once more to have the responsibility for constructing Heyerdahl's new boat.

As soon as the five Bolivians, four boatbuilders and an interpreter, arrived in Iraq, they began working with the Marsh Arabs to prepare the reeds. The long, cigar-shaped bundles made by the Marsh Arabs had to be much longer than the total length of the ship because they were to be curved upwards into a sickle shape at each end. The bundles were gathered into two large sausages of reeds that were to be used to form the hull. The work progressed rapidly, and in five weeks the boat was finished. It was a splendid sight, yellow and golden, where it lay ready alongside the bank of the river. The reed boat was named the *Tigris* after the river on which it was launched. The *Tigris* was eighteen metres long, six metres broad and three metres high. The weight of the tightly packed reed ship was about 33 tonnes. With its ten metre tall straddle-mast, sail, two enormous rudder oars astern and two plaited bamboo cabins on the deck, one large and one smaller, the *Tigris* was both larger and more handsome than either of the two *Ra* boats had been.

Twelve days after being launched, the *Tigris* was ready for departure. The crew, eleven men, moved on board with their personal belongings and several tons of food and water for the coming months. Only four remained of those who had taken part in both *Ra* expeditions. Besides Thor Heyerdahl, these were the American, the Russian and the Italian. Otherwise, the crew consisted of one Danish and one Norwegian student, a Mexican, a German, an Arab and an American photographer, who was to have the main responsibility for filming.

Tigris, the largest of the three reed boats, while it was being built.

"Let go the moorings! Hoist the sail!" Thor was filled with relief and pleasure when at last he was able to shout his orders to the crew. The boat began to get up speed. "Hurrah, we're sailing!", cheered one of the crew, as the wind filled the rectangular cotton sail. The crew rejoiced as the first Sumerian vessel in modern times passed the confluence of the Euphrates and the Tigris at a good speed. However their joy and enthusiasm were to be short-lived, for the boat proved to be extremely difficult to steer downstream. However they wielded the oars, the boat drifted towards one of the banks. The oar on the port side began churning up clay and mud like a plough. Horrified spectators on land helped to shove the heavy reed boat out from the bank. This resulted in the boat

Tigris anchored by the river bank while on its way to the open sea.

---

drifting at full speed towards the date palms on the opposite side. They continued in this way for a while, but were at least going downstream.

SAILING THROUGH GARBAGE

After a few days, the bow and sides of the golden reed boat had become very discoloured and dirty. The water in the river was severely contaminated. Indeed, the level of contamination was so high that the crew was worried that the reeds in the hull might lose their buoyancy as a result of all the chemicals and filth in the water. It was worst of all outside the port of Abadan, where the surface of the water between tankers and the quayside was a thick soup of black crude oil, sewage and garbage. The situation was not improved by the fact that a nearby cellulose works spewed out large quantities of a yellowish viscous mass. The

pollution here was certainly far worse than they had experienced on the *Ra* expeditions!

Always preoccupied with environmental issues, Heyerdahl thought this was dreadful. They tried using the oars to clear away the worst of the filth around the boat, but it built up round the hull as quickly as they shovelled it away. After floundering in filth for a day and a night, it seemed to them that the *Tigris* was already lying a lot deeper in the water. Some of the crew members were convinced that the chemicals in the contaminated water had penetrated the reeds and damaged their impermeability. They decided to dispose of everything on board that was not absolutely necessary, just as was done on the *Ra* expedition. They didn't think that they floated appreciably higher after carrying several hundred kilos ashore, but they were still floating so high that they were unable to touch the water if they leaned over the edge. This had been possible on the *Ra*.

Both the skipper and the crew felt great relief when, after several days, they were able to put the river behind them and sail out into the wide Persian Gulf. However, the passage

through the Gulf was to prove a great strain for both the ship and the crew. Firstly, because the geographical conditions were unknown to the men on board and, secondly, because it was not easy to navigate *against* the wind and the weather. On the *Ra* expeditions, they had crossed the Atlantic *with* the wind and the current. In the Gulf, they had to sail against the wind. This was an art they had not tried before. Moreover, the wind in the Gulf is capricious and unpredictable. They had still not learned the knack of using the rudder oars effectively. This resulted in a number of emergencies between the many sandbanks, rocks and islands in the Gulf. But practice makes perfect, and they learned gradually.

BREAKING NEW GROUND – AGAIN

As they sailed out of the outermost estuary, Heyerdahl stood on the bridge and felt that, once again, he was in process of breaching a scientific taboo, as if craft such as the *Tigris* had the right to come as far as this, but no further. At the moment they left the boundary of the river, they overstepped the limits laid down by the so-called experts for what a craft made of berdi reeds could be permitted to do. The experts held the view that the Sumerians, just as they had said of the Egyptians, had not ventured out into the open sea in their reed boats. According to the experts, these were used only for river transport, because the reeds absorbed water and the boats would sink. So, when Thor Heyerdahl ordered the hoisting of the sail outside Shatt-al-Arab, he knew that many scholars would regard this as a vote of no confidence in established dogmas. Perhaps that was exactly what it was!

Well out in the Persian Gulf, they found themselves in a calm belt that did not seem to belong there at all. Normally the north wind should have blown them straight out of the Gulf. The problem was that weather and wind were not behaving "normally". Heyerdahl and the crew of the *Tigris* knew perfectly well that the area of the sea where they were now becalmed was the only place in the world where the ocean currents change direction according to the time of year. The wind always blows from south to north in the summer, and from north to south in the winter. The alternations of the monsoon are part of the working of nature's clock, as regular

as the sun's shining during the day and the moon's at night. But not this time – the north wind did not fill the sail of the *Tigris*. Instead, it hung as limp as a dishcloth. It seemed that the god of the wind had forsaken the Gulf. They would have to make do with small gusts. Each time there was a movement in the sail, the men were filled with hope, but the hope vanished more quickly than it had come.

Suddenly, as if let out of a bag, there were several violent gusts of wind, not from the north, but from the south. They were so powerful that they threatened to send the boat back

The crew are relieved to be on the open sea.

towards Iraq and the shipping lanes. The wind forced them closer to Failaka's treacherous cliffs than they appreciated. The same night the steering watch woke the crew because he heard the sound of breakers through the darkness. The sound grew to a steady crashing and rumbling. Somewhere ahead in the pitch dark night there were cliffs or reefs waiting for them. Something had to be done. They had no motor they could put into reverse or any other way of avoiding shipwreck and disaster.

What does the crew of an unwieldy reed ship do in such a situation? They quickly reefed both sails, and dropped two anchors to stop the boat from drifting towards disaster. But the anchor cables broke. To prevent or delay running aground, they threw overboard a large canvas drag anchor. To their astonishment, the water was already so shallow that the canvas bag went to the bottom and dug itself into the clay so that the drifting gradually came to a halt. They began using their flashlights to send SOS signals out into the night, but there was no response. No-one came to their rescue.

At dawn it was high tide. This caused the drag anchor to loosen. The *Tigris* began to drift towards the cliffs again. What could they do to stop the uncontrolled drifting of the ship? The crew were at a loss, but something *had* to be done. The only course open was to hoist the sail. With the sail up, they would attempt to manoeuvre the boat along the cliffs towards the east coast, where they would have to face the lesser of two evils: they would sail even further into waters with cliffs hidden under the surface of the water and with treacherous shallows. In the pilot book they had on board, this part of the sea was stated as being unsafe unless accompanied by an armed escort. Now they were in such shallow water that the *Tigris* was churning up mud and seaweed.

It looked as if all odds were against them, when they discovered a black dot on the eastern horizon. Half an hour later, the 17 000 tonne Russian cargo ship *Slavsk* lay just beyond them. From the *Slavsk*, with which they had been in contact before, a lifeboat was lowered and immediately headed towards the *Tigris*. The men on board the reed boat began to glimpse a hope of being rescued from the dangerous situation they were in. A tow rope was brought on board the *Tigris* and the drag anchor was hauled back into the boat. Full to the brim of greyish sludge and mud, the drag anchor was as heavy as lead, but this was the very thing that had saved them from shipwreck in the dark. As soon as the anchor had been hauled

up and emptied, the lifeboat from the *Slavsk* began the job of towing them away from the shallows – or so they thought.

What happened in reality was altogether different. Instead of being towed away from the danger zone, from treacherous shallows and cliffs, quite the opposite was happening. Although the lifeboat had a powerful motor, the wind took such a strong hold on the tall reed boat that the *Tigris* was towing the Russians instead of the other way round. The lifeboat drifted backwards after the *Tigris* along the coast towards the dangerous shallows. The wind increased to 24 knots and, after a while, they completely lost sight of the *Slavsk*. Now they really were in a mess. The atmosphere on the *Tigris* was strained, and the Russians on board the lifeboat were not in the best of moods either.

PIRATES AND RANSOM

The situation was not improved by the appearance of a mysterious *dhow*, a local type of boat, which began circling around them. It was manned by a gang of dubious looking fellows, to put it mildly. No-one had seen where it came from. Suddenly, it was there. The dhow didn't draw much water and they could hear that it had a powerful motor. The mast was sawn off. What kind of boat was this? What was it doing there? What did the shady characters on board want? Suddenly it headed straight towards the *Tigris*, but stopped a short distance away; not surprisingly, for it was many generations since these fellows' ancestors had seen such a strange craft in these waters.

Thor sent his local interpreter over in a little rubber dinghy. He returned with a message that, for a thousand dollars, they were willing to tow the *Tigris* out of the dangerous area. Thor was prepared to negotiate, but the captain of the *Slavsk*, who was on board the lifeboat, indignantly refused on Thor's behalf. The Russian skipper offered instead to give them six bottles of vodka and two crates of wine. They responded by informing him that they were Muslims, and consequently did not drink alcohol. Without further discussion, the dhow withdrew.

The only course open to the *Tigris* now was to hoist the sail and give up making any further attempts at being towed back to the *Slavsk* , which had long since disappeared from view. The Russian captain had a walkie-talkie, which he used to speak to the first mate on board the *Slavsk*, who was able to

The dhow with the pirates who demanded a ransom.

tell him that, according to the radar, the *Tigris* – and the lifeboat – were rapidly approaching the dangerous area. The current was very strong. Mud from the bottom swirled around them from increasingly deeper troughs in the waves. Then another dhow appeared, and yet another. The men on board seemed not merely shady, they looked like thoroughgoing pirates. When the interpreter on the *Tigris* went to explain the situation to them, the towing fee had now been doubled to two thousand dollars. They were completely unwilling to bargain, and made it clear to the crew of the *Tigris* that, if they did not pay what was demanded, they would lose everything anyway as soon as the reed boat went on the rocks it was heading for. They received a cynical warning: "Without our help, you are all finished." This was pure piracy. Encouraged by the Russian captain, they still refused to pay. The dhows withdrew once

more, and anchored near the dangerous reefs, lying in wait for the *Tigris* to run aground like jackals waiting for a dying prey. If they were not paid the ransom, these pirates were surely capable of taking advantage of the darkness to rob them of all their valuables.

In an hour's time the sun would set. Heyerdahl *had* to make a decision. By refusing to pay "ransom" he would put in danger not only the lives of the crew of the *Tigris*, but also the Russians on board the lifeboat that was still attached to the reed boat's hawser. "I am in command of the boat, and I intend to pay the dhows." Thor had made up his mind, however bad it made him feel to have to swallow such a bitter pill. The *Tigris* was towed out to deeper water, to the Russian cargo boat that lay waiting. The local dhows disappeared into the darkness two thousand dollars richer. The cargo ship *Slavsk* sent over a long hawser and began towing the *Tigris* out to deep water. Such towing was certainly not good for the heavy reed ship, jerking and

The Tigris in the wake of Noah, by the coast of Bahrain in the Persian Gulf.

snatching at the boat as the heavy hawser slackened and tightened, but they had no choice.

IN NOAH'S WAKE?

Over three weeks after the launching, the *Tigris* approached the island of Bahrain in the middle of the Persian Gulf. Now they were in the waters where the story of Noah's ark began. The Sumerians were the first to tell the story of the Flood. In these waters, they said, a great ship was once built by the ancestor of all mankind on the orders of a merciful god who wished to save the human race from complete extinction in a fearful deluge. While houses and fields were flooded, the great ship floated on the waves until the flood had abated and the ship lay safe on land.

The ancient Mesopotamians believed that somewhere on the other side of the ocean "where the sun rises", lay the mysterious land of Dilmun. Dilmun was a sacred land for all

of the people of Mesopotamia. It was the original home of the gods, and it was in Dilmun that the Sumerian Noah settled down to multiply the human race after the Flood. According to scholars, Bahrain is the Dilmun of antiquity. It was here that the *Tigris* was heading, among other reasons, to have repairs done to a large hole in the bow, a hole "as big as a dog-kennel", as Heyerdahl was later to describe it. For days, fragments of reed had floated in their wake and, in front of the bow, the spiral ropes hung loose over the gaping hole. There was no immediate danger, but the reed boat needed to be repaired as soon as possible.

They lay at the quay in Bahrain for three weeks. While the boat was being repaired, Heyerdahl had plenty of time to study the archaeological remains of ancient Dilmun. He was able to inspect the world's largest prehistoric cemetery with about 100 000 burial mounds, temple pyramids with a special type of masonry, buried cities, harbours, ancient artefacts, etc. There could be no doubt that, thousands of years ago, Bahrain had been the site of a rich culture with many contacts overseas. Reed boats had been here before them! Dilmun had certainly not been out of the reach of the Sumerian reed boats.

After the boat had been repaired, not with reeds but with the slender mid-stems of date-palm leaves, the *Tigris* was able to set sail again. With "the bow once more as solid as a bird's breast with every feather in place", the people on board were thrilled when the wind filled the sail and gave them an uplift out of the Persian Gulf. They rounded the northern tip of the Quatar peninsula, and the *Tigris* sailed into waters teeming with extremely poisonous sea snakes. For two days, the sea around them was filled with the snakes, and no-one dared to take a bath from the side of the boat.

BETWEEN CLIFFS AND SUPERTANKERS

Now they had difficult waters ahead of them. They had to pass safely through the narrow Strait of Hormuz with its dense traffic. Tankers and bulk carriers from all over the world rushed day and night in both directions through the strait. This was an extremely hazardous playground for a reed ship that was not only difficult to manoeuvre but also had a crew that had not yet properly mastered the art of navigating it. Such thoughts tormented the crew of the *Tigris* as they sailed towards the strait. A couple of hours after midnight, they drew near to the dreaded area. Ahead of them they saw a jungle of red flares that appeared to block the fairway. The flares grew to threatening magnitude as they approached, is if they were heading for a burning battlefield. It transpired that a large area ahead was closed to all traffic because of ongoing drilling operations. They had to steer to the north of it all and into a narrow passage between another oilfield and an island called Abu Musa that was surrounded by reefs. To the north of this was the main shipping lane, which they had to avoid at all costs.

They sailed along the moonlit headland with the vertical cliffs of the Arabian peninsula until a chaos of ships' lights came into view. Soon they found themselves with their experimental reed boat wedged between supertankers and cliffs. Gigantic ships' hulls rushed past them with red and green lanterns and white lights. The *Tigris* danced wildly on waves that seemed to come from all directions. The men on board the reed boat waved feverishly with flashlights and paraffin lamps. It made no difference really, for there was nothing that the enormous ships could do. They could not swing away at such short notice. On the contrary, it was the crew of the *Tigris* that had to make sure to steer away from

them, and wriggle past this critical place with the help of their rudder oars and square-sail. It was not easy but, with the wind directly behind them, they came safely through the strait. Their speed through the Strait of Hormuz had been up to five knots, and added to this was the speed of the current. "Talk about sailing! We've managed to navigate!", exclaimed one of the crew when they had come through the strait. Soon they were sailing safely off the coast of Oman in open seas on their way to the Indian Ocean.

It was the last day of the year, and they were safely out of the Gulf. They had cause to celebrate. From his personal case under the mattress, the ship's Russian doctor, who in his native country was a space scientist, conjured forth the choicest dishes: Russian champagne, real Russian caviar, astronaut bread, turkey-a-la-space with moon cheese and a whole variety of Sputnik tubes from which they squeezed their mouths full of pastes, creams, jams, desserts and juices. They enjoyed gazing at the silver crescent of the moon against the star-studded Arabian night sky, as they squeezed astronaut mouthfuls between their jaws and toasted with champagne. Life felt good!

"If a railway engine were to come in through my door while I sat at breakfast I would be greatly surprised. But not more surprised than when the bow of a ship came in while I lay on my bed", writes Heyerdahl. It was 2.30 in the morning, but it was no dream. He heard a hoarse, hostile voice roar out something in the distance. Then the voices of some of his crew members: "Keep off! Keep off!" "What is this?" The angry question was shouted in English with an Arab accent. "A ship!" the *Tigris*'s Arab interpreter shouted back indignantly. "Get away! You are breaking our ship!" The bow of a police patrol boat filled the cabin door opening. A violent jolt went through the *Tigris*. At once everyone on board was awake. They reacted to the "attack" with wild war cries. "Tell them to scramble away, these are international waters!" shouted the Russian doctor. "They are not," retorted the Arab interpreter. "We are right up under the Oman coast, and besides, you don't tell people to scramble away when they are pointing a machine gun at you!"

They had received a visit from a patrol boat with armed police from Oman's coastguard. The crazy blips from their masthead, intended to warn other boats to keep away, had had the opposite effect on them, as moths are drawn to a light.

The Tigris in idyllic surroundings on its way out of the Gulf.

They had arrived for an inspection. But, coming close enough to see the strange golden reed boat, the policemen had been so surprised that they had forgotten to steer or stop. They had rammed the *Tigris* amidships so that reeds and bamboo shook. Never had the coastguards seen so many angry, bearded and drowsy men swarm out so fast on hands and knees from two small bamboo cabins. Confronted with eleven furious men raising their fists and roaring in a multitude of languages, the bewildered patrol-men backed away until they disappeared in the dark.

Shortly after, it happened again – another collision! Either patrol boats were difficult to steer or the *Tigris* affected them like a magnet. For the second time, the patrol boat rammed them and butted its bow through the cabin door. Yet again, eleven angry men roared in different languages, and the patrol

boat backed away and disappeared in the night for good. In daylight the following day, they were able to see that no damage had been done to the reeds by the collisions. The reed bundles were wet through and had become as pliant and tough as compact rubber fenders.

SUMERIAN FIND IN OMAN

Two days after the collisions, the *Tigris* lay at anchor in the picturesque seaport of *Muscat*, which was also the capital of Oman. At this time, Oman was closed to tourists but, through the Sultan, they were granted entry visas. In the interior of the country, a Sumerian temple pyramid had recently been discovered, over a thousand kilometres from Iraq (Mesopotamia), the site of ancient Sumer. This was a sensation, not least for an expedition whose objective was to establish how far a reed boat of the Sumerian type could sail. The following day, Thor Heyerdahl and his crew were taken into the country so that they could see for themselves the

Sumerian stepped pyramid or *ziggurat*. A stone's throw from the pyramid, they were also able to view 5000 year-old copper mines. This was where the Sumerians had obtained copper for weapons and tools. Over 140 000 tonnes of slag was left behind after mining activities, so enormous amounts of copper must have been transported from here. Heyerdahl was in no doubt that the Sumerians had had big, ocean-going reed ships. He knew of a clay tablet found in the Sumerian town of Ur, which tells of a ship's cargo of 18.5 tonnes.

When the *Tigris* sailed from Muscat, they had to follow the shipping lane. For several days, they lay in dense traffic fighting with sail and steering oars to get out of the way of fast ocean liners and tankers that thundered past them on both sides. They were painfully aware that their reed boat was not visible on the radar of the giant steel ships. One night, a big cruise ship with brightly lit decks several stories high brushed past them. The *Tigris* only just avoided being swept up by an invisible cable just in front of the bow. Immediately after, another big ship loomed out of the dark, passing so close to them that it seemed to be part of their own vessel. A vertical wall of steel rose against their bamboo cabin and was gone again before they had time to think, let alone steer away. They were only able to cling to reeds and ropes while the *Tigris* hopped and jumped like a cork on the big waves. This was dangerous, really dangerous. Heyerdahl brought to mind a story he had been told of the crew of such a ship that had found the sail of a dhow stuck to their bow. No-one on board had noticed a collision or heard screams from the crew on board the dhow. By now, the men on the *Tigris* had had enough, and got out of the shipping lane as soon as they could.

ON COURSE FOR THE INDUS VALLEY

After all of their hair-raising experiences and close shaves, they were at last clear of the heavy traffic of the shipping lane. A combination of planned, impulsive and involuntary manoeuvres had brought the *Tigris* further north than Heyerdahl had thought possible during the winter half-year, which is dominated by the north-easterly monsoon. Now it was actually possible for them to choose between the two sides of the Indian Ocean. Should they sail to Africa or to Pakistan? They had been in Bahrain, which must be the legendary Dilmun, and in Oman, which was probably the equally mysterious *Makan* referred to in Sumerian sources.

Now it was possible for them to visit the third place mentioned on the ancient clay tablets, *Meluhha* in the Indus Valley in Pakistan. Objects from the Indus Valley had been found in Mesopotamia. For Heyerdahl, the temptation to pay a visit there was irresistible. With unanimous support from the crew, he decided to sail towards Pakistan instead of Africa.

This was to prove to be the correct decision, a decision that was to create a thought-provoking new pattern and new prospects within the study of the oldest civilizations. There was of course no time for extensive archaeological research during the *Tigris* expedition but, as was later written, "… the voyage gradually became a string on which Heyerdahl collected pearls of research in a shining necklace. *Meluhha* and the Indus Valley were to constitute the finest jewel of the whole necklace and give meaning to all the others".

For ten days they sailed peacefully north-east. They had no difficulties of any kind and no dramatic episodes. Their only contact was with patrolling sharks, a faithful escort of dolphins, and brief visits from playful porpoises and a few curious whales of larger species. On the morning of 26 January there was a joyful shout from the top of the mast, "I have discovered Pakistan!" It was the eleventh day since they left Muscat. The first sight of Pakistan was Astola Island, an inhospitable place, which looked like a flat iceberg, teeming with small poisonous snakes. They did not go ashore!

As it began to grow dark, they caught sight of the distant inland mountain ranges of Baluchistan. To take advantage of a fair wind, they sailed along Pakistan's moonlit, white cliffs. The moment they passed the cliffs, they began to get a strong onshore wind. The wind increased in strength and the breakers along the coast grew to fearful heights. They had to find shelter! On the morning of 27 January they turned into a huge bay, Ormara Bay. Here there was a shark-fishing village surrounded by dreary desert. They waded ashore, where they were met by the village policeman, who told them that no foreigners were permitted to go ashore in this part of the country. However, since they were already there, they were welcomed. In the village there was a colourful fishing community. Isolated as they were, people here had to be more or less self-sufficient. The main street was shorter than the total length of the *Tigris*, and much narrower. The "shops" were tiny. Thor took an inventory of the smallest shop: seven

carrots and five potatoes. Nothing could be further from a supermarket.

IMPORTANT FIND IN MOHENJO-DARO

In spite of the friendly reception they had received, including a welcoming dance on the beach, this was no place for them to stay. They had to move on. A week later, the reed boat lay moored to a buoy in Karachi's busy harbour. Heyerdahl and his crew were visiting the famous ruin of the prehistoric city of *Mohenjo-Daro* deep in the Indus Valley. Like the great cities of ancient Mesopotamia, Mohenjo-Daro now lies far from the original course of the river. The mighty Indus River that once flowed lazily past the city wharves has since withdrawn. Only a small part of the once so important seaport has been excavated by archaeologists, but enough to confirm that the people who once made up the Indus civilization were culturally on a par with the civilizations of Sumer and ancient Egypt. Mohenjo-Daro's cultural zenith was reached around 2000–1800 B.C. Excavations have revealed that the city was rebuilt seven times following floods before it was finally abandoned in the 15th century B.C. No-one knows who founded the city, what became of the inhabitants or why it was abandoned. It may be that the population disappeared owing to unrest, for many of the skeletons found during excavations show signs of a violent death in combat.

Heyerdahl and several other scholars believe that the Indus civilization was probably the mysterious land of *Meluhha* referred to in Sumerian sources. In the ruined cities of the Indus Valley, terracotta figures of bearded men with distinctly Sumerian features have been found. Gold earrings identical to those found in the royal graves of Sumer have also been discovered. In a small field exhibit at the foot of the Mohenjo-Daro ruins, Heyerdahl saw, to his surprise, a ceramic seal with an engraved picture a sickle-shaped reed ship with a deck cabin between a double set of straddle-masts and two rudder oars aft. It was like seeing a picture of the *Tigris*!

Heyerdahl was in no doubt. There had been contact by sea between Mesopotamia and the Indus Valley in prehistoric times, contact which must have been based on reed ships of the same type as the *Tigris*. He was in agreement with the scholars who identified the Indus area with *Meluhha. Dilmun, Makán* and *Meluhha* belonged together. With the *Tigris* they had now visited all three. Now it was time for further odysseys, adventures, discoveries and reed boat experiences. On 7th February they sailed from Karachi. They were all eager to be at sea again. The Indian continent sank into the ocean in the north. Farewell Asia. Ahead of them once more was the Indian Ocean. All the men were in the best of spirits even though several of the crew members were ill. This happened every time they were ashore. The food and water they consumed was not always of the best quality.

Life on board now seemed free of problems. They had been at sea for almost three months since the launching in Iraq. The *Tigris* still floated higher in the water than the *Ra 2* had done after only three weeks. The Marsh Arabs had certainly been right when they asserted that reeds for boatbuilding must be cut in August.

The only thing that irritated them at this time was a number of false reports spread around the world by the media. Several times they had reported that the *Tigris* had gone down in a storm. Once it was reported that a member of the crew had been eaten by a shark, and that Heyerdahl had therefore been forced to call off the expedition. One day they were asked by the expedition's head office in London, "Why has the *Tigris* broken its back?" There was little they could do about negative rumours of this kind. The best they could do was to continue, thereby proving the seaworthiness of the reed boats, in other words letting the results speak for themselves.

TOWARDS THE RED SEA

Where were they headed now? They didn't know. Madagascar, the Red Sea or somewhere on the coast of north-east Africa

The ceramic seal from the ruins of Mohenjo-Daro with an engraved picture a sickle-shaped reed ship similar to the Tigris.

seemed the most probable or alluring destinations. Shortly after this they sailed into one of the worst storms Heyerdahl had experienced at sea. A roaring gale swept over the Indian Ocean. The waves towered over them like small volcanoes smoking with foam and spray. The thick topmast broke like a matchstick and the main sail hung like a water-filled parachute in the tempestuous sea. However, they didn't lose the rigging, which was the worst thing that could have happened. Then they would have been left adrift on a heavy reed ship with only the oars to propel them. The rudder oars were made fast and abandoned. There was nothing to do but ride out the storm just as Noah had done in his ark. All night the storm raged, but by morning it had abated. They had come safely through the furious storm, and now began rapidly repairing the mast and the other damage.

Heyerdahl now decided to head for the Red Sea. If he managed to navigate the *Tigris* into ancient Egyptian waters, there would no longer be any water in this sea that reed boats could not master. Then they would have succeeded in connecting together in one reed boat voyage all three previously known great civilizations of Mesopotamia, the Indus Valley and Egypt. What could be achieved by inexperienced modern men in a replica of a Sumerian reed boat should have been a simple matter for a trained reed ship's crew in prehistoric times. In Thor's view, the reed ship was ideal for sailing the oceans.

For several weeks they sailed south-west, apparently alone on the sea. The winds were unstable, and they were often completely becalmed. They made an average of two knots or approximately eighty kilometres a day. They spent their days fishing and studying marine life. Around the boat there was an incredible amount of fish. Looking over the side was like looking down into an overfilled aquarium. However, the hammerhead sharks created a certain amount of excitement. They were terrific hunters, a danger not only to other fish but also to the men on board. One day, one of the crew sat dangling his legs over the side of the ship. "Shark! Shark! Getup!", shouted another crew member, who had discovered an enormous man-eater with its dreaded fin above water going at high speed towards the dangling legs. When the owner of the legs looked up, he was staring straight at an ugly beast with small, cold eyes at the end of projections on either side of its broad, flat head. In the nick of time, he

The mountains of Socotra ahead. The African continent is within reach.

hoisted himself up at the same moment as the great hammerhead shark streaked past. The men who saw the episode estimated that waiting another second would have cost him his foot. Some days later another member of the crew was nearly eaten by an enormous man-eating shark while he lay in the water filming the colourful marine life. But that ended well this time too.

WAR ON ALL SIDES

The weeks went by without any contact with other people. They did not see a single ship, not even a fishing boat. They were completely alone in their own peaceful world. But this was a peace that was not to last long. They soon had other things to think about. During the first days of March they began to receive alarming radio messages. Ethiopia and Somalia were at war with each other. The countries they were approaching were now closed to them. They had to avoid the Horn of Africa. If they came too close, they would be arrested and interned. The Arabian side of the Gulf of Aden, South Yemen, was also forbidden territory. The communist

The Tigris on its way into the Gulf of Aden. A helicopter was keeping them under close surveillance.

government there was at war with both of the country's capitalist neighbours. Some days later, they received a direct message from the expedition's head office in London, "Please beware of political situation in this area as previously advised. We have had no cooperation from either the South Yemen or the Somalian Governments. Stop." What now? Where should they go? What should they do?

In Heyerdahl's view it should be possible for them to navigate and manoeuvre well enough to keep to the median line between the belligerent countries, directly on course for the narrow Bab-el-Mandeb Strait, which led into the Red Sea. They made an attempt at this, but then the wind died down completely. There was not a breath of wind from any

direction. A dead calm such as this they had never experienced. The sail hung dismally, like a wall carpet. Then they became the victim of the invisible ocean currents. The *Tigris* drifted inexorably closer to Socotra. This was a large island off the Horn of Africa, which now belonged to South Yemen. As a precaution, they asked for permission to land on Socotra. They received the following telegram in reply: "Tigris must not repeat not attempt to land on this island before written permission has been given. Stop".

Direct from a friendly western European foreign ministry came another independent warning: "Do not go to Socotra now, you may get into trouble." Unconfirmed radio messages said it was believed that the Russians were installing military bases on this strategically important island that belonged to their ally. Socotra controlled the entrance to the Gulf of Aden and the Red Sea. No aeroplanes or ships were allowed to pass within range of vision. Helpless without wind, they drifted still

closer to the island. They would probably be shot at or put before a military court. They did not know which was worse.

On 12 March Socotra's mountain skyline appeared in the distance. "Hurrah! We have reached Africa!" The exclamation came with mixed feelings. This was a great achievement. They had crossed the Indian Ocean, but the situation that they had involuntarily brought upon themselves cast a damper on their feelings of joy and triumph. To put it bluntly, there was not a trace of joy on board when, against their will, they continued to drift towards the forbidden island.

One night the watch shouted from the bridge that he could hear gunfire in the distance. The next day everyone on board heard the drone of an aeroplane. A twin-engined military plane was heading directly for the reed boat. They hurriedly hoisted the United Nations flag. The plane dived straight over the boat, turned and came straight back again. Were they going to be shot at? bombed? They stood ready to jump into the sea, when the American on board shouted: "Hurrah! It's American!" Just a few minutes later a military helicopter appeared, but this time it was French.

IN PORT AT LAST

Socotra was alarmingly close when they had a pow-wow on board. They decided to try to steer clear of the shore. If they didn't manage this, they would take the wind in from the opposite tack and sail back into Hadibu port. However, everything went well, and they continued towards the Gulf of Aden. It was time to open some bottles of red wine reserved for special occasions. On the night of 8 March 1978 they were able to drop anchor in the port of Djibouti. The *Tigris* had reached yet another continent.

They had planned to stay for a week in Djibouti in order to arrange for permission to continue to Massawa (now Mitsiwa), the Ethiopian port where Heyerdahl had loaded papyrus from Lake Tana for the *Ra* boats, and where for this reason Thor had hoped to end the *Tigris* voyage after another week's sailing. But this was not how things were to turn out!

When they came ashore they found that the war was still raging with unabated force. Russian and Cuban forces were supporting the Ethiopians in defending Massawa against Eritrean liberation forces that held the entrance to the port and the surrounding coasts. This mean that the whole area was a war zone. Where were they now to go? The solution came in the form of a friendly letter from North Yemen's ambassador in London, authorized by a minister, who wished their little expedition welcome to North Yemen on the other side of the Red Sea. The crew of the *Tigris* responded joyfully to this letter, but their joy and optimism was short-lived. Heyerdahl received a telephone call from London with the disheartening news that North Yemen had withdrawn its permission. For "security reasons", the *Tigris* was refused admittance to the country's territorial waters. This definitely meant the end for the expedition. Thor had to face reality.

What should he do with the reed boat? Speculators in many countries were ready to buy *Tigris* to put it on exhibition, but if there was one thing Heyerdahl did not want, it was that. It was not possible to take the boat to Norway to exhibit it at the Kon-Tiki Museum with the *Ra 2* and the *Kon-Tiki* because the museum did not have room. In Djibouti it would just lie rotting. He didn't want that either. It was then that he decided to burn the *Tigris*. The copy of an ancient reed boat was to be a fiery protest, an appeal to all sensible and responsible people to stop acts of war and the arms race. Heyerdahl informed his men of his decision as they ate breakfast on deck the next morning. The crew gave their wholehearted support to the plan. They sent an open letter to the Secretary General of the United Nations, underlining that their action was a protest against war, the supply of weapons and the development of weapons of mass destruction. The *Tigris* was towed out and anchored under full sail by a small coral island outside the harbour, then set alight. This brings us back to the episode described at the beginning of this chapter.

After over five months at sea and having covered a distance of approximately 6 800 kilometres, Heyerdahl had with the *Tigris* expedition once more disproved a scientific dogma. In a single expedition he had connected the Sumerian area in the Persian Gulf with the ports of the Indus Valley and the ancient Egyptian area by the Red Sea. Now he had proved by means of experiments on three oceans that it was possible for prehistoric vessels to sail from Asia to Africa, from Africa to America and from America to Polynesia. While the *Kon-Tiki* raft and the two *Ra* boats only drifted with the ocean currents and trade winds from east to west over the Pacific

the Atlantic Oceans, the *Tigris* was consciously navigated in extremely varying winds and currents. There is no doubt whatsoever that prehistoric reed boats must have been good and highly navigable ocean-going vessels.

Those who have watched the weather-beaten Norwegian, Thor Heyerdahl, cross the oceans in his primitive craft might well be tempted to think of him as an explorer, pure and simple. However, it is wrong to view Heyerdahl's travels as being primarily geographical. First and foremost, his life's work has been founded on travels *in time*. The historical dimension has been his guiding star more than traditional geographical exploration. Heyerdahl's unique position among Norwegian explorers is based on his travels through the collective memory of mankind. And it is here that his greatness lies. It is not without reason that he was recently elected Norwegian of the century.

LIST OF ILLUSTRATIONS

It began with a Boat: An Introduction

Bill, J., Poulsen, B., Rieck, F. og Ventegodt, O., *Fra stammebåd til skib, Danmarks søfarts historie 1*, Copenhagen, 1998.

Christensen, A.E., *Frå vikingskip til motorsnekke*, Oslo,

Grønnesby, G., *Sjø og land i bronsealderen*, Spor no 1, 19, pamphlet, 1995.

Grønnesby, G., *Sjø og land i bronsealderen*, Spor no's. 1, 19, pamphlet, 1995.

Hermanus-Audardottir, M., « The Early Settlement of Iceland», *Norwegian Archaeological Review* 34, 1991

Lillehammer, A., *Fra jeger til bonde – inntil 800 e.Kr.*, *Aschehougs norgeshistorie*, bind I., Oslo, H. Aschehoug & Co., 1994.

Molaug, S., *Vår gamle kystkultur*, bind I., Oslo,1985.

Rieck, F. og Crumlin-Pedersen, O., *Både fra Danmarks oldtid*, Roskilde, 1988.

Theodorsson, P., «Norse Settlement of Iceland – Close to AD 700?», *Norwegian Archeological Review*, 31:1, 1998,

Ottar – the viking

Blindheim, C., *Ottar: Handelsmann og oppdagelsesreisende*, Ottar 5, Tromsø, 1995.

Bratrein, H.D., *Bjarkøy og Finnmork*, Ottar 5, Tromsø, 1995.

Eldjarn, G., *Litt om båter og skip på Ottars tid*, Ottar 5, Tromsø, 1995.

Lund, N., *Ottar og Wulfstan. To rejsebeskrivelser fra vikingetiden.* Roskilde, 1983.

Sandved, A.O. Translation into Norwegian. *Ottars beretning*, Ottar 5, Tromsø 1995.

Storli, J., *På sporet etter håløyhøvdingen*, Ottar 5, Tromsø, 1995.

Leif Eiriksson and the Discovery of America

Brøgger, H.W. , *Vinlandsferdene*, Oslo 1937.

Brøndsted, J., «Norsemen in Norsk America Before Columbus». Annual Report of the Smithsonian Institution, 1953.

Hreinsson, Vidar, Gen. Editor, *The Complete Sagas of the Icelanders*, Volume I, Leifur Eiriksson Publishing, Reykavik, 1997, pp. 22-3.

Ingstad, Helge, *Oppdagelsen av det nye land*, Oslo, J.M. Stenersens Forlag AS, 1996.

Prytz, K., *Vestover før Columbus*, Oslo 1990.

Ramskau, T., *Solsteinen*, Copenhagen, 1969.

Rausing, G., *Bronzealderens Columbus*, Skalk 5, 1969.

Skaare, K., «An Eleventh Century Norwegian Penny Found on the Coast of Maine», *The Norwegian Numismatic Journal* No. 21, 1979

Jens Munk and the Hunt for the North-West Passage

Hansen, Thorkild, *Jens Munk*, Oslo Gyldendal Norsk Forlag, 1966.

Birket-Smith, Kaj, *Jens Munks Rejse og andre danske ishavsfarter underChristian IV*, Copenhagen, C.A. Reitzels Forlag, 1929.

Munk, Jens, *Navigatio Septentrionalis*, Copenhagen, 1624.

Kolltveit, Bård, «Nordvestpassasjens historie», lecture, Oslo 1999

With *Fram* Across the North Arctic Ocean

Nansen, Fridtjof, *'Fram' over Polhavet, Den norske Polarferd 1893 – 1896*, bind I. and II., Kristiania, H. Aschehoug & Co's Forlag, 1897.

Johansen, Hjalmar, *Selv-anden paa 86 grader 14'*, Kristiania, H. Aschehoug & Co's Forlag, 1898.

Johansen, Hjalmar, Diary from the Polar Expedition.

Borch Sannes, Tor, *'FRAM' mot Nordpolen*, Asker, Norsk Maritimt Forlag A.S., 1988.

Barr, Susan, *'FRAM' mot Nordpolen*, Oslo, Chr. Schibsteds Forlag AS, 1996.

Sørensen, Jon, *Fridtjof Nansen. En bok for norsk ungdom*, Oslo, Jacob Dybwads Forlag 1952.

Arnesen, Odd. *'FRAM' Hele Norges skute*, Oslo, Jacob Dybwads Forlag, 1942.

Article in *Morgenbladet*, 10th September 1896.

C.A. Larsen – The Pioneer of the South Arctic Ocean

Risting, Sigurd, *Av hvalfangstens historie*, Kristiania, 1922.

Risting, Sigurd, *Kaptein C.A. Larsen*, Oslo, 1929.

Sollie, Finn, *De store polaroppdagelser*, Oslo,1977.

Tønnesen, Joh. N., *Den moderne hvalfangstens historie*, bind 2 og 3, Sandefjord, 1967-69.

Various unpublished materials, Sandefjordmuseenes bibliotek (The Sandefjord Museums, Library).

Otto Sverdrup and the Discovery of New Territories in the North

Sverdrup, Otto, *Nytt Land*, Kristiania, H. Aschehoug & Co, Kristiania (Oslo) 1903.

Borch Sannes, Tor, *«FRAM»*, Asker, Norsk Maritimt Forlag AS, Oslo 1988.

Hegge, Per Egil, *Otto Sverdrup Aldri Rådløs*, Oslo, J. M. Stenersens Forlag A. S., Oslo 1996.

Barr, Susan,: *«FRAM» mot Nordpolen*, Oslo, Ch**r. Schibsteds Forlag A/S,** Oslo 1996.

Roald Amundsen Conquers the South Pole

Amundsen, Roald, *Sydpolen, Den norske Sydpolferd med FRAM 1910-1912*, Kristiania, Jacob Dybwad Forlag, 1912.

Huntford, Roland, *Scott og Amundsen*, Oslo, Aschehoug & Co (W.Nygaard), 1980.

Huntford, Roland, *Scott and Amundsen*, London, Hodder and Stoughton, 1979.

Gran, Tryggve, *Fra tjuagutt til sydpolfarer*, Oslo, Ernst G. Mortensens Forlag, 1994.

Amundsen, Roald, Antarctic Expedition, diaries.

Johansen, Hjalmar, Antarctc Expedition, diaries.

Hassel, Sverre: Dagboksnotater fra Sydpolen, diaries, 1911-1912.

Bjaaland, Olav, With Amundsen to the South Pole, diary, 1910-1912

Thor Heyerdahl and the Kon-Tiki Expedition

Dahl, Tor E./Øgrim, T., *Thor Heyerdahl og verdenshavenes mysterier*, Oslo 1995.

Evensberget, S., *Thor Heyerdahl Oppdageren*, J.M. Stenersens Forlag, Oslo 1994.

Heyerdahl, T., *Kon-Tiki ekspedisjonen*, Oslo 1948.

Jacoby, A., *Møte med Thor Heyerdahl*, Oslo, 1984.

Johansen, Ø.K, *Kon-Tiki-ekspedisjonen 50 år etter*, P2-Akademiet, Oslo, 1998.

Thor Heyerdahl – By Papyrus Boat Across the Atlantic

Evensberget, S., *Thor Heyerdahl Oppdageren*, Oslo 1994.

Heyerdahl, T, *Raekspedisjonen*, Oslo 1970.

Jacoby, A., *Møte med Thor Heyerdahl*, Oslo 1984.

Thor Heyerdahl and the Tigris Expedition

Evensberget, S., *Thor Heyerdahl Oppdageren*, Oslo 1994.

Heyerdahl, T., *Tigris. På leting etter begynnelsen*, Oslo 1979.

Heyerdahl, T. *I Adams fotspor. En erindringsreise*, J.M. Stenersens Forlag, Oslo 1998.

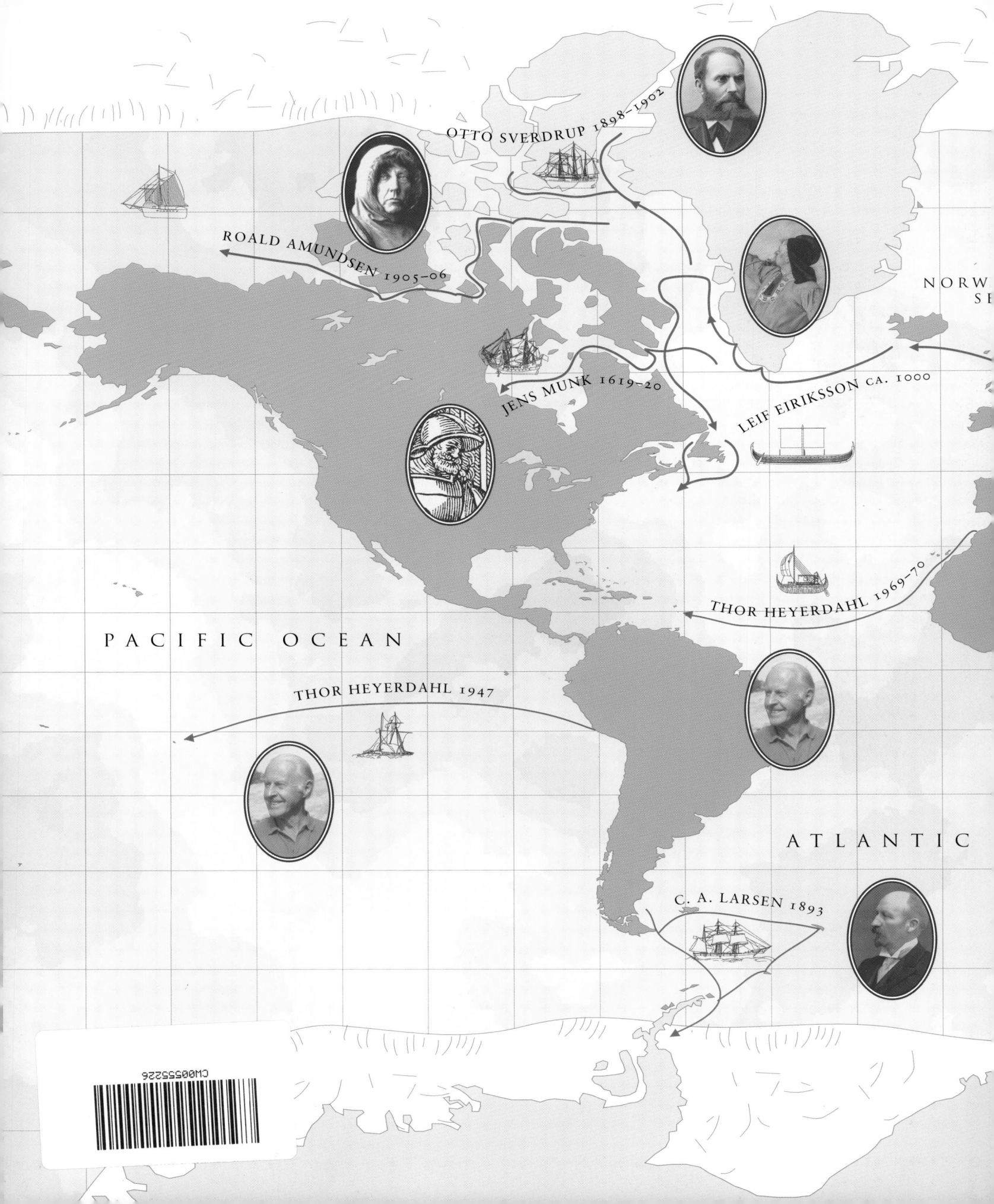

OTTO SVERDRUP 1898–1902

ROALD AMUNDSEN 1905–06

NORW
S

JENS MUNK 1619–20

LEIF EIRIKSSON CA. 1000

THOR HEYERDAHL 1969–70

PACIFIC OCEAN

THOR HEYERDAHL 1947

ATLANTIC

C. A. LARSEN 1893